Frieda A. Kiefer
Perkins In[stitution]
Nov. [illegible]

Frieda Kiefer Merry
19 Hilliard St.,
Cambridge, Mass.

HARVARD STUDIES IN EDUCATION

I. **The Oberlehrer: A Study of the Social and Professional Evolution of the German Schoolmaster.** By William S. Learned. $1.50.

II. **The Appointment of Teachers in Cities: A Critical and Constructive Study.** By Frank W. Ballou. $1.75.

III. **The Teaching of Economics in Harvard University.** (*Out of Print.*)

IV. **Relative Frequency of English Speech Sounds.** By Godfrey Dewey. $3.00

V. **The Intelligence of Continuation-School Children in Massachusetts.** By L. Thomas Hopkins. $1.75.

VI. **The Financial Support of State Universities.** By Richard R. Price. $3.50.

VII. **Individual Differences in the Intelligence of School Children.** By Mary M. Wentworth. $2.00.

VIII. **The Vocational Guidance of College Students.** By Lewis Adams Maverick. $2.50.

IX. **The Small Junior High School.** By Francis Trow Spaulding. $2.50.

X. **What Shall the Public Schools Do for the Feeble-Minded? A Plan for Special-School Training under Public School Auspices.** By Guy Pratt Davis. $3.50

HARVARD UNIVERSITY PRESS
CAMBRIDGE, MASSACHUSETTS

HARVARD STUDIES IN EDUCATION

PUBLISHED UNDER THE DIRECTION OF
THE GRADUATE SCHOOL OF EDUCATION

VOLUME X

LONDON: HUMPHREY MILFORD
OXFORD UNIVERSITY PRESS

WHAT SHALL THE PUBLIC SCHOOLS DO FOR THE FEEBLE-MINDED?

A PLAN FOR SPECIAL-SCHOOL TRAINING UNDER PUBLIC SCHOOL AUSPICES

BY

GUY PRATT DAVIS

PROFESSOR OF EDUCATION, STATE TEACHERS COLLEGE
INDIANA, PENNSYLVANIA

CAMBRIDGE
HARVARD UNIVERSITY PRESS
1927

COPYRIGHT, 1927
BY THE PRESIDENT AND FELLOWS OF
HARVARD COLLEGE

PRINTED IN THE U.S.A.

INTRODUCTORY NOTE

THE death of Dr. W. E. Fernald of the Massachusetts School for the Feeble-Minded at Waverley in 1924 robbed the medical and the educational world of one of its greatest benefactors. An untiring research worker in these two fields, he met and solved countless problems that confronted him in his attempt to establish a scientific procedure for the care and training of the mentally defective child.

Dr. Guy Pratt Davis had the rare opportunity of close association and study with Dr. Fernald and with his successor, Dr. Ransom A. Greene. Under their guidance and through their cordial coöperation, Dr. Davis has thoroughly studied the problems and procedures at Waverley, and in the present contribution has outlined the various needs and the great possibilities of public school coöperation in the solution of this pressing medico-educational problem.

In the face of such needs and possibilities, the suggestions of Dr. Davis evidence a practicability and conservatism that are extremely praiseworthy. I heartily commend this publication to those interested in any of the many phases of education. It should prove especially helpful to school administrators who are baffled by the presence of feeble-minded children among normal class groups.

EDWIN A. SHAW.

PREFACE

IN the fortieth annual report of the trustees of the Massachusetts School for the Feeble-minded for the year ending September 30, 1887, appears the following brief statement:

"After serious and prolonged search the Trustees have elected Walter E. Fernald, M.D., the first resident superintendent of the school. They need say no more about him than that his professional and personal qualifications appear to promise success in his responsible and delicate labors. He has had the varied experience which his post requires and will enter upon it, not to try his hand, but to bring his matured acquirements to our assistance."

Then, after thirty-seven years of intense labor, he laid down his work on the evening of November 27, 1924. The School, as he left it, is a monument to his life and work. Thus it was, that, on the first day of July, 1925, by legislative act, the Massachusetts School for the Feeble-minded became the Walter E. Fernald State School.

During his period of service as superintendent of this institution, he gained distinction as a builder, as an educator, as an organizer, as a scientist, and as an inspiring and lovable individual. Perhaps his greatest success as a builder was the library on Mental Defect, pronounced by experts to be the most complete to be found anywhere in the world. His achievements as an educator have been even more far-reaching than his achievements as a builder. He recognized early that the first step in the education of the feeble-minded, as with other people, was to make them happy; that the feeble-minded, like other people, are happy when they are doing something for which their capacity fits them. Hence he organized a twenty-four-hour program for every child under his care — a program in which the child was doing all the time whatever its needs and capacities required. The child was provided with the opportunity for play according to its capacity; work was likewise provided. Dr. Fernald was the first person to standardize manual labor according to intellectual levels in so far as the feeble-minded are concerned. He was able to find work that was nicely adjusted to the mental capacity of ever subnormal child. This made the work of these mental retardates a pleasure as well as a means of education.

Those who knew Dr. Fernald best, however, will remember him more because of his inspiring and lovable personality than because of his notable achievements. Since his death, literally hundreds of parents of children who had been under his care and guidance have testified that they loved him because they felt that he loved children. It was this, perhaps more than his professional enthusiasm, that drove him on. Sometimes those of us who sat before him in his classes felt that he permitted it to drive him too hard. Yet, who shall say? It may have hastened the bringing of his labors to an end; yet, in another sense, his labors can never end. For there is now and will be forever a living memorial to him in the lives of those children, men and women of feeble mentality, who will have a better chance in the world by reason of his having lived.

Dr. Fernald's death did not permit him to make the next application of his educational system of the feeble-minded — that is, an application of the training of mental defectives to the public school. It is this which we have endeavored to do. After a careful study of this system, we feel convinced that not only is the "salvaging process," in so far as it effects the problem of the feeble-minded, a necessary adjunct to the public school, but that the inauguration of the aims, content, and methods of instruction in the typical school would constitute a step in advance in educational procedure. We would prophesy that when the day arrives, and in the minds of some it does not appear long hence, when a child of even three or four years of age will be admitted to the public school, the instructional process which we have endeavored to discuss will become the basis of the work.

On the first day of July, 1925, Ransom A. Greene, M. D., was appointed Superintendent of the Walter E. Fernald State School. Too great thanks cannot be given to him or to the members of the school staff for the coöperation and aid which made this study possible. Likewise, we desire to express our appreciation to the members of the Psycho-Educational Clinic of the Harvard University Graduate School of Education — Professor Walter F. Dearborn, Professor Edwin A. Shaw, Professor Edward A. Lincoln, Dr. Daniel Prescott, and Dr. Harry F. Latshaw. Likewise, we are indebted to Dr. Stuart M. Stoke, of the University of Buffalo, for the summary of the laws of learning. To Charles Swain Thomas, of the Harvard University Graduate School of Education, who has given his time and coöperation unsparingly, we are especially indebted. It will be evident that material has been gained not only from these sources but from all courses which it has been our privilege to pursue in the School of Education.

GUY PRATT DAVIS.

CONTENTS

CHAPTER I

THE NEED FOR SPECIAL-SCHOOL TRAINING IN OUR PUBLIC SCHOOLS ... 1

A. Special-Training Facilities for the Mentally Retarded Child in the Public Schools ... 2
   The Need for Specially Adapted Training Facilities ... 4

B. The Criterion for Mental Subnormality and Some Related Problems ... 5
   The Community and the Problem Child ... 6
   The Criterion for Mental Subnormality ... 7
   Standardized Fields of Inquiry for Clinical Studies of Borderline Defectives ... 9
   The Feeble-Minded Child and the Present School Organization ... 11

C. The Purpose and Nature of This Investigation ... 12

CHAPTER II

SPECIAL-SCHOOL OBJECTIVES ... 16

A. Some Objectives for Special-School Training in the Public Schools ... 16
   The Need for Psycho-Educational Analysis of Individuals ... 17
   An Adapted Curriculum ... 17
   Prevocational and Vocational Training ... 18
   Mental Hygiene ... 20
   Health Education as an Integral Part of the Educational Program ... 21
   Social Conformity ... 22
   Guidance and Supervision ... 22
   The General Influence on Public School Organization, Administration, and Teaching Method ... 23

B. Conditions on Which the Efficiency of Instruction for the Mentally Deficient Depends ... 23
   The Learning Process of the Feeble-Minded Child ... 24
   Adaptation of the Educational Process to the Mental Level of the Mentally Deficient Child ... 26

xiv   CONTENTS

    Pedagogy for the Feeble-Minded 27
    General Methods of Instruction 27
  C. Summary and Conclusions 37

CHAPTER III

An Analysis of the Instructional Program for Mental Defectives 39
  A. Sense Training 39
    Meaning and Purpose of Sense Training 40
    Need for Sense Training of the Feeble-Minded 40
    Types of Sense Training to be Given 40
    Simultaneous Commissions 47
    Form of Report 47
    Fundamental Principles Concerning the Pre-Kindergarten Training (Seguin) 48
    Summary 50
  B. Manual Training 51
    The Aim and Purpose 52
    The Nature and General Content of Manual Training . . 52
    Occupational Sequence of Manual Training 54
    Elementary Handwork 55
    Summary 58
  C. Physical Training 58
    Physical Training as a Factor in Psychological Development 58
    Relationship of Physical and Intellectual Training in Dealing with Mental Defectives 59
    The Physical-Training Program 60
    Physical Training in Relation to Needs of Maturity . . . 63
    Summary 64
  D. Occupational Training 65
    The Relation of the Feeble-Minded to Industry 65
    Motor Training in the Education of the Feeble-Minded . 65
    Functional Occupations for the Feeble-Minded 66
    Pedagogical Sequence of Occupational Training 67
    "Peak" Mental Age in Occupational Training 68
      1. Occupational Training and Mentality for Girls 68
      2. Occupational Training and Mentality for Boys 69
    Purposeful Concepts Concerning Industrial Training . . . 70
    Summary and Conclusions 71

CHAPTER IV

An Analysis of the Instructional Program for Mental Defectives (*Continued*) 72
  E. Academic Training 72
    The Value of Academic Instruction 72

CONTENTS

Is There an Overemphasis on Academic Training of the Feeble-Minded?	73
The Character of the Special-School Academic Instruction	75
1. The Teaching of Numbers	75
General Competency of the Feeble-Minded in Number Work	75
Number Content for Mentally Deficient Children	76
2. Reading	79
Why the Feeble-Minded Should be Taught to Read	79
Methods of Teaching the Feeble-Minded to Read	80
Some Typical Devices for Teaching to Read	81
3. The Teaching of Music	83
Music and the Feeble-Minded	83
Musical Training for the Feeble-Minded	86
(1) Rote Singing	86
(2) Rhythmic Drill	87
(3) Musical Appreciation	88
4. Dramatization	89
Dramatization as a Factor in the Training of the Feeble-Minded Child	89
Dramatization as an Aid to Other Subjects	89
5. Language and Composition	91
Purpose of Language Teaching	91
Content of the Language Program	92
Purpose of Composition Teaching	92
Content of the Composition Program	93
6. History, Geography, and Civics	94
The Feeble-Minded and Historical Content	94
Geography for the Feeble-Minded	95
Civics for the Feeble-Minded	96
7. Moral Training	96
The Need for Moral Training of the Mentally Defective Child	96
Methods of Moral Training Available	97
8. Mental Hygiene and Mental Defectives	100
Mental Hygiene and Creative Activity	100
F. Summary and Conclusions of Chapters III and IV	101
The Problem of the Future Education of the Feeble-Minded	101
Previous School Education and Occupational Training	101
The Instructional Program Summarized	101
Results of Special-School Training	102

CHAPTER V

THE OBJECT LESSON	108
A. The Nature of the Object Lesson	108

B. The Teaching of the Object Lesson 109
   The Teacher and the Object Lesson 111
   The Object Lesson and Sense Training 112
   The Object Lesson and the Kindergarten 113
C. The Object-Lesson Program 116
   1. Classified Object-Lesson Program for Special-School Training 117
   2. Some Typical Object Lessons for Literary Instruction . . 123
      (1) Arithmetic 124
      (2) Reading, Vocabulary Building, Language, Spelling . 127
      (3) History and Civics 129
      (4) Geography 130
      (5) Nature Study 131
      (6) Dramatization 131
      (7) Music 132
   3. A Proposed Daily Object-Lesson Program for the Special School 132
D. Summary and Conclusions 136

CHAPTER VI

THE RESULTS OF THE SALVAGING PROCESS 138

A. The Social and Economic Possibilities of the Feeble-Minded . 138
B. After-Care of Discharged Patients 139
   Analysis of the Waverley Study 140
C. Analysis of Report on Supervision of Trained Male Defectives 146
D. A Study of the Social, Occupational, and Economic Efficiency of the Feeble-Minded 150
   A Study of Three Hundred Twenty-Eight Institutionally Trained Male Defectives 151
   A Study of Forty-One Institutionally Trained Female Defectives 154
E. Summary and Conclusions 159

CHAPTER VII

THE TRAINING PROGRAM OF THE SPECIAL-SCHOOL TEACHER . . . 161

A. Qualifications of the Special-School Teacher 162
   Good Physique 162
   A Wholesome, Well-Balanced Temperament and Disposition 162
   Character and Personality 163
   Social Outlook 163
   Skill in Teaching and Management 164
   Special Training 165

CONTENTS xvii

B. The Major Subjects in the Training Program of the Special-School Teacher 165
    The Normal School and the Special-School Teacher 167
    What the Typical Normal School Offers 167
    What the Typical Normal School Should Offer 168
    The College and the Special-School Teacher 169
    What the College Should Offer 169

C. Summary and Conclusions 171

CHAPTER VIII

A Proposed State Program for the Training and Instruction of Mental Defectives 173

A. The Mental Defective and the Public School 173
    Introduction 173
    The Mental Defective as a Potential Social and Economic Burden 173
    Reasons for the Lack of a Formal, Accepted Program . . . 174

B. A Proposed Program for the Salvaging of the Mentally Defective Child 174

C. The Early Recognition of Every Feeble-Minded Child in the Community and in the Public Schools 175
    The Keynote of a Practical Program for the Training and Instruction of Mental Defectives 175
    Rural-School Training of Defectives and Instruction of Parents 177

D. The Organization and Administration of Special Schools as Integral Parts of the Public School System 177
    The Special School and the Rural Community 178
        (1) The Consolidated Rural School 178
        (2) Country School Homes 179
        (3) The Colony System 179
        (4) Traveling Workshops 180
    Organization of the Junior School in an Urban Community 180
        (1) General Standards for Assignment of Pupils to the Junior School 180
        (2) Enrollment 181
        (3) The Special-School Curriculum 181
        (4) Physical Properties and Equipment 181
        (5) The Daily Program — Length of the School Day and Year 183
        (6) Discipline in the Special School 185
        (7) Qualifications of the Special-School Teacher 186
        (8) General Methods of Instruction in the Special School. 187
    The Special School as a Training Unit by Itself 187
    Social Supervision and Social Assistance 190

CONTENTS

The Special School as a "Clearing House" 191
Legal Provisions for the Establishment of Special or Junior Schools 191
E. Summary and General Conclusion 193

APPENDICES

APPENDIX I. The Object-Lesson Materials 197
APPENDIX II. "The Ten Fields of Inquiry" 205
APPENDIX III. Bibliography 222

LIST OF TABLES

TABLE:		PAGE
I.	Development of State Training School Facilities for Training Feeble-Minded Children	3
II.	Report of Special Classes for Feeble-Minded and Subnormal Children in Our Public Day Schools	3
III.	A Summary of the Economic Efficiency of Three Hundred Twenty-Eight Institutionally Trained Male Defectives in Its Relation to Mental Age	157
IV.	A Summary of the Economic Efficiency of Forty-One Institutionally Trained Females in Its Relation to Mental Age	158

LIST OF CHARTS

CHART:		PAGE
I.	"Peak" Mental Age for Boys in Occupational Training . . .	68A
II.	"Peak" Mental Age for Girls in Occupational Training . . .	68A
III.	Average Weekly Wages of Three Hundred Twenty-Eight Mentally Defective Males in Their Relation to Mental Age . . .	152A
IV.	Average Range of Weekly Wages of Three Hundred Twenty-Eight Mentally Defective Males in Its Relation to Mental Age . . .	153A
V.	Average Weekly Wages of Forty-One Mentally Defective Females in Their Relation to Mental Age	156A
VI.	Average Range of Weekly Wages of Forty-One Mentally Defective Females in Its Relation to Mental Age	156A

WHAT SHALL THE PUBLIC SCHOOLS DO FOR THE FEEBLE-MINDED?

A PLAN FOR SPECIAL-SCHOOL TRAINING UNDER PUBLIC SCHOOL AUSPICES

WHAT SHALL THE PUBLIC SCHOOLS DO FOR THE FEEBLE-MINDED?

CHAPTER I

THE NEED FOR SPECIAL-SCHOOL TRAINING IN OUR PUBLIC SCHOOLS

FROM the point of view of education it becomes important to know the number of children who are unable to profit by the usual type of school training because of mental handicaps. Today, we have 900,000 mentally defective or borderline children in the public schools of the United States, in addition to approximately 70,000 children now in special classes or in state training institutions for the mentally retarded.[1] The training of these 900,000 children is now being grossly neglected. Thousands of children are being kept in school, year after year, at great public expense, and yet the schools, as a system, do practically nothing worth while for them. The training processes used are of slight avail, doing little to organize their potential energies, limited even though they are, for the service of the community or for the welfare of these as individuals. Because we do not spend more wisely for their training, we are literally wasting what we do spend upon them; furthermore, we are actually wasting the children themselves. The work done in the little classroom of the distant country or in the big classroom of the great city is essentially the same — it is the work of changing American children into good American men and women, physically, socially, morally, economically self-sufficient, believing in equality because they have known it, believing in opportunity for others because they have experienced opportunity, and believing in each other, because, through childhood studies, they have been directly and intimately associated with each other as a part of the people.

[1] Haines, Thomas H.: "Special Training Facilities for Mentally Handicapped Children in the Public Day Schools in the United States, 1922-1923." *Mental Hygiene*, No. VIII, October, 1924, pp. 893-911.

Thus, the place of the special-school training in the public schools of our country.

Up to within a few years ago, the literature of the mentally subnormal emphasized three main aspects. The first was that nearly all feeble-mindedness was highly hereditary. The second was that the intellectually inferior were almost without exception vicious and immoral, indeed presumedly criminalistic. The third concept was that they were as a general rule vagabonds and paupers, not capable of being trained to support themselves by their own labor, and hence, of necessity, supported at public expense. However, within the past few years many things have taken place which cause us to believe that we have been rather too sweeping in some of our deductions and generalizations. Entirely new cross sections have been revealed by means of the study of the mentally defective in special-school classes, school clinics, out-patient mental clinics, in private practice, in community surveys, and in the army. Much has been learned regarding adult feeble-mindedness from the after-care of special-class pupils and observations of discharged inmates of institutions for such. But before entering into the details about these matters, let us turn our attention to the special-training facilities for the mentally retarded child in the public schools.

A. Special-Training Facilities for the Mentally Retarded Child in the Public Schools

Public school facilities specially adapted to meet the developmental needs of mentally handicapped children have developed rapidly in recent years. Many states now have special statutory requirements for the organization of such special classes in all school districts in which the feeble-minded children of school age exceed a specified small number. In some states, aid is given from the state school fund to meet the higher costs of special-school classes as now organized.

The development of state training school facilities for the training of feeble-minded children has proceeded more rapidly during the past few years than in the early years after the middle of the nineteenth century. Data from the reports of the United States

Bureau of Education indicate this growth. A summary of these data follows in Table I.

TABLE I

DEVELOPMENT OF STATE TRAINING SCHOOL FACILITIES FOR TRAINING FEEBLE-MINDED CHILDREN [1]

YEAR	STATE TRAINING SCHOOLS	NO. OF INMATES	TEACHERS EMPLOYED
1900	19	9,792	
1918	43	35,968	
1921–22	51	38,761	492

The Bureau of Education also reports data, from 1913, on special classes for feeble-minded and subnormal children in our public day schools. These facilities have developed very rapidly during the past ten years. A further investigation was made in 1923, which shows the same tendency toward rapid growth, a summary of which follows in Table II.

TABLE II

REPORT ON SPECIAL CLASSES FOR FEEBLE-MINDED AND SUBNORMAL CHILDREN IN OUR PUBLIC DAY SCHOOLS [2]

YEAR	PUBLIC DAY SCHOOLS	NO. OF PUPILS	INSTRUCTORS IN SPECIAL CLASSES
1913	52	9,357	586
1914	72	10,890	650
1915	72	12,795	797
1916	118	16,524	939
1918	131	18,133	1,134
1922	133	23,252	1,132

(Adapted from Haines.)

In the mental health surveys of 52,269 public school children conducted by the National Committee for Mental Hygiene,

[1] *Schools and Classes for Feeble-Minded and Subnormal Children, 1918.* Department of the Interior, Bureau of Education, Bulletin, 1919, No. 70, pp. 6–7. *Ibid.*, 1922, 1923, No. 59, p. 2.

[2] Haines, Thomas H.: "Special Training Facilities for Mentally Handicapped Children in the Public Day Schools in the United States, 1922–1923." *Mental Hygiene*, No. VIII, October, 1924, pp. 893–911.

from 1914 to 1924 inclusive, in 15 different states, 1,636 children were diagnosed as "mentally defective," and 1,619 as "borderline mental defectives." These 3,255 children all need special-school training. They constitute 5.49 per cent, or 549 in each 10,000 of the 59,269 children included in the studies. These children were found in states as widely separated as Rhode Island and Arizona, North Dakota and South Carolina, Wisconsin and Mississippi. They may be considered, therefore, as representative. Thus, if this percentage holds throughout the United States, there were among the 18,102,792 children from seven to fifteen years old in school on July 1, 1923, some 993,843 who needed special-school training because of their mental handicaps.

These 70,000 who were being trained in special classes or in state training schools constituted approximately 7 per cent of the entire 993,843. The shortage of special-class or special-school facilities in the United States, as of July 1, 1923, left 923,843 children unprovided for. Over 900,000 children, handicapped in the use of imagery, symbols, and concepts to the degree whereby they could not pursue successfully the course of study or follow the daily program of the ordinary primary or grammar grades, were being pulled and pushed through this, to them at least, meaningless and useless procedure. Nothing in the plan of activity of the school seemed especially designed to bring out or develop the individual capacities of these 900,000 mentally-handicapped children. Our training facilities have not been utilized for their benefit.

The Need for Specially Adapted Training Facilities. — These mentally defective or borderline defective children in our public schools should have training facilities especially adapted to their peculiar needs. These facilities should be at least as good as, and in some respects better than, those which are now provided in the common type of school training, or even in the majority of special classes or state training schools. Until such facilities are afforded them, our public schools cannot seriously undertake the instruction, training, and socialization of these mentally handicapped children. It seems evident, then, that until such provisions are made, we are clearly neglecting one of the most logical means of preventing the expensive delinquencies of older defectives. Not only does our general present neglect cost us enormous amounts of money in courts, jails, poorhouses, and other charitable institutions, but we are neglecting to make these mentally subnormal children economically and socially efficient, as well as keeping them from that opportunity and contentment which is theirs by right.

It is particularly in the public schools that this neglect is most apparent. It is not only in inheritance that the troubles of this world are to be sought — they are quite as much the result of improper and insufficient training. In other words, whereas such factors as delinquency and crime are commonly thought of as the inheritance of an emotional and affective deficiency, intelligence tests have revealed at least to us that they are quite as much a matter of training and environmental conditions. The schools either treat these children as though they were not mentally handicapped, expecting them to share the opportunities offered the normal individual, opportunities which their incapabilities do not allow them to grasp, or blindly pass over their delinquent and truant complexes. It is, in fact, the attitude of the school, one which held that if sufficiently urged they could be brought up to grade, which is in part responsible for their rather usual classifications as truants and disciplinary cases. It is a sad comment upon our public schools when we view the large proportion of mental defectives who go to prison or who become human derelicts; it is but evidence of their failure in the task of adjustment or readjustment and training.

B. The Criterion for Mental Subnormality and Some Related Problems

Considerable variance of opinion has existed concerning those methods best suited to the needs and capacities of mentally subnormal children. There has been uncertainty as to where and how such children could be most efficiently trained, and how much training they could profitably make use of, and by what methods or means they can be managed best, once they are trained. Even today some educators gauge capacity for training by capacity for learning to read and write and figure; they seem to have no other measure of mental function and personality growth. Furthermore, some educators and administrators seem to maintain that mentally subnormal individuals as such cannot be molded into conformity with community life. Others hold the view that even though such extra-institutional life may be possible for some of the intellectually inferior beings, only by means of a properly organized state or boarding institution can they be trained; that is, no feeble-minded child is a proper subject for training along with so-called normal children. According to this view, feeble-mindedness takes on the nature of an affliction, a disease, so handicapping the child that the training problem becomes something absolutely differentiated from that of the average child. Thus it is argued that he has no place in the ordinary public school, even though he may be given a place within the haven of a special class, or within the walls of a school organized and equipped along lines which shall be indicated in our discussion. It may be said in passing, however, that such persons fail to recognize those indistinguishable degrees of variability in mental level by which one passes, in any large and unselected group of human beings, from that intellectual status known as "normality," to one designated as "feeble-mindedness" or mental subnormality.

The Community and the Problem Child. — Views such as those expressed above are illustrative of a misuse of a concept and a general lack of proper understanding. It is true that we are accustomed to think of the different mental levels as more or less hard-and-fast entities, and the individual who falls into the class known as "feeble-minded" is "different," much as the insane were regarded as "different" a century ago. As a matter of fact, these classical divisions have been devised and used rather as a matter of convenient designation; and, furthermore, each problem child, whether his particular problem consists in some special mental defect or in some unusual or troublesome organization of personality, is, *sui generis*, a special problem for the home, the school, and the community. So long as children and schools continue to exist, every community will have its problem cases. The public school is responsible for the training of the children of the community. The responsibility for the training of problem children can not be shifted upon any other agency or institution unless such agency or institution is equipped for the special service. If the community is to give the mentally subnormal individual what he really needs, special-school training facilities and specially adapted training opportunities are required. Either, therefore, the school should be so equipped and organized that these opportunities are offered, or else see to it that the child has them offered him in a suitably equipped training school.

As early as 1850, Dr. Samuel G. Howe, superintendent of the first training school in this country, the Walter E. Fernald State School (established in 1848 and now located at Waverley, Massachusetts), saw that this work was an integral part of public education. In one of his early reports he says: "The (state training) school for the feeble-minded is a link in the chain of common schools — the last, indeed, but still a necessary link in order to embrace all the children of the state." As a general rule, the state training school for the feeble-minded in the United States is quite independent of public instruction and of the community or public day schools of the state. The public school tends to look upon the education of mental retardates as a special duty and privilege of the state training school. And since this necessary last link in our educational system is specially charged with the training of mental retardates, the argument seems to be that any child who can reasonably be classified as an intellectual defective should be sent away to a state training school for all his training. Several fallacies underlie this kind of reasoning.

The Criterion for Mental Subnormality. — One of these fallacies is involved in the broadening of our viewpoint with respect to mental defect; its connotation has been greatly enlarged during the past few years. In addition, while these training schools were established for the training of imbeciles and idiots, in actual practice these institutes have received principally emotionally and mentally unstable children even of the higher grade of intelligence. From the outset, delinquent mental defectives have been in the majority among these populations.

Since the introduction of the Binet-Simon individual tests of general intelligence (first published in 1905), the mental deficiency concept has been broadened to include far more than mere idiocy and imbecility; in fact, it is beginning to include more than mere mental defect *per se*. Under this new concept of what constitutes mental deficiency, mentally handicapped children are far too great in number to be given a place in our present state training schools, even though this were deemed advisable. Furthermore, it would be impossible to determine any process whereby any community could be persuaded to raise taxes for the purpose of constructing and operating boarding schools for the training of all its feeble-minded children. And even though this were possible, to recommend such training schools, *i.e.*, boarding institutions, for many children who are really seriously mentally deficient would be ill-advised. Since any properly organized home is an educational and socializing agency of the greatest importance, it is an inestimable educational advantage for the feeble-minded child, as also for the normally minded child, to remain in his own private home — or even in a good foster home. Institutionalization, wherever possible, must be avoided, in the case of the normal and the feeble-minded alike.

What, then, constitutes, our concept of mental subnormality? Seventy has been commonly accepted as the I. Q. arbitrarily marking the upper limit of feeble-mindedness, but it seems too high, and an I. Q. of 50 squares better with the economic and social criteria by which the feeble-minded are ordinarily differentiated. That is, the criteria for feeble-mindedness are, in the last analysis, the social-economic, as well as the psychological, since the latter have value only in so far as they correlate with the former. It is true that a child with an I. Q. between 50 and 70 will profit little by instruction in the three R's, yet he will often learn enough about some occupation to care for himself and to manage his affairs with ordinary prudence.[1] That is, strictly

---

[1] Dearborn, Walter F.: *Intelligence Tests: Their Significance for School and Society*. Lowell Institute Lectures, 1925, to be published by Houghton Mifflin Company.

speaking, no one would be called feeble-minded who can compete on terms of equality with his normal fellows and manage himself and his affairs in terms of socially acceptable principles, irrespective of what his mental age might be as measured by tests of general intelligence. In other words, we do not seem justified in diagnosing an individual as feeble-minded solely on the basis of mental age, for there does not appear much doubt but that emotional instability, for example, is just as important, and in some cases a more important factor, than inferior intelligence. And yet, in selecting school children for the special classes, the determining factor seems to have been inferior intelligence. This means that the special classes in our public schools contain many children who are not really feeble-minded, even though they do not have an I. Q. any higher than many of the feeble-minded. Enough placement and follow-up work has been done already with special-class children who have left school to establish this point beyond reasonable doubt.[1] In fact, although we can gauge pretty accurately the scholastic limitations of any mentally retarded child, as yet we are in no position to be absolutely positive with respect to the social-economic limitations of such until, from the beginning of his school life, and as much earlier as possible, we succeed in giving him a type of training that is as well adapted to his particular needs as the regular course of study to the needs of the typical child.

Standardized Fields of Inquiry for Clinical Studies of Borderline Defectives. — Even in cases of very slight mental defect some of the cardinal symptoms of imbecility are usually found in lesser degree. That is, from a clinical point of view, the borderline case of the " moron " grade differs from the case of actual imbecility quantitatively rather than qualitatively. In a paper entitled, *The Diagnosis of the Higher Grades of Mental Defect*, Dr. Fernald said: "There are generally evidences of physical inferiority, certain 'stigmata of degeneracy,' and defective muscular and motor coördination. There is usually a history of delayed dentition, late walking, delayed speech, and relatively long continu-

---

[1] Barry, C. S.: *The Mentally Retarded Child in the Public Schools.* National Committee for Mental Hygiene, Reprint No. 186, 1923.

ance of anti-social habits. The individual lacks the expression or appearance of normal mentality. There is frequently a history of mental defect or mental disease in the family. Unmoral and anti-social tendencies are often present. There is a history of school retardation and poor scholastic ability on examinations, with special difficulty in arithmetical and practical computations, and a lack of general information and knowledge. The patient is unable to apply himself continuously in any one direction for any considerable length of time and is willing to risk severe penalties for some very slight gain. His actions and conduct indicate a lack of good common sense.

"An accurate and incontestible diagnosis of one of these borderline cases can be made satisfactorily only after a thorough-going physical examination, knowledge of the family history, personal history, especially the story of his infancy and early childhood, school history and records, social and moral reactions, sex habits, emotional stability, associates, interests — the fullest inquiry as to his general information and practical knowledge."[1]

The charts included in the Appendix show the inclusiveness of the *Ten Fields of Inquiry* which furnish a working basis for individual case study at the Walter E. Fernald State School. Every possible bit of evidence is presented, not only in its proper field but in relation to the evidence in the other fields of inquiry. It is primarily a means of summarizing the pros and cons from a great mass of testimony. It is the same principle as that used in psychological experiments, where the summation of stimuli, each too slight to be perceived, nevertheless brings about a maximal reaction. From a study of the fields of inquiry of 860 cases, it appeared evident that no single symbol like the Binet mental age, or any more or less arbitrary coefficient or formula, could adequately express or represent the complete mental or intellectual status of an individual. Instead of being represented by a single symbol or by the sum total of the varying degrees of ability in certain directions, the mental capacity of a

---

[1] Fernald, Walter E.: "Standardized Fields of Inquiry for Clinical Studies of Borderline Defectives." Reprinted from *Mental Hygiene*, Vol. I, No. 2, pp. 211–234, April, 1917.

given individual can be more correctly expressed by a formula similar to an algebraic equation, including the additions and deductions representing his various reactions, capacities, and deficiencies. It is clear, therefore, that a measurable intellectual level is not the only factor of importance in any study of the feeble-minded and in the working out of the type of care and training they need. To summarize — ordinarily, in a definitely feeble-minded person, evidence of mental defect will be found in most of the ten fields of inquiry; and even in the so-called borderline cases where the mental defect is slight, as a rule, definite evidence of mental defect will be found also in nearly all fields.

The Feeble-Minded Child and the Present School Organization. — As at present organized, the academic courses of the upper grades and of the high school are closed to the feeble-minded child; and the opportunities of the ungraded classes are for the recognized defective. The trade schools, with their "more or less snobbish airs," desire only those successful students who might attend high school, but who, because of economic factors, prefer that type of school. The doors of such schools should be opened wide to the feeble-minded child who is at all educable, just as they are to those who later become continuation-school pupils. Special teachers should be found who not only understand the attitudes, interests, needs, and capacities of these mentally defective children but who, with their feet firmly upon the ground, could "make a science out of the art of plumbing." Our reform schools in many cases offer curricula more suitable to the abilities of these children; and if these schools, or similar ones, were made a part of the training equipment of the fourth to the sixth grades of our public schools, there would be practically no need for them under their present designation and purpose. Cyril Burt, the English psychologist, in commenting upon the same problem in the schools of London, says in part: "By providing occupations and duties, in nature more congenial, and in difficulty more advanced; by granting freer outlets for emotional tendencies and a fuller play to the spirit of activity, many instinctive propensities may, when emancipated from repression and adroitly re-directed, yield energy for legitimate purposes and enthusiasm for nobler ideals and strenuous work."[1] It should be remarked, in passing, however, that the problem of misbehavior and delinquency and its prevention or correction is not entirely one of the public school. Thus, a child of average intelligence brought up in a superior family desirous of having him fill a high professional niche in life may be just as badly off as the mentally incapable child. Or a child, who because of greater intelligence and better training is superior to those about him, may oftentimes come to an equally unhappy end.[2] Relatively few studies have been made with respect to what the public school has actually accomplished, not so much in terms of education in its narrower interpretation, as in the sense of education for life. We shall endeavor to show, therefore, not only what the instructional and training process of the feeble-minded should be, but we shall devote considerable attention to what the "salvaging process" has actually accomplished — more especially with respect to social rehabilitation and economic efficiency.

These special-school facilities for the training of mentally subnormal boys and girls may be costly — we shall show that they need not necessarily be so — but what comes to the community by way of delinquency and crime, is indeed far more costly than any educational system which could be considered. And, what of the individual?

3. The Purpose and Nature of This Investigation

Special-School Training in Content and Theory. — The general needs for special-school training, together with the criterion for mental subnormality, have been presented above. It now becomes our purpose to present in detail the theory and practice underlying special-school training, as exemplified by the Walter E. Fernald State School, in its application to the public school system. We shall consider, therefore:

(1) The objectives for special-school training in the public school system, together with the conditions on which the efficiency

---

[1] Burt, Cyril: *Mental and Scholastic Tests*, p. 189. P. S. King and Co., Ltd.
[2] To Professor Walter F. Dearborn I wish to acknowledge my indebtedness for the principles contained in the section *The Feeble-Minded Child and the Present School Organization*.

of instruction and training of mental defectives depend. We shall endeavor to show that the point of emphasis should be placed, first, upon the acquisition of right and orderly habits, and, secondly, upon the acquisition of knowledge and information of a rather specific kind. In terms of this general aim, as a pivotal point, we shall consider the more specific aims of special-school training, including, (*a*) the need of a psycho-educational analysis of each individual who for any reason is unable to profit by the usual type of public school training; (*b*) the adaptation of a curriculum to the needs, capacities, and life-interests of mentally deficient children; (*c*) prevocational and vocational training, the primary purpose of which is to cultivate an attitude of work — following directions, coöperation, dependability, cheerfully sustained effort, and the like; (*d*) mental hygiene, including sex hygiene; (*e*) health education, as an integral part of the special-school program; (*f*) social conformity, that is, the molding of the subnormal child into an individual who appears and acts in just about the same way that any ordinarily intelligent person appears and acts; (*g*) guidance and supervision, both during and after school life; and (*h*) the influence the special-school may exercise upon the trend of elementary education for all children, irrespective of intellectual capacity.

In considering the conditions on which the efficiency of instruction of the mentally deficient depends, we shall present the following: (*a*) the learning process of the feeble-minded child, showing that, in general, the learning process of the mental defective does not differ materially from that of the normal child, since education is primarily a matter of adjustment or accommodation of the individual to his environment; (*b*) the adaptation of the learning process to the mental level of the subnormal child, necessitating freedom on the part of the teaching staff from all unnecessary restraints tending to be detrimental in any way to the intellectually inferior child; (*c*) the pedagogy for the feeble-minded, showing that whereas the general principles are the same as for the normal child, the conditions are very different; (*d*) the types of teaching processes in the special school, the most important being the "object lesson"; and (*e*) the size of the class, including both general and specific considerations in this connection.

(2) Classification for instruction and training of mentally defective children, including the fundamental principles involved, showing that the ultimate classificatory decision must be scientific, diagnostic, composite, and in terms of the individual child.

(3) An analysis of the instructional program for mental defectives. Herein, the training process has been divided into two general divisions, the first including sense, manual, physical, and occupational training, the second, the more important phases of "literary" or academic training or work of the special school. Although each of these phases has been considered in terms of specific aims, content, and teaching method, an endeavor has been made to correlate them around one central core of development, namely, the mental aspect of life.

(4) The "object lesson," including (a) the nature and purpose of, and the theory underlying, this means of instruction; (b) a classified object lesson program for special-school training; (c) some typical object lessons for literary instruction; and (d) a proposed daily object-lesson program for the special school.

(5) The results of the "salvaging process," in three sections, as follows: I. *After-Care Study of the Patients Discharged from Waverley for a Period of Twenty-five Years* (Fernald, Walter E., M.D.); II. *One Hundred Institutionally Trained Male Defectives in the Community under Supervision* (Matthews, Mable A., Head Social Worker of the Walter E. Fernald State School); and III. *A Study of the Social, Occupational, and Economic Efficiency of the Feeble-Minded.* In toto, our combined study has included 1116 mentally deficient individuals, 898 males and 218 females, showing the work of the Walter E. Fernald State School in its social-rehabilitation and economic-occupational efficiency program for mental defectives.

(6) The training program of the special-school teacher, including (a) the qualifications of the special-school teacher, and (b) the major subjects in this training program from the standpoint of (1) the normal school, and (2) the college. And, finally

(7) A proposed state program for the training and instruction of mental defectives, which includes four main premises, as follows: (*a*) early recognition of every mentally defective child in the community and in the public school; (*b*) training and instruction in terms of the child's needs, capacities, and interests, emphasizing the acquisition of socially accepted habits, attitudes, ideals, and skills, over and above the acquisition of knowledge *per se;* (*c*) long-continued industrial and vocational training, thus, the organization of the special school, or the "junior school," as an integral part of the regular school system; and (*d*) social service during the school-life of the child and after-supervision and continued guidance.

CHAPTER II

SPECIAL-SCHOOL OBJECTIVES

A. Some Objectives for Special-School Training in the Public School System

It is a truism of all educational procedure that the organization and administration of the school, together with its curriculum, should be adapted to the varying needs, capacities, and interests of the individuals directly concerned, in content, method, and rate of potential progress. Any curriculum which is characterized by uniformity can result in a classification of children only through frequent and numerous failures to promote and less frequent and also relatively few extra-promotions, thus rendering the twin problems of retardation and elimination very serious ones. Even though differential curricula were so organized that the three mental levels — superior, median, inferior — may each benefit, there remains that group of individuals found at the lowest points of the intellectual ladder, who, even in the curriculum for the inferior group, are unable to make satisfactory progress. In general, it may be said that the greater the degree of curricular differentiation, the fewer cases of limited educability there will be. Even so, it is seldom less than from three to seven per cent of the typical elementary-school population.

The general aim or objective of special-school training is to make of the individuals directly concerned in our study law-abiding members of the community in which they may live, socially adaptable, and economically self-sufficient, capable of complete or at least partial self-support through worth-while labor and productivity. By some it may be thought that the mentally retarded child is a potential sinner; it is likewise true that he is a potential saint. Which one he becomes will depend primarily, perhaps entirely, upon the type of training he receives in the home, the school, the church. It follows, therefore, that the point of emphasis should be placed, first of all, upon the acquisition of right and orderly habits, and, secondly, upon the acquisition of knowledge and information of a rather specific kind.

The Need for Psycho-Educational Analysis of Individuals. — A psycho-educational analysis of each individual, who for one or many reasons is unable to profit by the usual type of public school training, is the first specific objective which we desire to present. The details of this mental, physical, social, economic, and moral analysis have been considered in Chapter I, under the *Ten Fields of Inquiry*. It should be concerned with a most thoroughgoing examination of all phases of child nature, remedial measures following, where possible — as, for example, in the case of emotional instability or certain physical defects. Upon the basis of this inquiry, including mental age, previous training, scholastic record, and teachers' estimates of intelligence, a tentative classroom placement and procedure should be determined, accompanied by diagnostic instruction and training of a special-class teacher.

An Adapted Curriculum. — From the first objective the second is but a natural outgrowth, namely, the adaptation of a curriculum to the needs, capacities, and interests of these mentally deficient children. In order to bring this about successfully, from an academic point of view, school progress must of necessity be of an extremely elementary character, since experience and experimentation have shown that proficiency in the three R's is seldom attained beyond that of the fifth or sixth grade at the most. The steps in the educational procedure must necessarily be small; the instructional materials of a concrete and objective nature rather than of an abstract content. A considerable portion of that found in the standard curriculum at the present time should be omitted. Motor and sense training, more especially in the case of the younger children, and prevocational work in the manual and industrial arts for the older children should receive a greater proportion of time, attention, and effort in the program of studies than is now customary.

The mental-age levels of the individuals concerned will range from three or four to eleven or twelve years. Yet pupils with the same intellectual level will differ greatly in mental function — that is, they will vary in ability for various kinds of instruction and training. Thus, although group instruction is to be continued were it only for the social benefits to be derived, yet the group should be small enough so that a considerable degree of individualized instruction and training is possible.

Prevocational and Vocational Training. — Upon leaving school these mentally subnormal boys and girls will presumably enter the unskilled or semi-skilled occupations. These occupations are of such a varied character that, it is generally believed, it is usually impracticable to attempt vocational training of a highly differential character. The trade skills, except for the increased efficiency which comes through training on the job, are not complicated or difficult in most of these occupations. It is therefore apparent that the industrial-arts work of the special school should be principally prevocational rather than vocational in the strict interpretation of the term. For example, the girls may receive training in sewing, cooking, general housework, certain phases of cafeteria work, nursing in its elementary form, in addition to a modified form of academic work and physical education, including health and mental hygiene. The boys, likewise, while receiving training in physical education and a modified form of the customary academic training, may receive instruction in carpentry, painting, shoemaking, masonry (including cement-mixing), toy-making, broom and mat construction, drafting, household mechanics, auto mechanics and the repairing of machinery, the use of the lathe and printing press, and the various aspects of agriculture and horticulture, where the local community makes these latter possible and feasible. In so far as the individual's ability will permit, opportunity should be given for each pupil to undertake work in each of these fields mentioned.

After these have been covered and a fair degree of mastery attained by the student, provision should be made for concentration on the particular type of work toward which his particular aptitudes, capacities, and interests seem to draw him. Here it may be suggested that, after all, we are not endeavoring to make skilled artisans out of these boys and girls. Even though such may be a possibility, it is not primarily our purpose. If the mentally subnormal individual is to enter into successful competition with normal individuals in either unskilled or semi-skilled labor, he must receive that type of training which will prepare him for such competition. By receiving this rather diversified type of preliminary training he is enabled to compete on equal terms in a particular type of work with the normal individual who has not had the opportunity of such instruction. Furthermore, it becomes possible for him to perform unskilled or semi-skilled work in several different fields rather than being limited in a larger degree to one field, as would be the situation were he trained to do but one thing. This is highly essential, if not absolutely necessary, in the training of those who lack initiative and natural versatility. The real advantage which comes from this more general type of training is to be seen especially when hard times come, for during such periods the more or less unskilled worker finds opportunities more restricted in some fields than in others. Educationally, the principle of a broad, basic training seems sound; economically, it functions in the majority of cases.

If we admit that by means of special-school training the mentally retarded child has received the requisite training whereby the skill and strength necessary to enter into some gainful pursuit have been acquired, even though he were so equipped, he could not hold any position for any length of time without having formed the habit of regularity. That is to say, unless he went to work regularly, day after day, unless he were there on time, unless he remained on the job until he saw it through to completion, unless he had acquired social adaptability — that ability which enables us to get along well with our fellow men — he could not succeed, however excellent may have been the training. But these habits, so very essential in the work of everyday life, are equally necessary to success in school. How often, for example, do teachers repeat instructions because the child was inattentive? How often do they tell a child to do a task before it is finally done? In this insistence, perhaps, the teachers do not realize that they are really the ones who are directly responsible for the formation of habits which if continued hinder the child from becoming a coöperative, adaptive, economically self-efficient member of society. Without this latter result, the salvaging process of human potentiality is very much reduced in its possibilities. All this is essential in the case of any child, irrespective of its mental level; it is, however, more essential for the feeble-minded child, since it is as difficult for him to unlearn a habit once formed as it is for him to learn it.

After all, the primary object of prevocational training in the special school is the cultivation of an attitude of work — following directions, coöperation, dependableness, cheerfully sustained effort, and interest in the particular task. With these assets the defective child will be able to compete successfully with normal individuals and so become worth-while individuals in community life.

Mental Hygiene. — Special-school instruction and training cannot afford to neglect the importance and possibilities of mental hygiene, including sex hygiene. Both preventive and corrective work can be accomplished. An even temper, a pleasing and controlled disposition, a desire to please, dependableness, and a responsive personality are certainly worth more in terms of social adaptation, both in school and in after-school life, than a working knowledge of square root and historical dates. In nearly all cases, shyness, emotional instability, sullenness, and related social disfigurements, may be corrected or at least beneficially modified. It follows that, irrespective of the degree of individual training which appears necessary, there must be a large amount of concerted activity so motivated that the children will participate eagerly, earnestly, and happily. We wish for a schoolhouse with a cheerful, sunny room, with plants and pictures and whatever possible pets; a program, varied with short periods of sustained effort, followed by periods of play; and a teacher, modestly but well dressed, possessing a well-modulated voice and a reasonably pleasing personality. All these have their part in the functioning of a mental-hygiene program for the mentally deficient child. Individuals who are incapable of profiting by favorable conditions of this type should receive especially careful consideration. Problem children may be psychopathic, it is true, but very often their complexes are the resultant of inadequate and unintelligent home training plus a failure of the school to understand them. One of the major functions of the special school is to stabilize these boys and girls who are mentally retarded.

As previously noted, these habits which the mentally retarded child is to form by means of special-school training are of much greater importance in the determination of his future than is the knowledge he acquires in school. However, this does not mean that the mentally subnormal child is not to participate in the wisdom of the race to the limit of his mental capacity; it simply means that his mental saturation point is much more easily and quickly reached in the realm of understanding than in the realm of habit-formation. Thus, through the acquisition of right habits he may do what is considered right and refrain from doing wrong without being able to give any comprehensive reason why.

Health Education an Integral Part of the Educational Program. — Health education should constitute an integral part of the educational program; it should not be looked upon as an added or extra-curricular activity. Through well-directed physical exercises, such as games, supervised play, dramatization, and dancing, the mentally deficient children improve not only with respect to general health and general physical vigor, but they at the same time acquire motor coördination, social adaptation, self-control, a sense of fair play, and a degree of initiative. In the formation of habits of personal cleanliness and attention to factors of personal hygiene, the majority of these children can compete on terms of practical equality with normal children of equivalent age and maturity. A considerable proportion of the content of the present course in health education can be adapted to their needs, with this proviso — that it be presented and developed within the range of their mental level. Much of this content is within the sphere of comprehension of an eight-year-old mental level. No one of the health phases usually stressed in such a course of instruction need be omitted. For instance, girls of the moron type can be taught to differentiate between wholesome and unwholesome food-stuffs, to know the importance and need of a constant supply of fresh air, and why we should have a pure water supply; they can learn also to care for younger children and to practice some of the relatively simple phases of first-aid work.

Social Conformity. — One of the chief objectives of many private institutions for mentally subnormal children is to make these individuals inconspicuous by making them as nearly like normal people as possible. From this objective at least one conclusion of great importance to the special school can be drawn. Courteous manners, becoming yet inconspicuous clothing, speech clearly understandable, erect carriage, exact motor coördination including a normal gait — all these most surely and inevitably count much in everyday life. Any child who is well-mannered, whose rating on a social conformity scale is high, including manners, speech, morals, and conduct in general, to a very considerable degree may counterbalance his handicaps of limited mental development. Much of the training in good citizenship of the usual curriculum can find a welcome place in special-school training. Speech-correction work must be persistently but patiently applied; unstable motor coördinations of the body can to an appreciable degree be overcome by physical exercises. Moral training can advance considerably without any really clear comprehension of vital moral principles. This makes it apparent that special-school training should offer as one of its contributions social conformity, the making or molding of the mentally deficient child into an individual who appears and acts in just about the same way that any ordinarily intelligent person appears and acts.

Guidance and Supervision. — Much of the success of the special-school training for mental defectives will depend not only upon the nature of the training itself but also upon guidance and supervision which should come particularly after the close of school-life and entrance into some form of remunerative work. In the cities the trained social workers, in the smaller communities a representative of the special-school staff, should be primarily responsible for some guidance and supervision after these mentally handicapped boys and girls leave school. Some placement work should be done, and even training on the job should find a place. Where the teacher has made the home-contacts which should have been made while the child is attending school, through periodic visitations, she can impress the parents with their responsibility, especially with respect to home supervision. If, for example, the person concerned is unfit for marriage and ultimate parenthood — that is to say, for independent life — this should at once be made clear to the parents. Should the home possess an influence of a negative and undesirable nature, as is many times the case so far as the feeble-minded child is concerned, supervision through some welfare agency in a boarding house might offer a possible solution. However, there may be extreme cases; for these the only recourse may be some more or less permanent institutional care.

The General Influence on Public School Organization, Administration, and Teaching Method. — Although this last objective, which we desire to present briefly, may appear to have relatively little to do with special-school training as such, it is nevertheless of real importance because of its intimate relation to elementary education in general. It seems to us that one of the objectives of special-school training should be the influence it may exercise upon the trend of elementary education for all children, without regard to intellectual capacity. That is, it should direct attention to the needs of normal children who differ among themselves quite as much perhaps as do mentally deficient children. It may tend to stimulate every teacher to consider the child as of first importance rather than making curricular content the chief point of emphasis in the organization and administration of the school.

B. Conditions on Which the Efficiency of Instruction for the Mentally Deficient Depends

The successful organization and functioning of the training program for the feeble-minded depend not only upon those factors considered in the preceding section, such as the recognition of certain fundamental and specific educational objectives, the alleviation of physical and mental handicaps, adequate differentiation for instructional purposes, and the like, but also upon the presence of certain teaching conditions upon which the ultimate value of the training process, either directly or indirectly, depends. It becomes therefore our present purpose to discuss some of the more important factors determining the efficiency of instruction for the mentally deficient.

The Learning Process of the Feeble-Minded Child. — The feeble-minded differ from the superior and normal children only in degree, but not in kind, a premise which has been summarized as follows: "Born alike but different." Thus it would appear that the learning process of the mental defective does not differ materially from that of any normal child. From a psychological point of view, all behavior may be considered and analyzed from the standpoint of more or less definite responses to given situations. Certain responses, such as reflexes and instinctive tendencies to reaction, are commonly spoken of as unlearned, that is, they are held to be innate in the individual; other responses, such as habits, are learned reactions. It is the function of the educative process to modify and extend these responses whereby the individual may be able to adapt himself to that form of society of which he is a member as fully and beneficially as possible. Education as a process thus becomes a matter of adjustment of the individual to his environment. In the light of present-day psychology and from the viewpoint of original endowment factors, the following principles [1] seem tenable: (1) Instincts do not determine many or important human activities; (2) Human beings, irrespective of their mental level, are endowed with a stimulus-response mechanism; (3) The behavior of an organism is due to its tendency to maintain or restore its previous physiological equilibrium; and (4) Individuals vary widely with respect to their receptivity to stimuli (*i.e.*, to situations) and their ability to make responses. Learning *per se* is the selection of the con-

---

[1] For much of the substance in this paragraph I am indebted to Dr. Stuart M. Stoke, of the University of Buffalo.

summatory response to a given situation and takes place mainly by means of two general methods, namely, association wherein temporal contiguity is the conditioning factor; and trial-and-error involving problem situations primarily, responses which are usually overt, and solutions attempted with random responses. In both types of learning, the same laws control alike the responses selected by the feeble-minded and by the normal child. In general, all learning is habit formation, habits being formed upon the basis of these laws or principles. The kinds and complexity of habits which any individual can form depend, then, not only upon the functionality of these principles but also upon the sensitivity and complexity of the nervous system. Thus, human beings learn whatever they are capable of learning according to the same general laws, although not all are apparently capable of learning the same things and in the same way even under optimal conditions. Up to the limitations set by limited endowment of a mental sort, the feeble-minded child is usually found to be able to do the ordinary kind of school work quite accurately correlating with mental age [1] and by means of the same intellectual processes. To a very considerable degree what he learns depends upon the nature and the rate of the intellectual or learning process.

The mentally retarded child if given only ordinary school opportunities seems to get about all he is capable of getting by way of scholastic achievements. This principle we believe tends to show that, in the past, the scholastic training of the feeble-minded, whether under public, private, or institutional auspices, has been somewhat overevaluated; and that far too much consideration has been given to the more purely literary or academic instruction and too little to social, moral, habit, and occupational training. This principle, if it is true, shows that a great deal of money can be saved in the education of large numbers of mentally defective children in our public schools through the incorporation of special-school training in the educative program. Since the intellectual factor, that is, the factor of mental level, is a relatively fixed one, and since, speaking broadly, the school cannot

[1] See Correlation Charts, Appendix, II.

increase this, the teacher's chief function and privilege seems to be that of exercising whatever intelligence the child has and expressing it in terms of school work. In other words, the real educational opportunity of the special school rests not upon an endeavor to increase mental level but to increase mental function. It is perhaps comparable to the carpenter who by virtue of necessity and circumstances has but few tools; these, however, he has been trained to use well in the usual constructional operations. Indeed, he is often a better workman than the carpenter with many tools who has really never learned to use them properly. Likewise the defective child who, although of relatively low mental capacity or level by virtue of its development, is superior morally, socially, and occupationally to his normally endowed brother.

Adaptation of the Educational Process to the Mental Level of the Mentally Deficient Child. — In order that the instructional process may be adapted to the needs, capacities, and interests of the feeble-minded child, it becomes necessary that a relatively large degree of teaching freedom be given the teachers in the special school. This freedom has to do more especially with the general management of the details of the program, the time for scheduling the various subjects to be taught, the length of the class-period, the degree of efficiency essential for individual advancement or promotion, and the interchange of subjects on the part of the individual. This does not mean, however, that the instructional staff is to follow no program at all or a more or less purposeless or meaningless form of procedure. It does mean that individual pupil-advancement must be uppermost in the teacher's plan of instruction, that the mental defective must be placed where he will receive the most beneficial training, and that the method of presentation must be adapted to the mental and educational level of the child. Furthermore, as we shall show in Chapter VIII, there is to be a daily program for the special type of school as there is in other divisions of the public school system. However, the teaching staff must be freed from all restraints that tend to hamper the development of the mental defective.

Pedagogy for the Feeble-Minded. — Broadly speaking, there is no special pedagogy involved in the training of the mentally defective child. The general principles are the same as for the normal child. However, the conditions are very different, the rate of progress and the teaching "pace" much slower. To maintain a rather continuous interest on the part of the mentally deficient, use should be made constantly of graphic, concrete school material. Specifically, the special type of the teaching process is the "object lesson," although simple projects are of value. There is no particular difficulty attached to the planning of the schoolroom education of the subnormal child, since he will do well usually wherever placed, provided he is understood by the school, the work is adapted to his mental age, and the teacher is instructed to be satisfied with the best that the child can do. It is not his liabilities which should be catalogued and indexed; rather, his assets should be appraised, approved, and developed to the utmost.

General Methods of Instruction. — The technique of instruction should be adapted to the mental and educational level of the child. The educational principle that the technique of instruction, including the methods and devices of the teacher, should be adapted to the mental and educational level of the child has found a place in all educational literature, irrespective of the type of individual concerned. In order that the individual pupil may be reached, methods adapted to the particular child's difficulties and deficiencies must find their application. For example, the alphabetic method of teaching to read, now in many systems relegated to the limbo of past pedagogy, as an initial method of instruction, will be found superior to the present-day phonic, word, or sentence method with many mental defectives. This does not necessarily mean, however, that these latter methods are never to be used in the special school; as a matter of fact, once the reading foundation has been made secure through the alphabetic method, it is, in the best of our special institutions, builded upon by the phonic method. When the special difficulties of the child have been discovered, a simple change in method may often bring about really remarkable results.

However, remedial or corrective methods do not function according to an automatic or self-application principle. The classes of the special school should be in charge of highly trained teachers who are able to diagnose and analyze the child's disabilities, and, once having done this, to so adjust the teaching procedure and instructional content to meet the individual needs and capacities. Whether or not it is financially justifiable to give all feeble-minded children the advantages not only of group instruction but more especially of a rather high degree of individualized instruction may be questioned. It seems plausible to state that when a mentally defective child shows very definitely an incapacity or an inability of making further academic progress, he should, wherever possible and practical, be given some form of occupational training and an opportunity to develop personal attitudes and ideals and healthy habits, although none of these phases of the training process should ever be absolutely separated, for they will find their greatest value in the degree to which they are interrelated and interwoven. It is certainly true that children who appear unable to receive further profit from an instructional process of a literary sort are much better off in school under proper supervision and with minds occupied with meaningful and purposeful acts than they would be in some of their own homes or on the streets, where numerous serious social complications are bound to arise sooner or later.

Although the most important teaching process in the special school is the object lesson, there are certain other processes that have a place in the training program. Such instructional means include (*a*) educational tests and measures, the purpose of which is both diagnostic and prognostic — that is, to determine what the child already knows, what he does not know, and the scholastic progress being made from time to time; (*b*) oral and written reviews, stressing the former in the case of the feeble-minded, for the purpose of integrating or unifying the elements of any subject, on the one hand, and of all the related subjects on the other; (*c*) drills, either by means of formal repetition or through the application of similar principles or elements in terms of new subject matter, for the purpose of content fixation and habit formation; and (*d*) teaching in the narrower sense — including the use of books, simple talks and discussions, questions, topics, outlines, drawings, pictures, objects, maps, stencils, exercises, simple experiments, the solution of simple problem situations, and concerted activity or group instruction — a method of procedure more commonly spoken of as the "socialized recitation."

Many things must be taught the feeble-minded child which need not be taught the normal or superior individual, as such, since the latter acquire them more or less incidentally in the teaching process. Much more repetition, drill, and work of a formal nature are necessary with mental defectives than with other children, for whereas the normal and superior grasp the significance upon one or two presentations of the facts, the feeble-minded need many presentations of the same or similar principles. Whatever may be the reason for this — whether drills develop the mental functions or increase the intellectual capacities, or merely develop good study habits, habits of attention and application, or develop a certain physiological capacity for memory or various other skills, or develop a certain mental technique which may function in many situations — whatever be the reasons, formal drill in the case of the feeble-minded children is very effective.

It follows, therefore, that formal exercises and drill should not only be a teaching device of first importance but that the drill processes employed should be made especially interesting, vital, and dynamic. Also, these more formal processes should be supplemented by methods of incidental instruction, by the object lesson, and wherever possible by simple problem or project work.

The so-called "developmental method" of the instruction of mental defectives can be made excellent use of, although in this instance more use must be made of telling, directing, and demonstrating. Further, the process must be of extremely slow procedure, going on by means of very short, related, integrated steps. Although many, possibly the majority, of the children in the special school will be unable upon their own initiative to make any considerable progress, nevertheless if we have as our teaching ideal the development of those powers and capacities of the child which will function, later, independently of the teacher, we should give them the opportunity, with much direction, supervision, and guidance, to attempt the solution of simple problematic situations or even projects commensurate with their motor skill, understanding, and interest range.

The learning process of the feeble-minded child has previously been considered. The first law of learning, that of reintegration, is of particular value. For one of the first and main problems of the teacher is to find out what the child knows and does not know, what he can do and cannot do, what is inclusive and what is exclusive in his range of comprehension, and on the basis of this information, through or by means of similar situations or identical elements, pass on to the following step in the learning procedure. In the teaching of the feeble-minded, it becomes primarily a question of simple gradation, slow procedure, adaptation of the technique of instruction to the mental and educational level of the child, and teaching method, if some degree of success is to be achieved every day.

It has been found advantageous to begin the training of these mentally deficient children with simple exercises which involve the use of the large or axial muscles; exercises such as walking, running, skipping, hopping, going in and out the rounds of a ladder horizontally placed, or up and down steps; simple rhythmic games; dusting, sweeping; handling large tools; driving nails into a section of wood with or without the use of lines to guide the procedure; constructing a crude table or bench; braiding with heavy twine; sewing with a large bodkin or making a design with a large needle on sewing cards; making mats — first, small and coarse, later, larger and finer ones; and numerous other exercises of a rather similar nature. The purpose of these is not the acquisition of skill but the development of bodily and muscular coördination — something in which mentally defective children are almost always deficient. This type of training thus prepares the way for more refined, more complicated, and finer movements and adjustments.

Systematic, orderly progress, the achievement of some degree of success each day are very essential in special-school training. Whether we follow the logical, the psychological, or the so-called "natural order" of learning, some semblance of progress must be adhered to in the development of facts, interests, attitudes, or skills, whatever may be the nature of the activity involved.

The mental level of the children considered in our study necessitates the use of objective, concrete methods of instruction, predominantly. Successful teaching in the case of the feeble-minded involves, therefore, not only a simple gradation of work and slow instructional procedure, as indicated above, but instruction and training by means of group activities, dramatization, field trips, objects, things, and the like, rather than by means of pure abstractions, words, symbols, rules, and formulae. Some one, in this connection, has characterized the feeble-minded as being "thing-minded" rather than "thought-minded." They are not predisposed toward reasoning, cognition, or reflection; rather they are interested in seeing and doing things, in whatsoever is concrete and objective. That is, as a group, they may be characterized as being "eye-minded," "ear-minded," or "muscle-minded." It would appear that, being thus attuned, the actual handling of things and the doing of things tend in themselves to create problem situations and so are of greater value in motivating the work than would be the mere reading or thinking about various situations, or of working out mental solutions of which the feeble-minded are as a rule incapable of determining the correctness.

Nevertheless, in so far as possible, the mentally deficient child should be trained to become as efficient in abstract thinking, in the forming of correct concepts, and in making correct applications as he is in concrete thinking. Progression from the latter to the former must be made by simple, slow gradation from the more concrete to the less concrete. It should be noted, however, that it is never entirely safe to abandon wholly the visible, the tangible, the concrete, the objective; where abstract quantities are used, they must be constantly re-vitalized by concrete reference and application.

Teachers will take constant care to see that interest and attention do not flag. Fundamental interests are those which arise from internal, definite stimuli. New interests are added through old ones by the discovery of those elements which are common to both the old and the new. Attention follows interest; passive attention, a response to but one stimulus, or undivided attention, is of much greater value than active or forced attention, a response given in the presence of conflicting stimuli and hence divided. The things taught best in the special school are those most nearly related to the child's interests, both fundamental and acquired. Thus it is that manual work makes a strong appeal to the subnormal child, appealing as it does to certain instinctive tendencies and interests, such as play, constructivity, manipulation, activation, and muscular exercise.

In order, then, that the work of the school might be organized in accordance with the doctrine of interest, the idea seems to have arisen that children should commence their training with problem- or project-work — for example, the making of useful things — rather than with single operations or formal drills. This is of course a very commendable tendency, but many authorities possessing extensive experience with mental defectives of low grade or with serious muscular incoördinations, feel that better results are obtained by formal drills on simple processes. To start the child who has no control of the tools or of the elementary processes on complicated problems will cause blundering, the spoiling of tools and materials, confusion, and the loss of confidence. We should emphasize that the purpose of manual training at the outset for these cases is to improve muscular coördination, to develop hand skill, to acquire dexterity in handling tools, rather than to produce an artistic product, that these results are achieved most rapidly by repeated drills, and that the method is not contrary to the doctrine of interest or of the psychology of habit-formation, in so far at least as the mental defective is concerned, since as a rule he enjoys repetition.

The "object lesson" is a teaching device which has for its main purpose an increase of knowledge by means of the direct study of materials, processes, or conditions; it is an application of the concrete, an endeavor to subordinate the printed page to the use of the individual's sense, and the repetition of mere words or abstractions to relatively clear ideas concerning real things. Thus, by means of the object lesson when properly presented, the mentally deficient child gains a first-hand acquaintance as well as an understanding of the concrete factors which make up his environment. From the point of view of our discussion, this method or teaching device seems to present three values of importance: (a) it is a dynamic means of presentation, being vitally motivated and so arousing a high degree of interest, causing the interest thus aroused to be maintained for a considerable length of time; (b) when taught in its relationships, the information which the child gains takes on a new meaning. Thus, when presented in terms of unification of the more important aspects of the educative process, it takes on many new meaningful aspects. Instead, then, of these various aspects being pure abstractions, the child comes to view them as real means of obtaining a mastery over his environment. At the same time an opportunity is presented whereby the knowledge thus obtained becomes functional. Transfer of training takes place by means of the common elements in the activities involved; hence, whatever direct training of a practical kind the child receives is dependent not only upon the conscious effort of the teacher but also upon the resemblance, *i.e.*, the identity of elements, between the objects, materials, or activities under consideration and the later everyday life of the child. And (c) the feeble-minded child requires repetition and constant drill throughout the training period. Since the object lesson presents a vitalized situation involving like processes in the various phases of the activity, many means are given for practice and habit formation.

In terms of the feeble-minded and the training process of the special school, two suggestions of considerable practicality follow. First, those activities which make an appeal to both fundamental and acquired interests should be used, since attention and coöperative effort follow interest. Secondly, object lessons should be selected on the basis of continuity of application.

As previously stated, with the mental defective, it is not so much the acquisition of knowledge that is of value; it is the habits, attitudes, and skills formed. Many subnormals are natural drifters, due in many instances to the fact that they were inadequately trained in continuity of application.

Where there is departmentalized instruction, proficiency can be attained by means of complete coöperation and conferences among the teachers concerned; otherwise, the teacher can present the object lesson in a relatively independent manner, although at all times considering what has gone before and what is to follow, and so teach it in its ultimate relationships. With feeble-minded children, materials must be of a simple, concrete, and highly practical nature, and throughout the process much suggestion and guidance must be exercised by the teacher. From the present point of view the project method *per se* is an advanced step in the teaching process, being, as it would appear, especially applicable to normal and superior children, although possibly feasible for the mental defective if presented in the simplest of terms free from complicated abstractions.

Constantly teachers must develop the technique of lesson planning. Opposed to the rather common opinion, it is probable that lesson-planning is of greater necessity in the work of the special school than in the regular grades — assuming that instruction is to proceed on a basis of equal efficiency. In contrast to the many aids and devices at the command of the regular-school teacher, under present conditions the program of the special school appears to be organized in a fairly general way and the teacher is expected to exercise considerable freedom in the planning and presentation of details, subject to certain general restrictions. The real teacher will not only adjust and shift the training procedure in accordance with the varying needs and capacities of the mentally defective child at the time of entrance in the class, but more especially as his developing requirements present themselves to view — a really difficult task in itself. It is apparent that this cannot be done satisfactorily except through constant study of the many problems involved, through careful preparation, and through daily lesson-planning. For the trained and experienced teacher an outline form is usually sufficient; for the inexperienced teacher an elaborate plan, involving leading questions, teaching devices, means of approach, and processes, is usually necessary.

Whatever seat-work there may be should include matters of a simple problem-solving nature which tend to challenge thought and necessitate continuity of application — all interrelated with the actual work of the recitation itself. Further, it should offer an opportunity for application of principles learned during the recitation.

In spite of their intellectual handicaps, in spite of what we hear from various sources, these children continue to present many unsolved problems both to the educator and psychologist. Even so, in spite of the reputed simplicity of this particular teaching process, it cannot be overemphasized that the real teacher, aware of the wonderful opportunity and imbued with a true professional spirit, will receive her greatest reward in the satisfaction of a task well done, namely, the positive social, moral, occupational, and economic transformation she has helped to bring about in her pupils. Thus she will not shirk her responsibilities.

With mentally deficient children, praise and encouragement are very effective incentives to best efforts. Small rewards — candy, for example — given at the completion of the activity, are usually as effective with children of this type as are rewards of intrinsic value among normal children. Many times, simply a word of commendation or an encouraging glance is enough to bring about redoubled efforts and assiduity. It is true, of course, that herein rests a danger. Mental defectives are very commonly self-centered and egotistical; hence, these propensities may be very easily overstimulated by such means. Properly used, praise and encouragement are legitimate and worth while for bringing forth the best in feeble-minded children; and so, if understood, these rewards may find an important place in the pedagogical category of the special-school teacher.

Size of the Class. — A factor most frequently emphasized for successful special-school training is that the size of the group for instructional purposes be small. It would appear that in actual practice the enrollment in classes for mental defectives varies from 8 or 9 to 20 or 25 in different cities and countries. A recent investigation concerning the practice in American cities has revealed that the established enrollment was 15 pupils per class in 42 cities, 20 in 9, 12 in 6, 10 in 3, 15 or less in 67, and 20 or less in 92 cities. In only five cities was a registration exceeding twenty pupils found. State laws in Massachusetts, New Jersey, and New York limit the number to fifteen. On the other hand, there are found those who feel that there should not be more than four or five pupils per teacher, upon the supposition that under such conditions the teacher would be able to give these subnormals more attention, assistance, encouragement, drill, stimulation, and supervision, thus enabling the pupils to progress more rapidly.[1]

In connection with the training of feeble-minded boys and girls certain objections to small instructional groups are obvious. Under present conditions, it is too expensive to provide four or five of these children with the proper form of instruction and educational equipment necessary — as well as high-salaried teachers. However, in segregating the mentally deficient children, the progress of the normal and superior children is facilitated. Further, educationally speaking, the very small class is not justifiable. The intellectually subnormal child can very easily be overwhelmed by too much instruction. After the intellectual saturation point has been reached, the law of diminishing returns becomes functional in so far as instruction and drill, on the one hand, and labor, on the other, are concerned. It takes the mentally defective child a much longer time to acquire and digest information and to form his "hierarchy of habits." However, whatever merit attaches itself to these arguments against very small classes for the feeble-minded, we feel that the third point is of much greater importance from the point of view of our discussion. Children, more especially mental defectives, gain a great deal of benefit, particularly of a

---

[1] Wallin, J. E. W.: *Education of Handicapped Children*, pp. 134–135. Houghton Mifflin Co.

social sort, from the reciprocal give-and-take, from the stimulation, and the arousal of interest, which come from an orderly and well-conducted classroom procedure. Feeble-minded children learn the necessary lessons of practical life much better from contacts with numerous companions than from two or three classmates. In fact, what the typical subnormal child needs perhaps most of all is social adaptation. This is best developed through actual contacts in the classroom, the gymnasium, on the playground, and in the shops. Instruction of a highly individualized type, supplemented by concerted activity, is to be desired with the normal and superior; for the feeble-minded the point of emphasis should be on group activities of all feasible kinds.

It would appear that the size of the class for mental defectives will depend upon the degree of deficiency, mental, social, moral, or otherwise; upon the degree of homogeneity within the class; and upon the nature of the subject-matter to be presented. The teaching of a group of twenty rather evenly graded subnormals would presumedly be no more difficult nor heavier from the point of view of the teaching load than would be the instruction of fifteen children of varying mental levels. For our purposes, therefore, an instructional group of approximately twenty, organized upon the basis of sex, may be suggested as typical of our special-school training program.

Summary and Conclusions. — The general aim or objective of special-school training is to make of the feeble-minded children coming under its instruction law-abiding citizens, socially adaptable, and economically self-sufficient through worth-while labor and productivity.

The specific aims are: (1) The need of a psycho-educational analysis of each individual in accordance with the plan advocated under *Standardized Fields of Inquiry* (Chapter I, pp. 9-10); (2) An adapted curriculum, suited to the mental and educational level of the children concerned, with well-trained teachers and well-equipped classrooms; (3) Training of a prevocational and vocational nature, with an emphasis on the former of a more or less diversified type. In other words, provision should be made in the special school for a broad, basic training, rather than a highly specialized type, the primary aim being the cultivation of a right attitude of work; (4) Mental hygiene, including sex hygiene, the aim being emotional stability and normal social relations in simple life situations; (5) Health education, as an integral part of the educational program rather than an extra-curricular activity, the purpose being the development of physique and habits of health; (6) Social conformity, including good citizenship; a knowledge of moral principles; stable motor coordinations; courteous manners; clear speech; and the like. Specifically, the making of the feeble-minded child to act in accordance with the recognized principles of society and to appear and act in just about the same manner that any ordinarily intelligent person appears and acts; (7) Guidance and supervision, since much of the success of the special school will depend upon the responsibility for the mental defective exercised after he leaves school at the age of sixteen or before; and (8) The general influence upon public school organization, administration, and teaching method by an endeavor to fit the school to the child rather than the child to the school.

The learning process of the feeble-minded does not differ materially from that of the normal child. In teaching the mental defective, it becomes a question of simple gradation, slow procedure, adaptation of the technique of instruction to the mental and educational level of the child, and teaching method. Thus, systematic, orderly procedure, and the achievement of some degree of success each day, are particularly important in the special-school training. Likewise the size of the class is an important question for consideration. For our purposes an instructional group of approximately fifteen to twenty, organized upon the basis of sex, may be suggested as typical for our special-school training program.

With these objectives for special-school training and the conditions upon which the efficiency of instruction for the mental defective depends in mind, it now becomes our purpose to consider the classification for instruction and training of the intellectually handicapped.

CHAPTER III

AN ANALYSIS OF THE INSTRUCTIONAL PROGRAM FOR MENTAL DEFECTIVES

In the present and following chapter it is our purpose to present an analysis of the instructional program for mental defectives. The training process has been divided into two general divisions, the first including sense, manual, physical, and occupational training; the second, the more important phases of academic work in the special school. It will be seen that an attempt has been made to consider each of these phases with respect to specific aims, content, and methods of actual teaching involved, and to interrelate these around one central core of development — more especially the mental aspect of life. No one factor of instruction should be interpreted as an isolated unit in itself, although it presents apparent specific objectives, but only as a means of a well-rounded development of the individual child, socially, morally, occupationally, and economically.

A. Sense Training

In the introduction of the English translation of *The Montesori Method*[1] credit is given for the fact that "much of the material used by Dr. Fernald at Waverley is almost identical with the Montesori material," and then, parenthetically, "it may interest American readers to know that Dr. Seguin, upon whose work that of Dr. Fernald is based, was once head of the school at Waverley." In other words, the Montesori material is almost identical with that used at the Walter E. Fernald State School and the "physiological method" which we shall discuss, with certain modifications and extensions, is one which for seventy

[1] Montesori, M.: *The Montesori Method*. Macmillan.

years has been used at Waverley. The impress that Dr. Seguin and Dr. Fernald have left on that school is still shown in the methods and materials used there, especially in the training of the extreme low-grade feeble-minded. The discovery of the moron groups by means of improved diagnostic and psychological methods has made possible the approach to rehabilitation, not primarily perhaps by the method of psychological education, but through social education. The primary object has been to enable these individuals to get along in the world by making the most of their innate capacities.

Meaning and Purpose of Sense Training. — Sense training is not a process or system whereby the sense organs are perfected or refined, although it may render perhaps the nervous pathways or arcs more permeable and so improve their conductivity. Its chief function is mental, developing what we may choose to term the "sensory consciousness" of the child. Where properly directed, sense training should increase the speed, accuracy, and range of observation. It should also help the child to discriminate more fully between stimuli, to notice small differences, to acquire facts regarding varied situations, to compare and contrast facts, to draw correct inferences and conclusions from the facts thus compared, to classify facts and organize and arrange them in logical sequence, and to give the right names to those facts discovered. Indeed, one of the most important objectives of sense training is the development of systematic and methodical observation.

Need for Sense Training of the Feeble-Minded. — The normal child — through his play, games, playful occupations, and constant experimentation — may secure all the training of a sensory and motor nature required in his contact with the environment. But with the mentally subnormal child the case is radically different; he must have such experience, contacts, or training literally thrust upon him.

Types of Sense Training to Be Given. — Owing to the fact that scholastic work even in its simplest and most elementary form is impossible with the lowest grades of mental subnormality, *i.e.*, the idiot and the low-grade imbecile, exercise must predominate in the training of such, preferably as a part of the daily routine. If the energies of the children can be consumed by simple forms of work and outdoor recreation, they will not have much time for conduct of a disorderly nature which might otherwise arise in the earlier stages of the training process. Besides long walks under the guidance of a teacher, certain exercises can be brought into use in a methodical way.

Two of the best forms of this nature and for this purpose are found in the stone pile and the "walking ring."

(1) *Stone Piles.* — This consists simply of two rings or squares placed a considerable distance apart. Stones, whose size varies according to the needs of the class using them, are placed in either ring or square. The exercise consists in carrying them from one ring to the other.

(2) *Walking Rings.* — These walking rings are an excellent source of exercise for the low-grade defective. The better ones are made of cement, drained so they can be used both summer and winter, with a covering similar to that of the top of a tent or an awning. No standard size would be adhered to necessarily, since size is conditional upon conditions and available space. The exercise consists in walking around the ring or pavilion in single file, by twos, by threes, and so on, varying the line of march as much as possible.

In pre-kindergarten work, a walking ladder, a balance beam, and steps are used.

(1) *The Walking Ladder.* — The walking ladder is built upon stands so that it can be readily placed upon the floor. It is eight feet long, twelve inches wide, and with rungs placed about one foot apart. The child is taught to walk, placing the feet alternately in between the rungs, or upon them.

(2) *The Balance Beam.* — The balance beam is eight feet in length and four inches in width. The child is taught to walk in a manner similar to that of walking a rail.

(3) *Steps.* — The steps consist of three steps, each six inches in height. Special care should be taken that the child goes up and down these steps in a proper way — not, for example, going up in the usual manner and down backwards using both

hands and feet. Any incorrect movement should be rectified at the earliest possible moment.

For sense training proper,[1] the work is directed along the following lines:

(1) *Touch.* — The material for training the sense of touch is usually kept in a large bag. One of two methods is ordinarily followed. With the material in the bag, the child is asked to put in his hand and grasp one of the objects. Or else, with the material upon the tables, the child is blindfolded and then places his hand on objects and substances of contrasting qualities. At first, he is expected to notice only the different sensations produced by the contrast; gradually he is asked to select various objects by the sense of touch alone. Later he is asked to name them. When the object has been identified, it is brought out in full view, as in case of the material in the bag, and a minute or two is taken during which it is discussed — the use which is made of it, where it is to be found, etc.

The materials used in this training should include practically all the common articles which the child is likely to meet either in the school or out of it. A list of those articles which have been found practicable follows:

baseball	buttons	soap
worsted ball	nails	mitten
doll	tablespoon	saucer
china egg	teaspoon	faucet taps
domino	knife	screw driver
chalk	fork	spool
tin box	butter knife	croquet ball
hairbrush	shoe laces	bottle
small brush	suspenders	cork
sandpaper	pocketbook	thimble
lead pipe	toothbrush	screws
stone	comb	hook
wooden block	kid glove	shoe
tin cups	handkerchief	garters
safety pin	hammer	door knob

(2) *Hearing.* — For the development of the sense of hearing the classroom should be provided with a small, serviceable screen.

[1] See Seguin, Edward: *Idiocy, and Its Treatment by the Physiological Method.*

The teacher first gives the sound from behind the screen; the children are then questioned as to what animal or instrument is associated in their minds with the sound. As in touch training, the children will notice at first the contrasts, gradually coming to distinguish the various sounds so as to be able to name them. When once the children have named the particular sound successfully, a short discussion is held relative to the object under consideration. If an animal, questions regarding its use, appearance, and the like, are asked; if a means of conveyance, often the pupils can tell much about it. Sounds representing the common things of life should be presented, of which the following may be considered typical:

tambourine	siren whistle	dinner bell
cymbals	rooster crow	watchman's rattle
drum	bird	hen cackle
tin horn	ordinary whistle	sleigh bell
triangle	ordinary bell	cowbell

(3) *Smell.* — The material for this phase of sense training should be contained in small glass-stopper bottles. The bottle is passed around the class by the teacher and each child receives a good whiff of its contents. By gradual steps they soon come to name it, either, in the lowest mental cases, as pleasant or unpleasant, or by actual name.

Although the list of materials used should obviously include only those things common to the present and future experiences of the children, yet it ought to be made as complete as possible. Some of the things which may well be used are as follows:

ammonia	gasoline	oil of lavender
vinegar	camphor	peppermint
vanilla	sachet powder	oil of wintergreen
iodoform	formaldehyde	perfume
coffee	kerosene	extract of lemon
cinnamon	turpentine	tea

(4) *Taste.* — As in the case of smell, the materials used in the training of the sense of taste should be contained in small bottles with glass stoppers. Small sticks can be used as a means of placing a small portion of the substance into the child's mouth.

Both ends can be used and then it can be thrown away. After the children have tasted the substance in question, their facial expressions will usually express the result — whether pleasant or unpleasant. Gradually they acquire the ability to name it, after which a short talk can be given as to its usefulness.

Again, common substances should be procured for use, the objective being to acquaint the child with that with which it will most likely meet in everyday life. The following is suggestive of the materials to be used:

quinine	sugar	cinnamon
salt	ginger	vinegar
mustard	tea	molasses
coffee	alum	pepper
tannic acid	cocoa	cloves
peppermint	castor oil	wintergreen

It will, through patient and persistent instruction, be possible to train the children so that they are able to classify the various tastes. Upon questioning, the teacher will receive such descriptions of the taste as sweet, sour, bitter, tart, and salty.

(5) *Color.* — Sense training with respect to color differentiation is to be given with all the individual attention to the children possible. Various methods may be employed, of which the following may be considered basic and suggestive.

Place a large field of color, preferably a square piece of cloth, before the child. In the center of the table have a pile of small pieces of cloth of various colors. The exercise consists in having the child pick out and place upon the large field in front of him the pieces of cloth which correspond or "match" the one he is given.

The teacher may pick up a piece of cloth of one color and ask a child to get her another piece just like it.

The children can also be asked to name the colors. In this exercise three questions can be asked: "Is this color blue?"; "What color is this?"; "Get me a piece of blue."

The materials for this type of work should include not only various colors of cloth, but colored sticks, blocks, beads, paper strips, and bean bags. The applications should be simple but as practical as possible. For example, a particular application may be in the form of comparison with the child's clothing — his blue hat, his white blouse, his red necktie, for example.

(6) *Plain Form.* — For this phase of the sense-training process plain figures only are used. Two of each kind are spread at random over the long table. The teacher, for example, points to the figure and asks the child to get her one like it from the table. A wall chart can be used in connection with this training. The teacher centers attention on a particular figure on the wall chart, and directs the child to bring a duplicate of it to her. Practically every geometrical figure is used in this work. For the solids the dimensions should be about two inches in height and two inches at the base.

cone	rectangle	hexagonal cylinder
pyramid	cube	sphere
cylinder	square	ellipse
triangle	half cylinder	double cone
half sphere	trapezoid	circle

(7) *Color and Form.* — The same geometrical forms as used in the "plain form work" are used in "color and form," but in this case they are of the four colors — red, blue, green, yellow. Duplicates of each type should be placed upon the table and the same procedure followed as outlined under "plain form." The use of a chart is of advantage in this work. The figures are colored to correspond with those upon the table.

(8) *Color, Form, and Position.* — Four rectangular blocks are placed in front of each pupil and also before the teacher. The blocks should be uniform in position — that is, the order of colors should be the same.

The teacher stands in front of the class, which is assembled about the large table, and her movements are to be followed by the class. For example: she stands the red block on end; the class does the same. At first some of the children will set up a green block. In such a case rectification should follow immediately, whereby the child in error may come to distinguish between red and green. She can place the red and green blocks crosswise upon the yellow and blue. The children do the same. Thus

46   WHAT SHALL THE PUBLIC SCHOOLS DO

any number of combinations can be obtained, by means of the four colored blocks' placement.

A convenient size for these blocks is eight inches long and one and three-fourths or two inches square. Four colors are used, viz. — red, green, blue, yellow.

(9) *Form Boards.* — These inset boards should be used in connection with the Form Table. Three of the original boards used by Dr. Seguin are still in use at Waverley. Other form boards which can be used are: the Dearborn 3c; the Shaw Picture; and the Lincoln Hollow Square.

(10) *Common Object Table.* — On this table it is desirable to have small models of the common objects with which the child is likely to come in contact in the world outside of the school-room. The articles selected may be left to the teacher's judgment, for she is acquainted presumedly with the child and its environment.

Much time and patience are required to give the child a clear idea of each one of the objects. Various devices and methods may be employed, some of which are as follows:

The teacher holds up model and asks what it is. There follows a discussion on the subject.

The teacher asks a child to bring a specific object.

Some of the objects which may form a nucleus of this division are:

ships	coffee pot	rolling-pin
rowboat	frying pan	plates
clothespins	broom	cups
pitchers	knife	saucers
table	fork	dustpan
hairbrush	spoon	pail
comb	bed	washboard
mirror	chair	toothbrush
automobile	street car	sled

In fact, most of the common objects can be added to this table with which, in the judgment of the teacher, the children are likely to need an acquaintanceship.

(11) *Animal Object Table.* — On this table, similar to that of the common object study, small models of the most common animals are scattered about on the table. The same procedure

follows as noted in the preceding section, with a brief but definite discussion upon the animal in question.

A few suggestions are given below but these can be changed at the discretion of the teacher in charge.

fish	horse	elephant
turtle	cow	bear
giraffe	sheep	mouse
pig	donkey	rat
monkey	dog	frog
hen	cat	lion
squirrel	tiger	camel
buffalo	goat	rabbit

Simultaneous Commissions. — Once the varied senses have been sufficiently trained, the requisite motor coördinations formed, and the various objects differentiated to a fairly successful degree, the Seguin method presents an admirable opportunity for training the mentally retarded child in simultaneous commissions. The commissions must be very simple, direct, and within the range of the child's mental and physical experiences. Some samples of these commands follow:

(a) "Walk the ladder; put a yellow block on the window sill; and bring a red one to me."

(b) "Walk the balance beam; close the door; and place the red block on the chair."

(c) "Put the red block on the table; open the door; and bring the blue blocks over to me."

It will be recognized at once that the foregoing commissions are similar to year V, 6, in the *Stanford-Binet Individual Test of Intelligence.* Obviously, children on the average, with a mental age of less than five years, will be unable to put into operation three commissions, although they may be able to carry out two. Care should be taken, therefore, to put the commissions in the form of the mental capabilities involved, gradually where possible leading up to commissions such as those noted above.

Form of Report. — The form of report used for the pupils of the Pre-Kindergarten Room should be as specific and comprehensible as possible. In filling out this report, unmeaning terminology should be carefully avoided. Clear, concise, accurate descriptions of the child's ability should be found in each report. A convenient and helpful form of report is found below:

REPORT FOR PRE-KINDERGARTEN (SEGUIN) TRAINING

Name   Date
Sex
Date of admission to School
Age (at date of admission)
Mental Age
Coöperation   Application

SPECIAL GRADING

I. Sense training
   Touch
   Taste
   Smell
   Hearing
   Color
   Form
II. Dictation and Imitation with colored blocks
III. Hand Training
IV. Balance Beam   Walking Ladder   Steps
V. Deportment
VI. Personal Habits
VII. Special Notes

                                   Teacher
                                   (signed)

Fundamental Principles concerning the Pre-Kindergarten (Seguin) Training. — One hour is a convenient period for the class to remain in the classroom. Usually this is not too long. Since the work is varied, the children do not become tired or inattentive. As their powers of concentration are necessarily weak and uncontrollable, care must be taken that the child is not kept too long at one task.

In conducting the class it is well to keep the following items in mind:

(1) *Bulletin Boards.* — These constitute a large factor in the educational system. They contain special notices to the teachers and lists of classes with specific mental ages. Likewise, everything of importance to the class can be posted on this board.

(2) *Use of Object.* — Try not to talk to a child about anything unless it is possible to show him a picture or model of the thing in question.

(3) *Roll Call.* — At roll call the child is taught to stand up when he hears his name called.

(4) *Bearing of Pupils.* — Some form of discipline should prevail in the Seguin Room. Marching from one table to the other; hands off the table except when following out some command of the teacher; standing erect at the table; no loud talking or laughing; sitting quietly when necessary. These are a few of the things which will help keep the class in good order.

(5) *Competition.* — The spirit of competition should be encouraged whenever possible. When a child has accomplished successfully the task given him by the teacher, it adds a lot of interest to the class by allowing the other members of the class to clap for him.

(6) *Aid.* — The teacher in her enthusiasm for her work is liable unconsciously to aid the child too much. Try to help him a little but teach the child to do it himself. Never do it for him.

The chief requisite is a true missionary spirit on the part of the teacher. She must have the child at heart, first, last, and all the time. No child can be repulsive to her. Filthy habits, dirty faces, disgusting appearance — all must have a power of attraction to her rather than that of repulsion. Progress is slow; the pupils exasperating; obedience to commands reluctant. Yet through all this she must love the children, see them as they are, and work toward their betterment. A young inexperienced teacher desirous of learning, anxious to be trained, who loves the children and who in turn is loved by them, can do miracles where a trained teacher of the old pedagogical school would fail utterly.

Summary. — Thus, long before the children are prepared to enter upon the work of even the kindergarten, they are practiced in sense training in the Seguin Room, as it is designated at the Fernald State School. From a glass case filled with toys the teacher takes out, for example, a miniature hen. "Have you any feet?" she asks the immobile group before her. Most of them do not know. Next she inquires, "What do you eat with?" This they know, and so she talks about the hen's bill, its eggs and chickens, as the pupils learn to recognize pictures of the barnyard and to crow and cluck. Toy kitchen stoves and tea sets furnish a dolls' tea party, and through those and similar objects there is imported a knowledge of the names and purposes of the things concerning everyday life. Such exercises or training processes would be needless for normal children of ten years, the average age of those of the Seguin groups. The recognition of different pieces of wood, by their shapes, for example, constitutes an advanced lesson. The teacher holds up a longitudinal piece, and a child matches it from the pile lying on the table, while another child tries to make a square piece fit a circular one. "When do you see stars?" is the next question, as the teacher holds up a star-shaped piece of wood. Often it is two or three months before there is any clear comprehension of this or a similar question. As time goes on, an unusually bright child, relatively speaking, when asked to find a ball like the one shown him, finds a solution in its double or a dumb-bell.

Earlier than all this instruction and its accompanying moral lessons is the hand training "Put your hands together; put your fingers in and out; put your hands in a circle; put up your thumbs; close your other fingers; open them." For each of these seemingly simple exercises the teacher, day after day, for months even, takes the flabby nerveless hands of each child in her own and goes through all these maneuvers of progress with them. When the hands are partly trained, the children are taught to pick up pins from the floor. Then they wind string from one ball to another, and put little sticks in a board pierced with holes, both exceedingly difficult feats for them to accomplish. They learn to recognize objects inclosed in a bag by feeling their shape, and to know the difference between various sounds. Through spices and bottles containing liquids of various kinds they acquire a sense of taste and smell.

The chief function, as previously noted, of this hand and sense training is mental, developing what we have chosen to call a "sensory consciousness." When a sufficient degree of progress has been attained, the child enters the kindergarten, where the occupations and games are largely modified to meet the capacities and needs of these children. As would be expected, at the F. S. S., there is not such a wide or marked division between the kindergarten and the primary school as among normal children, a principle which of necessity should be carried out and paralleled in the type of special-school training advocated in this discussion.

B. Manual Training

Handwork, or manual training, deals with things rather than ideas. It is the objective way to make these children think, learning to do through doing. Dr. Fernald has said, "In this education by doing, we not only have a very valuable means of exercising and developing the dormant faculties and defective bodies of our pupils, but at the same time we are training them to become useful men and women." Dr. Goddard has said: "The one thing that fits all these children, the one thing that draws out whatever is to be drawn out of them, is training of the hand, manual training, industrial training."

Manual and industrial training are rapidly becoming the most prominent feature of the educational training now being given in our best schools, public or private, for the feeble-minded. Here are being carried on by the pupils themselves carpentry, painting, brick-making, shoemaking, tailoring, dressmaking, broom and mattress making, domestic work, and, where conditions allow, stock raising, poultry culture, dairying, farming, and other industries. These not only prove profitable in the way of financial return to the community involved, but offer a splendid outlet for the overactive and disciplinary cases, besides offering, as we shall later show, an occupational basis for those who are later to be placed under supervision in the community.

Aim and Purpose. — The aim and purpose of all handwork should be:

(1) To develop that muscular coördination and control which is lacking in most low-grade cases.

(2) To increase ability for social adjustment or adaptation, through experience in coöperation.

(3) With the higher groups, practical experience should lead toward vocational training.

(4) To cultivate self-reliance and keep interest and attention cheerfully engaged.

(5) To develop habits of observation, accuracy, and neatness.

(6) To develop imagination, originality, judgment, selection, and discrimination in so far as each child is physiologically and psychologically capable.

(7) To satisfy the inner urge of constructivity.

The Nature and General Content of Manual or Hand Training. — Having educated or trained the various senses, we can pass on to the training of the hand, or manual training, as it is called. In ordinary kindergarten work much attention is paid to the training of the hand, but, previous to the time when this was first brought into use, Seguin was at work training the hands of the feeble-minded, and his methods have to a great extent been incorporated with those which are now in use.

If we notice a feeble-minded child who has received no training at all, we usually find that there is a great lack of muscular coördination; the hands perform with difficulty such simple acts as buttoning a coat or even picking up a pin. In the case of the normal child this power is acquired early in life; but with feeble-minded children, particularly if they have had no previous education, it is not acquired until late — and if education is discontinued too soon, it may never be acquired at all. Many parents have the idea that our only object is to teach their feeble-minded children to read, write, count, paint, etc. The idea that manual training, first as training, later perhaps as production, is required, never enters their minds. No doubt this concept is due to the fact that the ordinary child acquires manual training almost without any direct training; whereas feeble-minded children do not acquire it unless specifically instructed in it. The hand of the mentally subnormal child is exceedingly soft and supple; in directing the child to use the fingers it will be seen that the muscular movements are badly directed, since the coördinating power which directs these movements is not properly developed. How, then, are we to develop this coördinating power? By means of manual training, we believe. The training of the hand to useful occupation is simply a later stage of the cultivation of purposive movements aided by the progressive development of the senses and the intelligence. If one notices a baby, a number of spontaneous movements will be seen — movements which are apparently quite purposeless; but as age and intelligence commence to dawn, these responses or spontaneous movements are intuitively or under direction brought gradually into useful coördination. In some low-class idiots we detect quite purposeless or automatic movements — such as rocking to and fro, flicking the fingers before the eyes, and so on. Such movements have to be replaced by purposive movements. Again, there are children who suffer from spasmodic or convulsive movements. Some children suffer from athetosis, an affection producing constant, slow, irregular movements, and in such cases it is essential to bring about through proper exercise a coördination of the muscular movements. For example, a child suffering from this athetosis should be set to pick up and place in their proper cavities the marbles on a solitaire board. Afterwards, what is termed a "peg board" will be found useful. The pegs first have to be grasped by the thumb and forefinger and then inserted into the holes in which they fit tightly. Then come exercises in threading beads and perforating picture cards, and the building of bricks into various forms. All these exercises are exceedingly useful for children lacking muscular coördination, as well as for those restless children who are often met with in this class. In all these exercises the hand is supplemented by the eye, since, as a rule, the hand and eye work together.

Form boards will be found useful in cultivating accuracy in grasping objects. These are flat pieces of wood with circular, triangular, square, oblong, etc., cavities into which correspondingly shaped pieces of wood have to be placed. At first, the tendency is for the feeble-minded child to put the square in the circular hole, but as time advances he comes to distinguish the varieties of shapes and sizes, placing the square in the square hole, the circle in the circular hole, the triangle in the triangular hole, and so on. The size-board may also be used. This is a flat piece of wood in which there are rounded cavities of various sizes into which circular pieces of wood have to be placed so that the small inset goes into the small cavity, and the larger circles into the larger cavities. Another method is to have a cushion covered with spots into which the child sticks pins; this will be found useful in training the hand for the more refined muscular movements.

Easy drawing lessons, painting, and making pictures with colored crayons, are also of value. Dressing lessons may be given with advantage, not only as an individual but as a class exercise, in order to assist the children to put on their clothes. Buttoning and unbuttoning clothes, lacing shoes, and tying bowknots not only effect this but secure that finer adjustment of the fingers so essential to the development of the feeble-minded.

Occupational Sequence of Manual Training. — With respect to industrial training, many of the pre-kindergarten and kindergarten occupations are very serviceable preliminaries to handicraft. Paper-weaving is a splendid preparation for sewing and darning; and the instrument which pricks perforated pictures will, in the hands of a fairly skillful pupil, often result in employment in the shoemaker's shop; sloyd-work, or simple manual arts, may in time lead on to carpentry. It is to be remembered that these exercises do not merely train the fingers but also through them the intelligence as well. Clay modeling, variegated paper mats, and bead necklaces not only train the fingers and the fine musculature but serve as stimulants to the spirit of emulation. There are many children who seem to learn more with their hands than with their heads, and with these industrial training has a distinct advantage over book learning. However, the actual employment to which the child is put will depend to a considerable degree upon his personal likes and dislikes. Some, for example, will prefer carpentry; others, cane-making; others, gardening. For children who live in cities certain of these occupations cannot be made use of. For these, there are many kinds of work which will be found useful for the employment of manual-training. Cane-weaving and basket-making are easily learned; knitting, crocheting, and darning and laundry work should be learned, since these will serve useful purposes in the home.

Elementary Handwork. — Handwork offers many opportunities to busy children. All simple work may be done at the large table, including zig-zag puzzles, peg-boards, weaving, lacing, etc.

The following is a list of those activities which have been found useful in the *Pre-Kindergarten and Kindergarten Rooms:*

bead stringing	sewing cards
building blocks	paper cutting
lacing strips	button stringing
braiding strips	cloth cutting
(These may be hung on the table)	pin frames
	large peg-boards
large sewing cards	button straps
objects to pick up	button mold
jig-saw puzzle	stringing
knitting	darning frames
sock knitting	small peg-boards
top spinning	animal peg-boards
worsted sewing	spool winding
plain sewing	ruling
shoes to lace	weaving frames
shoes to button	hand looms

For boys, training and not production in its strict interpretation is the aim of the elementary handwork. The activities or exercises of an elementary nature we may note as follows:

(1) *Pounding blocks.* — Here the children are given hammers and allowed to pound at random — first, with the right hand, then with the left, and then with both. The teacher should see that they keep in one form of rhythm, notwithstanding the random results.

(2) *Color table.* — This table is conducted similarly to that in pre-kindergarten, and so need not be elaborated upon at this point.

(3) *Sandpaper table.* — Here the children sandpaper at random the playroom blocks used in sense training.

(4) *Cane-seating table.* — Here the seats are made with rope rather than with cane. The weaving process involved is, however, the same in the case of either material when the child completes a seat. The rope can be taken out and done over again.

(5) *Rag sewing.* — All the rags of every size and description are gathered together in the lower-grade room, and the boys sew them together, later rolling them into balls. They are sent then to the proper room where they are used in making rugs.

(6) *Individual Work Benches.* — At these benches is done the planing, sawing, whittling, etc.; first, at random, and later more or less purposive.

The two following schedules comprise the work done in the elementary handwork for boys:

Schedule A	Schedule B
Pounding at random	Driving nails to a line
Crosscutting at random	Crosscutting to a line
Splitting at random	Splitting to a line
Planing at random	Planing to a line
Using hatchet at random	Using hatchet to a line
Whittling at random	Whittling to a line
Sandpapering at random	Definite sandpapering

The classes in this work are approximately one hour in length. A sample of an hour's activity in this phase of the training process shows clearly that considerable variety is essential with children, especially with the mentally subnormal: *hammering; color sorting; planing; sawing; cane seating; rag sewing.*

It will be noted that the activities listed under Schedule A are random activities; those under Schedule B, definite or "to a line." By the former, muscular coördinations and neuronic coördinations tend to be developed and formed. When these have taken place sufficiently, definite activity, as opposed to random activity, is undertaken, involving the same common elements of movement and material. This process leads to purposeful activity of a pre-vocational nature.

When we come to the girls, we find that this elementary work is solely for those whose mental level prevents them from starting in at the regular industrial work. That is, training, not production, is the primary aim in view. In this class, the girls can be kept the entire day, a half day, or two hours, although variety of occupation should be an important matter for consideration. The purpose of this work, then, is not to produce a finished piece of material, but rather to train the pupil to know and handle the work done later in the regular manual department.

Three looms are used in the room which has been set aside at the F. S. S. for the elementary handwork for girls. Here, for example, is made toweling for the institution. Other work done in this room is as follows: *fancy needlework; stenciling; crocheting; hand loom weaving; rag sewing; knitting; bandage making.*

Among the purposeful activities of this phase of the work are:

(1) *Dressing.* — Following the shoe-lacing and buttoning-strip exercises, classes are to be formed where the child can be taught to dress and undress herself.

(2) *Sweeping and Dusting.* — Training in this work can be given to a low-grade individual. This work can be given in the classroom or in any other of the rooms of the school building.

(3) *Bed-Making.* — In the special school a room or a portion of a room should be set aside where materials are at hand for training in this household duty. Regular classes should be held, the work being done under the strict supervision of the teacher in charge.

(4) *Rubbing.* — This form of activity combines both exercise and school work for low-grade children irrespective of sex. Large pieces of wood are covered with coarse carpeting, with a rag attached to both ends. Five or six of these are put in line and drawn by ten or twelve children. Thus the floors of the school building, especially the halls, are polished and repolished each day. Periods for this work are about thirty minutes long, twice a day.

(5) *Scrubbing.* — In this class the low-grade boys are taught to scrub properly. After they have had training and the teacher in charge considers them competent, they can be set to do the work in various parts of the building.

Summary. — Purposive activity is the key-point of the instructional process so carefully worked out by Dr. Fernald. His underlying motive of utility in all his teaching is especially well shown by such a simple operation as the lacing of a boot. Rather than teaching this theoretically on two perforated, upright pieces of wood, as in Sweden, the children at the F. S. S. learn on a real boot, perhaps on one worn by a member of the same group. However, the art of buttoning and unbuttoning, as pointed out, is acquired on strips of cloth, and is then transferred to each other's garments. It is all slow, indeed very slow, work, demanding energy and animation from the teachers who by means of a brisk manner and clear voice, must create and hold the attention of children whose actual physiological capacity is slight.

Likewise, the personal duties of everyday life, just because they are necessary, are taught as educational objectives. Thus, a toilet class, a bed-making class, a sewing class — each contributes its part to the development of a well-rounded personality and social adaptability, mental, physical, and moral.

C. Physical Training

Physical Training as a Factor in Psychological Development. — Many years ago, it may be recalled, Froebel wrote: "We cannot separate the body from the mind and soul, of which it is the outward expression, but in the beginning of life the intellectual and spiritual nature exists only in the form, and the physical nature plays the most important part. If, then, education is to act as a guide to natural development and not as a hindrance, it must take this fact into account, and, during the first years of life, devote itself chiefly to calling out and cultivating the minds and senses, which are intended as organs of the mind and spirit, so that when the latter begin to act they may find fit instruments to work with." Such were the words of Froebel, written more than a half century ago.

It is pretty generally conceded that the brain is an organ of the body, of the physiological nature of the body, like other organs, and it is likewise recognized that there is a very close and significant interrelationship of the body and mind. It is now known how physical impairment affects the quality and tone of the thinking mind and how the life of physical activity as carried on by the normal individual in childhood especially develops and coördinates the mental and muscular systems. The feeble-minded child is notably awkward in the manipulation of his muscles, whereas the development of the normal child is indicated by an increasing accuracy and fineness of muscular control. Thus it is that physical training becomes to a very considerable degree mental training. And so through manual training, occupational training, vocational guidance, etc., in training the child to do things we are but recognizing that what have seemed the humblest functions of the human organism are intimately and closely related to the highest powers, the mental.

Relationship of Physical and Intellectual Training in Dealing with Mental Defectives. — The close relationship now recognized as existing between physical and mental training is probably most clearly shown in dealing with the mentally subnormal, where the development of feeble minds has been hindered greatly and is perpetually being hindered by the many infirmities of feeble bodies and of imperfect sense avenues. It is apparent that movement is the first real manifestation of life; moreover, movement is so very closely connected with life that in some hidden way muscular activity carries with it the essence of life itself, creating ever-expanding stages. Proceeding upward step by step from the lowest stage of defect, the idiot, to the normal, we can see the importance of this concept.

(1) *The "Profound" Idiot.* — "Helpless, as it were, as an infant crying in the night, with no language of an articulate nature but a cry," the profound idiot leads merely a breathing, sleeping, eating — hardly a feeding — existence. For neither tissue, nerve, nor muscle may respond to or derive complete nourishment from food and exercise, and even response to secondary movements is impossible. Under ordinary conditions he is and must necessarily remain an institutional case. The functionality of training is absolutely negative in his case.

(2) *The "Superficial" Idiot.* — First, a step removed from this perpetual infancy, there is the "superficial" idiot. He may be

coaxed into voluntary movement by means of imitation unceasingly prompted and aided. With this feeble spark of humanity fostered and fed by daily bathing, rubbing, and massage, observation may be incited by the presentation of bright-colored objects, thereby inducing efforts to crawl, to creep, to roll, to seek after, and finally to walk. Such exercises repeated many times, at intervals not causing fatigue, are no less necessary than nourishing food in the work of nerve, muscle, and tissue building, by and through which the individual finally becomes capable of walking and feeding himself. Possibly, after a time, he may even aid in the care of young children of equally limited mental endowment, receiving stimulation from their care. This condition of early childhood is the extent of his power — a power gained through the most simple of physical movements.

(3) *The Low-grade Imbecile.* — The near idiot and the low-grade imbecile are the first to whom we can apply any definite system of training other than the mere movements of early childhood. Here too, however, deficiency of quality and tone forbids any exercises not directly associated with objects or strong incentives. Exercises with ladders, timed races up-and-down hill, or spaced walking, climbing, leaping, swinging, lifting of weights, grasping, catching, and throwing of stones — all are valuable adjuncts in correcting faults of gait, carriage, and grasping power. The utter inability to take hold of and retain objects is very characteristic of the imbecile.

(4) *Children of Middle and High-Grade Intelligence.* — Possessed of greater intelligence, children of middle and high-grade intelligence and those backward individuals just across the mental "border line" not only get more out of the same exercises and occupations than do the duller ones, but, capable of responding intelligently to commands, they gain from the various phases of physical training a benefit which is invaluable to them in attaining accuracy, precision, and skills in the arts and crafts, and this attainment, as we have previously pointed out, is one of the ultimate objectives of the training process.

The Physical Training Program. — Active sports should have an important place in the physical training program, being especially important and essential as an incentive to effort and right living. There should be planned an extensive program of active, stimulating amusements or recreations — from the most simple plays of infancy, the kindergarten games and outdoor sports of early childhood, and the evening dances, in which all should be encouraged to join, to the baseball, basketball, and football matches of the strongest and brightest of the middle and high grade. Brisk walks through the parks or out in the country, wherever possible, for those who cannot participate in these more active exercises, are indispensable parts of the daily routine of the feeble-minded — as is a constant life in the open during the milder seasons of the year. However, eternal vigilance must be the watchword; separation into mentally equal groups aids; protection to the weak prevents unfair competition and precludes bullying.

Side by side with the training afforded by the classroom should go the calisthenics, the plays, the games, which may be conducted in the classroom, in the gymnasium, or on the playground. Play, in itself, whatever may be its psychological basis, functions in terms of social adaptation of the child, besides resulting in physical development and betterment. In nearly all games, perhaps excepting the case of the very small child, concerted activity, so extremely essential in the training of the feeble-minded child, is called forth. Thus the child is practically forced to curb and subordinate his own desires and coöperate toward a purposeful end. The games in which he joins will exert a positive psychological and educational influence. Those who are slow and dull, apathetic in seeing, observing, thinking, doing, may be rather quickly benefited by the playing of games. Another advantage gained through playing games is that, as sensory perception is quickened, a player comes to see more quickly that the ball is coming toward him; that he is in danger of being tagged; that it is his turn; or in many other ways be aroused to quick responses to things that are taking place round about him. Perhaps of more importance in the training that comes through games is the development of that mental function formerly classified as "will power," the courage to take a dare or

62 WHAT SHALL THE PUBLIC SCHOOLS DO

a reasonable risk in determination to reach the goal or to win a game honestly. Likewise, there comes the power of self-restraint. With smaller children few rules are necessary; but as the players grow older more rules appear, requiring greater self-control and mental power.

In giving mentally retarded children games to play and exercises to perform it must be kept constantly in mind that the majority of them require the very simplest. Some of the games which have been found to be of real value to these children are suggested below:

GAMES ADAPTED TO MEDIUM-GRADE CHILDREN[1]

circle 10 pins	spin the plate	kangaroo jumps
chair relay	chase ball	merry-go-round
musical chair	somersaults	fly little birds
roll ball target	jumping	beanbags with targets
slap Jack	lassie	toss-and-catch beanbag
kick ball	garden scamps	handkerchief race
bend and stretch relay	circular relay	hopping
obstacle race	catch ball	button
line block race	balance beam	center base
ladder	train relay	leap frogs
tag well relay	hoop relay	black man
zigzag ball race	bell relay	horse trot
bat ball	all-up relay	teacher ball
skipping	musical blocks	bowling relay
monkey race	dictation block race	jump the beanbag
toss-and-catch ball	farmer in the dell	jump the rope

The above games are adaptable to the medium-grade children found in the special school. For those of a very low grade the few following simple games can be used: *carrying blocks to a table; knocking down block with ball; rolling large balls* (children in circle); *running for balls* (plain and colored); *kicking down blocks; kicking football.*

For the very low grade a red string can be tied to the left foot; then, in teaching them to march, they can be told to raise the foot with the red string on it. The marching consists of simple fancy drills, marching by twos, by threes, by fours, diagonally

[1] See, also, Superintendent's Bulletin, #54, p. 23, Oakland, Calif., Public Schools, for list of typical rhythmic activities.

across the room, and around the room. One half hour is a good period to devote to calisthenics or marching exercises, the remaining part of the period being given over to games. In playing the games it is well to develop the spirit of competition. For instance, wherever possible, sides may be chosen, the winning group cheering when the game is concluded. The use of drums in this work, especially in the pre-kindergarten room, has been found very useful, being used in marching and drilling. In practical work they are superior to a piano in putting enthusiasm and spirit in the children.

Physical Training in Relation to Needs of Maturity. — Enough has been indicated perhaps to show what can be done by way of active sports, plays, games, and exercises, whereby the mental development of the feeble-minded can be brought about as far as possible through its correlation with the physical. With these children, a much greater proportion of time must be spent on analysis, demonstration, repetition, and on individualized attention. Constantly the teacher must be an active and painstaking leader of her group. Otherwise the general pedagogical procedure is rather similar to the methods used in training mentally normal children. Each pupil must be considered separately, his mental attitude toward his environment studied, and those exercises and games selected which will tend best to develop what he needs most. The teachers of the special school must be all things to these children, with the idea of developing, in so far as possible, a readiness to meet the usual demands of life. And it seems to be a rather well-established fact that training or treatment along motor lines is one of the well-marked pathways to this attainment.

In combining mental and physical training in our program of study for the special school, we are guiding and organizing these activities in their relation to the needs of maturity. Even thinking is primarily a physical process and draws upon the vital stores of every organ; the energy, then, that makes clear thinking possible, depends largely upon the vigor of the body. Enthusiasm, self-confidence, the spirit of adventure, alertness, promptness, unselfishness, quick judgment — all these are to be learned on the field of games and sports; and every argument for such training of boys applies with equal force to girls.

Summary. — In the gymnasium the first attempts of these mentally subnormal children at conscious physical self-culture are very crude. They must learn to walk without shuffling, the training being often accompanied by the rather uneven beating of a drum struck by a member of the group. Here, likewise, are received the first lessons in patriotism by carrying a flag, honor dictating that under no circumstances should it be allowed to drag on the floor. The stronger members of a particular group assist in straightening the arms and legs of the weaker associates, and with sudden thrusts poke at the chins and heads of the lazy who will not look up. As a lesson in self-control, for example, a halt is called suddenly, and all sit, for a few moments, with arms folded. Strongly accentuated music arouses their dormant energies, since it is useless to expect the low-grade feeble-minded to go through a progressive series of physical exercises merely upon hearing the word of command. The physical exercises at the F. S. S. have been arranged as schedules of movements required in the doing of common things. In this way sense training is subserved by the physical training, as the child gains the will and desire to do any given exercise. First the teacher goes through the exercises step by step. These are then imitated by the class, until, by persistent and unwearied training, many of the children are able to execute the spoken commands. But to make it of real value and significance to the feeble-minded one must have faith in the value of such gymnastic training.

Further, we have shown the place and purpose in the physical training program of active sports as being especially important as an incentive to effort and right living; of plays and games functioning primarily in terms of social adaptation besides resulting in physical development and betterment; and of the very intimate and close relationships of the physical and mental, as also of their relation to the needs of maturity.

D. Occupational Training

The Relation of the Feeble-Minded to Industry. — One of the principal phases of the problem of the feeble-minded is the relation of the mentally subnormal to occupational efficiency. What is the mental defective capable of doing? What conditions are most favorable for his maximum production? What are the results of his endeavors to compete with normal individuals? It is the purpose of the present section to consider the first two points, the third question being considered in detail in Chapter VI.

As previously inferred, there are three more or less distinct "types" of the feeble-minded; namely, the very low-grade of mental defective, commonly termed the "idiot"; the slightly higher type, designated as the "imbecile"; and the still higher class in the mental scale, now known as the "moron." In our consideration of occupational training we are not concerned with those in the first class; they are not ordinarily trained or are so defective in motor coördination and hence control that it is an impossibility to develop them into useful individuals. Thus, they must remain typically cases of dependency. Unless there is some very serious physical disability, the other two types can almost always be trained to work in some way. It is with these two latter groups we are most especially concerned in special-school training.

Motor Training in the Education of the Feeble-Minded. — Because of the negative development in the more complex or higher mental processes, such as, for example, reasoning and judgment, it is necessary in practically every case to adopt motor training in the educational program of the mental defectives. As a rule, verbal instruction makes little impression on imbeciles and morons; nevertheless, they are easily stimulated when shown how an act is to be performed, and generally the response is fairly satisfactory. By using motor training based as it is on the imitative response of the individual, it is possible to engage them in some form of serviceable manual work. As we shall show in our instructional program for the feeble-minded, this training is a combination of instruction in the elementary-school subjects (such as reading, writing, simple arithmetic, and geography), and training in some of the general fields of industry, mainly in those involving manual work. It would seem inadvisable to make any attempt to train wholly incompetent functions; rather, whenever this can be definitely determined, it seems wiser that they be abandoned and thus apparently sacrificed in the interest of the more potent ones. Any peculiar capacity, bent, special inclination, or native ability should be tested out particularly, and studied for any unusual occupational possibility.

Functional Occupations for the Feeble-Minded. — It would appear to be a rather well-established point that the best occupation for the feeble-minded is general farm work. For this there are several apparent reasons; first, farming occupations do not require an especially high degree of intelligence; the usual rural environment does not present the degree of complexity of city conditions; men and women are happier and more contented under the changing routine of rural labor, where fresh air and out-of-door exercise are conducive to good health. However, in the majority of communities wherein the special school is likely to be established, occupational training in agriculture will not be feasible; but besides this occupation there are many others, as experience has shown, in which the feeble-minded can be trained in the excellent results. Among the occupational pursuits which may be presented are carpentry; chair-caning; brush-making; weaving (mats, rugs, hammocks, and towels); knitting, sewing, embroidery, printing, shoe-repairing, painting, plumbing, the simpler elements of tailoring, basketry, general housework, laundry work, cooking, millinery, paper-tearing, cutting, and construction work. As previously noted, just as it is possible to analyze the mentality of the normal individual and place him at work for which he seems best fitted and so most likely to succeed, so it should be possible likewise to detect such inherent or potential characteristics as will make the feeble-minded individual better fitted for one line of occupational training than another.

Pedagogical Sequence of Occupational Training. — In order that we may train the feeble-minded for general industrial employment, the program of studies must be based upon the broadest sense training, as indicated in Section I of this chapter, and a wide "experience training." The poor perceptive and associational powers of the mentally retarded, the defective and fickle memory, the slow processes of reaching a judgment, the inability to concentrate — these and other mental inferiorities may suggest failure. However, the experience of some thirty-five years at the F. S. S. has shown rather definitely that, in spite of the limitations in mental endowment of the feeble-minded, an organized, coördinated, and well-defined "experience training" is feasible and possible — not only from an intellectual point of view but from social and economic ones as well. The environment of the normal child furnishes him with these bases of education; yet even for him an intensive course in sense training would add much to his development; and how much more is this needed for those of limited mental capacities. We must therefore provide purposeful, intelligent, and systematic sense training as well as basic experiences in large numbers.

Superimpose upon this the general occupational training which has been shown possible at the F. S. S., and a foundation will be laid for those mechanical trades best suited to the feeble-minded. Where feasible, bricklaying, masonry, and other trade activities may be added. Such a program offers a good selection, well adapted to a wide range of possibilities.

With this general training of an occupational nature the work of the school will presumedly come to its close. Under present educational organization, it seems prohibitive for the public to maintain shops in which to teach all or even a selection of trades. Thus we feel that upon the close of his school career, the mental retardate should be sent to a shop where he can be taught a trade as a component part of the training process. Due to the training received in the special school it may not, however, be felt necessary to do this in all cases. Wherever it is felt essential, the shops of the industrial world should be included in the program of studies, the trade shops being persuaded to help by taking the pupils not as employees but as pupils — the teacher to continue the supervision of the pupils through coöperative efforts with the employers.

"*Peak*" *Mental Age in Occupational Training.*[1] — As one of our contributions to the subject of special-school training, we are presenting for the first time the "Peak" mental age in occupational training, Chart I. Here are the results of many years of occupational experimentation in its relation to mentality under the supervision of the late Dr. Fernald. This chart shows graphically the mental ages necessary for doing certain types of work. For example, a boy with a six-year-old mind could not run a printing press without spoiling a great deal of valuable material. Likewise, a boy with a ten-year-old mind would be intensely unhappy if required to do sandpapering rather than painting, or something equally difficult. The mental ages found by our psychological tests give very reliable information regarding the kind of work which can be profitably and agreeably done by mentally retarded boys. Chart II shows that the girl with a mental age of four or five has been found most successful and efficient in cutting and sewing rags, in bandage winding, and in work upon the Todd looms. At the other extreme of our mental age "peak" there is found a rather numerous group of operations for the girl with an intellectual capacity. So far, then, as our data enable us to determine there are three fairly distinct groups in the occupational training of subnormal girls, the general overlapping of occupational pursuits being due principally to the large number of common elements involved in the processes — and perhaps to the greater vocational versatility of girls as compared with boys. Not only do we find these children doing their best work, as indicated by Charts I and II, but they are more contented, happier, more coöperative and socially adaptable.

1. *Occupational Training and Mentality for Girls*

(1) *Four- and Five-Year-Old Mentalities:*

Cutting rags; sewing rags; Todd looms; bandage winding; begin plain sewing.

[1] See Appendix for correlation of chronological, mental, and school ages.

CHART I

"Peak" Mental Age for Boys in Occupational Training

(From Walter E. Fernald State School Data)

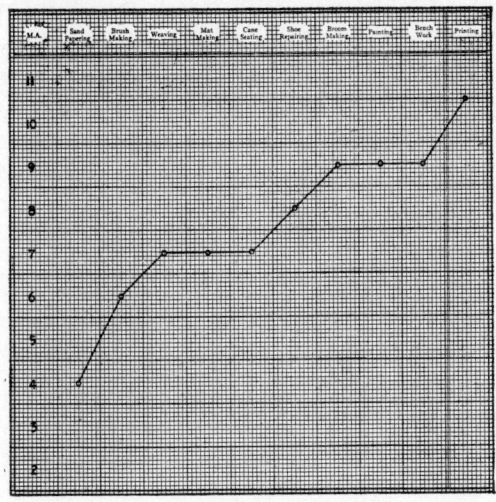

CHART II

"Peak" Mental Age for Girls in Occupational Training

(From Walter E. Fernald State School Data)

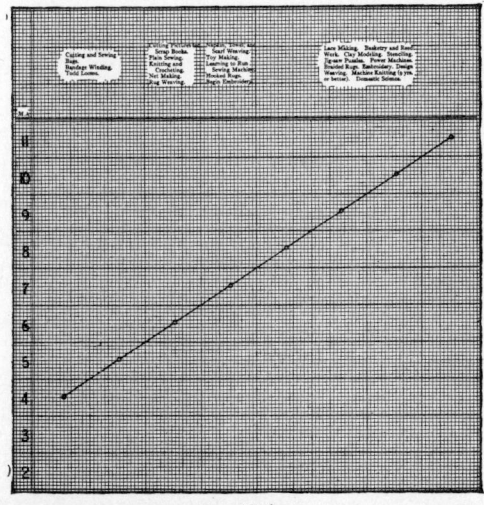

FOR THE FEEBLE-MINDED? 69

(2) *Six-Year-Old Mentalities:*

Plain sewing; knitting — plain; crocheting — plain; net making (stuffing and outlining); cutting pictures for scrap books; rug weaving.

(3) *Seven-Year-Old Mentalities:*

Napkin and towel weaving; scarf weaving; scrapbooks; bead stringing; crocheting; knitting; net making; toy making — complete process; plain sewing; learn to run sewing machine; hooked rugs; braid rags for rugs; begin embroidery.

(4) *Eight- and Nine-Year-Old Mentalities:*

Lace making; basketry and reed work; clay modeling; stenciling; jig-saw puzzles; design weaving; braided rugs; embroidery; power machines; machine knitting (nine years); domestic science.

Children over the nine-year level do all of these occupations.

2. *Occupational Training and Mentality for Boys*

(1) *Five-Year-Old Mentalities:*

Sandpapering; brush making; cutting rags; sewing rags; pounding at random; pounding nails to line; sawing at random; sawing to a line.

(2) *Six-Year-Old Mentalities:*

Sandpapering; sorting and tying bristles; brush making; practice painting; cutting coir yarn an equal length; making coir brush mat; rug weaving.

(3) *Seven-Year-Old Mentalities:*

Sand papering; cane seating; painting boxes, blocks, chairs; making coir brush mats; making coir braid mats; weaving — towels and napkins; begin shoe repairing.

Learn the use of tools and making of simple objects, as animals, coat hangers, etc.

(4) *Eight-Year-Old Mentalities.*

Cane seating; painting furniture and outdoor painting; weaving; Coir braid rugs; brush mats; shoe repairing; making boxes, bread boards, coat trees, bird houses, sleds; making brooms — begin process.

Children over the eight-year level do all these things plus sign-painting and printing, furniture repairing, inside painting and varnishing, and running printing press.

Boys of ten- and eleven-year mentality may be taught to set type and care for printing press.

The Charts give, for girls and boys respectively, the type of work of a manual or an industrial nature which best correlates with a specific mental age, as found by means of investigation of the data furnished by the F. S. S. From a psychological viewpoint we believe these to be of great importance to the special school, because, in general, the adherence to these correlations will result in much better and more purposeful occupational training, make for greater vocational efficiency, and also for real social adaptation, coöperation, contentment, and happiness.

Purposeful Concepts concerning Industrial Training. — Pupils should be classified into working groups according to mental ability and industrial capacity. With these groups in mind, the occupational training is to be organized from the simple to the complex, from those activities which involve the use of the large muscles, coarse materials, and large tools to those involving the use of the finer muscles, finer materials, and more detailed work.

The psychological time to begin any particular piece of handwork is when some real need necessitates its use. For instance, toy making may well precede the Christmas recess; a household article, when there is a need for it in the home; a dress, when the approach of the May Day festival is at hand. In so far as possible every project, simple though some of them most certainly will be, should come forth as the result of the individual child's present need and interests. In many cases this will involve coöperative effort which is particularly essential with the feeble-minded, for what they need, almost without exception, is real social adaptation.

Greater interest, zest, and enthusiasm will result if working models of the article to be constructed are presented to the mentally retarded child, since there seems to result far greater joy and satisfaction when he has visualized the objective to be attained.

A concerted discussion may well precede each lesson, involving the materials to be used, the best way of handling these materials, and why it is better to use one sort of material than another.

Every special day can be made a real teaching device to motivate and intensify the usual school routine. Each room may present the entire program or part of the program of the special-school day in its own room, and these in part or in whole may be given before the assembled school population. In so far as possible, every child should be an active participant in these projects, doing something whereby he may feel the satisfaction which comes through the achievement of success.

All manual or occupational work should be purposeful and practical. Feeble-minded children, as well as normal children, can be taught the right use and care of all equipment, and be held responsible for the neatness and orderliness of the workroom, including in this the benches, the arrangement of the various closets, lockers, and condition of the tools. "A place for everything and everything in its place" should be a guiding principle in all occupational training.

Summary and Conclusions. — The chief reason for emphasizing industrial and motor training is that it functions in actual life. Experience has shown that the mentally subnormal child is actually benefited more by physical, manual, and occupational training than by academic instruction. Motor education gives excellent opportunities for mental training, the two being very closely correlated. It gives opportunities to compare, judge, analyze, and to solve new problematic situations, to adapt means to ends, and to coördinate movements toward the attainment of desired objectives. Primarily, motor education consists in the development and refinement of muscular coördinations; intellectual education has to do largely with the establishment of associations between related ideas and with the proper coördination of mental processes. And since the child is, fundamentally, a motor being, it is by means of movement that the child acquires a knowledge of the world about him, or social adaptability.

CHAPTER IV

AN ANALYSIS OF THE INSTRUCTIONAL PROGRAM FOR MENTAL DEFECTIVES (*Continued*)

E. ACADEMIC TRAINING

Value of Academic Instruction. — It has often been stated that to teach the principal academic subjects, including number work, reading, writing, language and composition, geography, and history, for example, is actually a social, an economic, and an instructional waste in so far as the training of the feeble-minded is concerned, since they do not acquire sufficient facility or competency in classroom arts to make any real or practical use of them. It seems evident from our data that an intellectual capacity as represented by an I. Q. of less than 70 is insufficient for any type of arithmetical procedure; that an I. Q. of around 90 (80-90) is required for skill in arithmetical computation; and that an I. Q. of better than 90 is a necessary prerequisite to the successful solution of problems. Discrepancies will always appear, and although much is being done along the lines of computation in arithmetic in the schools for the feeble-minded, these general conclusions, we feel, may be applied in the usual public school. A slowing down of educational procedure would help, but it cannot make up entirely for limitations of mental capacities. With respect to reading ability we would note that children with I. Q.'s of over 100 will rarely ever find difficulty in reading fluently and with comprehension. It is likewise true that children with an I. Q. of less than 70 will never be able to gain a mastery over the essentials of reading, although it is quite possible that some of these defectives may be able to make habitual the automatic elements involved in the process, but will not acquire power to comprehend. In general, an I. Q. of less than 70 is indicative of a general inability to learn to read; and an I. Q. of 100 or better, other things being equal, means that the child will be able to learn to read well; and from 70–100 I. Q. there is a gradual overlapping between ability to acquire the automatic elements of reading and the perceptual elements involved. The same conclusions are borne out by our study of the correlation of I. Q. and the most usual work as determined by teachers' marks.[1]

It seems apparent that even the highest grades of mental defectives, assuming proper classification, do not make any considerable practical uses of the academic skills and habits acquired. Many children of this mental level gain a mastery over the mechanics of reading fairly well up to third-grade competency; a few possess special talents along reading lines and read more difficult matter with fluency and readiness. Nearly all, however, score lower on content reading than on word reading, very few being able, where the subject matter is at all involved, to read by paragraphs or even lines from the printed page. Moreover, we are told, few seem to acquire the desire or the permanent habit of reading, although there are many exceptions, particularly where adventure, exciting narratives, and life according to the idea of the feeble-minded, is portrayed. They enjoy rapid-moving scenes, conversation, etc., though in a relatively simple degree.

Is There an Overemphasis on Academic Training of the Feeble-Minded? — Experience tends to show that, on the whole, the feeble-minded are benefited more by physical, manual, and occupational training than by the usual type of academic instruction. It is generally believed that the mentally subnormal children throughout the country are being over-instructed in the academic subjects, not only in the case of those who are in the regular classes but also in the case of the larger proportion of those in the special classes of the public schools. On the whole, the program of studies of the special classes is organized on the same principles with respect to subject content as are the regular grade curricula; however, more elasticity is permitted and more emphasis is placed on the various phases of motor training. It should be

[1] Davis, Guy P.: *The Relation of General Intelligence and the Ability to do School Work.* (Unpublished) Harvard Graduate School of Education, 1925.

noted that, under such conditions, motor training is commonly considered, not as a major and integral part of the program, but rather as an adjunct or supplement to the orthodox academic subject matter. Shall we, then, in view of our preceding considerations, eliminate all forms of literary instruction — as some would have us do? We do not believe this should be done; rather we would posit a re-emphasis of all forms of motor training, including sense training, sublimating academic instruction to still purposeful and practical usages to the feeble-minded. On the one hand, parents desire, irrespective of their children's mental capacities, that these individuals should receive some elements of academic instruction; and, in our inauguration of the special schools in the public school system, we need and desire their coöperation. This feeling on the part of the parents seems to come from the rather common but no less mistaken notion that academic instruction as mental training possesses greater value than does motor training, and also because they desire the eradication of illiteracy if possible, since the latter stigmatizes the child — perhaps more than anything else. However this may be, whether academic instruction possesses transfer value in so far as common or identical elements are concerned — and we believe it does although we do not know how much — it does not seem that literary instruction is devoid of some intrinsic value. It does lead to the development of habits, attitudes, and skills of a practical value and does give a command of certain literary tools — a command which we feel will ultimately make the feeble-minded child happier, more efficient, and, indeed, more human.

Thus, we believe that although motor training, in its close and intimate relationship to mental development, should receive the major emphasis in the training process of the special school, we owe it to the mentally subnormal to give a reasonable amount of time, energy, and thought to literary pursuits. We desire to do each day the very best for him we know how, and the means seems to us to be a special-school training whose content will be both motor and academic, suited to the needs, capacities, and interests of our feeble-minded children.

The Character of the Special-School Academic Instruction. — Whatever be the content and specific character of this academic instruction, it must be made vital and purposeful to the feeble-minded through oral, visual, manual, and concrete presentation. It should, moreover, be very closely interwoven and interrelated with all the child's activities and experiences both in and out of school. The usual means and methods of instructional procedure should be enriched by incidental discussions relative to the question or project under consideration and by object lessons, by means of which, because of their practical value, these children through the special school may gain adjustment and social adaptation. As we shall show presently, the academic instruction will be confined more particularly to the rudimentary subject matter and to those elements thereof which are within the comprehensive horizon of, and which have the greatest utility for, the mentally subnormal.

1. *The Teaching of Numbers*

General Competency of the Feeble-Minded in Number Work. — The higher grades of mentally subnormal children can be trained to count, and some can obtain a mastery over the mechanics of figuring, in so far as concrete applications are concerned. As a rule we find them most competent in addition and subtraction; some learn to repeat the multiplication tables rather glibly; they are least competent in division and fractions. Many can manipulate the operations involved in concrete problems with considerable facility, such as buying, selling, and measuring, provided the conditions, in their essential details, remain unchanged. Mentally retarded children can master concrete number work, wherein the concrete elements involved are familiar objects. It would seem to follow, then, that the teaching of number work is successful only when it is really a part of some other field of endeavor — not number work *per se*. Even then the less proficient of the group are often unable to carry this information over to concrete work in another department. For instance, here is a boy who can tell you how many horses are in each barn and how many in all barns put together, or any other simple, concrete problem dealing with the barn or perhaps with the horses; but he could not tell you how many books there are in a room if there are three on one table and four on another. Another boy may be able to do excellent wood work; he can measure, count his inches, and rectify his errors, which will be very few; but in all probability this same youth would be unable to add 5 and 2 at the blackboard. This perhaps seems strange; however, it is simply a question of interests, needs, range of experiences — as well as mental incapability. Few are able to solve problems of any degree of complexity; they do not know what process to use; they tend to lose sight of the problem involved, and so get the processes confused; or they are unable to think clearly in terms of abstract numerical relations, or acquire thorough-going abstract numerical concepts so as to be able to generalize. Few of the feeble-minded can satisfactorily bridge the gap between the concrete and the abstract.

Number Content for Mentally Deficient Children. — By virtue of necessity all number work for these mentally handicapped children must be concrete, simple, and based upon experiences within the range of activities and the capacity of the pupils concerned. In reality, these children do not care to have any relations with numbers until the time arrives when they have some vital need to use them. If we teach number work as a part of manual training, reading, geography, etc., these children soon acquire a rather satisfactory knowledge of the numbers they actually need. Frequent repetition and drill are necessary, especially in the four fundamentals. All exercises should be short and "snappy," with emphasis upon accuracy rather than speed.

Simple, practical problems should be based upon the daily activities of the special-school children, such as the cost of sewing or cooking materials, and manual-arts supplies; calculating grocery, fuel, and clothing bills; earning, spending, and saving money. Fractions involving the use of $\frac{1}{2}, \frac{1}{3}, \frac{1}{4}, \frac{1}{6}, \frac{1}{8}, \frac{1}{12}$, and such decimals as are involved in the use of money, should be taught. By the use of simple projects the children should acquire a working knowledge of the more common measures —

FOR THE FEEBLE-MINDED? 77

$\frac{1}{2}$, $\frac{1}{4}$, $\frac{1}{8}$ inch, foot, yard, acre, $\frac{1}{2}$ mile, $\frac{1}{4}$ mile; pint, quart, gallon; pound, hundredweight, ton; dozen, one-half dozen. The names of the coins from one cent to one dollar should be learned; the use of money in buying and selling, making change, and keeping accounts at a model store or restaurant, should form the subject of frequent drills. The square, the circle, the triangle, and rectangle may be used in measuring problems.

Such details indicate in a rather general way what we may expect to teach children who have a mental age of six years or higher; below this we find no evidence of any competency in number work whatever.

Each teacher, it follows then, must use her own originality in finding out what things the child would like to count or add. Situations or experiences should be devised and arranged whereby the boy or the girl will get only that type of concrete number work which he desires. Perhaps we shall not even call it a "number class" or an "arithmetic class" or let the child know he is learning number relationships. After he has been drilled on concrete things until he has a reasonable mastery of those things in which he is interested, provided he is not too far below the border line of intelligence, he may be very gradually led away from the realm of the concrete to the simple abstract. In all number work we should rest content to progress slowly. The main thing is to make progress even though it is by means of short steps each day. Likewise, we, as teachers, must be extremely patient, always keeping it uppermost in our minds that we are trying to teach the feeble-minded child to understand certain things well enough to be able to use them in actual life.

The following outline may prove suggestive:

The Kindergarten

Count objects with crayon
Trace figures with crayon or yarn
Ruling
Begin time telling — hour and half hour
Picture number cards

First Grade — Six-Year-Old Mentalities

Count by 1's to 100, 2's to 20, 5's to 100
Write numbers to 10, names and figures
Do four processes to 10, first with, then without objects
Simple concrete problems of one step
Learn pt., qt., in., ft., cent, nickel, dime

Second Grade — Seven-Year-Old Mentalities

Count by 3's to 100
Learn Roman numerals to XII
Do four processes to 20
Name and express in figures and words to 50
Learn coins from one cent to one dollar
Learn ft., yd., qt., and gal.
Add columns in 50 limit
Subtract without borrowing 97 — 35
Do concrete problems of one step

Third Grade — Eight-Year-Old Mentalities

Learn units, tens, hundreds
Write numbers in figures and words to 100
Learn $\frac{1}{2}$, $\frac{1}{3}$, and $\frac{1}{4}$
Read numbers to 100
Multiplication tables to 7
Do problems in four processes in hundreds
Do short division
Do a two-step concrete problem

Fourth Grade — Nine-Year-Old Mentalities

Learn Roman numerals
Complete addition and subtraction drill
Multiply and divide by numbers of 2 and 3 order
Drill in long division
All multiplication tables
Add and subtract simple fractions
Frequent use of ruler and yardstick
Add and subtract problems in dollars and cents
Concrete reason problems of three steps

2. Reading

Why the Feeble-Minded Should be Taught to Read. — If the feeble-minded child will learn to take pleasure in the simplest reading material, there would seem to be sufficient justification in the teaching of it, since then it will tend to function in terms of the individualistic-avocational aim of education — and this notwithstanding the rather prevalent feeling that mental defectives with a maximum degree of intelligence less than eight years, who have learned to read, seldom if ever use their knowledge of reading in after life except perhaps under compulsion. Furthermore, in addition to the pleasure and happiness which may come from an ability to read, even a slight ability in reading tends to make the subnormal child seem more like other children; and when he is a high-grade deficient, he should be given an opportunity to show how much he can master. In brief, we owe it to him that he may have an opportunity to learn to the very best of his mental ability and understanding, irrespective of their limitations.

The objectives of reading, as taught in the special school, are the same for the instruction of the feeble-minded as for the normal; they may be and have been expressed in many ways, but among them we would present the following: the development of power to recognize the printed symbols of language; to pronounce and read the words fluently and with expression; to extract the thought from the printed page; to secure pleasure as well as information from reading; and to acquire a taste for worth-while literature. However, to whatever degree we may be able to do this, the first and most important concern in teaching feeble-minded children to read is to develop a reading vocabulary for the common terms which they may be expected to meet in their daily life and occupational contacts, including the automatic recognition of the words and the interpretation of the thought of matter within the realm of their reading ability and comprehension; they are thus trained to read and understand notices, street signs, street car signs, figures, the months and days of the year from the calendar, the time of day, simple orders and bills, their signatures, and like matter of everyday concern.

Methods of Teaching the Feeble-Minded to Read. — In selecting the material for reading, the teacher must naturally be influenced by the type of child, his environment, needs, and interests. The content should be simple, being concerned with the events and experiences of everyday life, and unusual words passed over without emphasis. Although basal readers and supplementary reading material will probably be used, it should cause no surprise or concern if they are not, especially at the commencement of the learning process. Furthermore, perhaps above all else, we should begin at the child's own level, and not where, under more fortunate circumstances, we consider he should be.

Any one of a number of methods or a combination of them can be used in teaching the feeble-minded to read. Some teachers find one reading method superior to others; but so far as we can learn, there is no general agreement on any single method. Thus it follows that the method which the teacher finds yields the best results is the best method for her to use, although it is likewise presumably true that a general method should be used throughout a particular special school. No teacher should rest content with simply hearing the children read from books; in fact, there should not be too great haste to have the children read from books at all. Perhaps the best foundation work is laid by means of a large amount of blackboard reading, which may be based on the language lesson and interrelated with dramatics and music. In fact, before the mentally subnormal child can be taught to read, we must create a real desire and a real need.

Even though methods must necessarily vary because of the variation in interests, needs, and capacities of these children, we are offering some more or less general suggestions concerning the ways and means of teaching reading to the feeble-minded. In this phase of the academic instructional process, use should be made of cut-out letters, words, and phrases (for matching), elevated or depressed letters for supplementing the visual with the factual impressions where necessary, blackboard and chart work, the use of illustrated elementary readers and story books in considerable quantity, loose-leaf readers (both individual and collective) constructed by the pupils and teacher in the class, in which the "stories" recount the experiences of the children in the class and home — for example, charts or "movies" portraying actual or imaginary experiences of the Christmas season, the first snowfall, etc. The use of pictures and games, together with a great variety of the recognized methods of teaching — the alphabetic, syllabic, word, sentence, phonic, phonogrammic, rhyming various action words and sentences, dramatization, flash cards, and dictionary charts with illustrative pictures. While the word-and-sentence method (in connection with the use of illustrative material and motor expression dramatization, writing words, and pronouncing phonic elements and words) will probably prove most valuable in the majority of cases, other methods — especially the so-called "archaic" alphabetic or syllabic method — will function to best advantage in exceptional cases.

Some Typical Devices for Teaching to Read. — (1) For the child who is continually losing his place in reading, use may be made of a cardboard slip about the size of a post card to place below the sentence that is being read or studied.

(2) For children who are learning "sight words," the following game, or similar ones, may be tried. Draw on the blackboard a three-foot square and write in it at random the words to be drilled on. The children stand in single file facing the blackboard, the leader ten feet away. On a desk beside the leader place a damp towel in a basin. Give the first child a soft rubber ball which he wets by rubbing on the towel. He then throws it at the blackboard and calls out the word he hits. The leader then goes to the rear of the line. An older child may assist by returning the ball. A variation of this game is to use figures rather than words.

(3) For impressing new words upon the children's minds, a story is written on the blackboard introducing several words the children have difficulty in remembering. Each child is in turn called upon to go to the board and erase a given word.

(4) A set of animal stamps made of rubber and a set of A. B. C. printing blocks furnish very interesting seat work for the children who are learning to read. The children stamp an animal and then, underneath, print its name. As they become somewhat more expert they will be able to copy simple stories from the blackboard.

(5) The objects or activities connected with the schoolroom, the playground, the neighborhood, stores, streets, cars, etc., may be made the source of supply for additions to the vocabulary.

We may use cards upon which commands are printed — for example, *Bring me a pencil; Get my chair; Close the door.* A printed word symbol may be attached to an object — for example, the printed word "horse" is attached to a small model of a horse — and the child told to do something with this object. The majority of these objects or models will have been learned by means of the "animal object table" in the sense training, although from time to time new ones should be added. Each word to be drilled upon is written or printed on a small card about $3'' \times 5''$ and a complete list of the words is written on the blackboard. Each child is given a card, and, as the teacher calls for a word, the child holding the card goes to the board, points out and pronounces the word and then gives his card to the teacher. After one round the cards are mixed and again distributed. A similar device is to use cards on which short sentences have been printed, with corresponding sentences on the blackboard.

Use may be made of the "Fish Pond." — The "fish" in this case are small cards about $1\frac{1}{4}'' \times \frac{1}{2}''$ on which words are written (or printed) and which have a paper clip on the end of each one. The fish poles are short sticks about one foot long with a cord for a line and a bent pin for a hook. If a "fish" is caught which cannot be identified, it must be "thrown back" into the pond. One child keeps score, and each of the others tries to get the largest "catch," the teacher acting as referee.

Jingles make a great appeal to feeble-minded children, since activity is involved. Mother Goose is always good, and one may find or adapt several other rhymes, any one of which will furnish enough material for several weeks. The following is illustrative

> Blow, wind, blow, and go, mill go!
> And the miller will grind the wheat.
> Then the baker will take it
> And into bread make it
> And bring me some good bread to eat.[1]

3. The Teaching of Music

Music and the Feeble-Minded. — Harmonious integration and coöperation are essential factors in bringing about a successful adaptation to the environment. Thus, the problem resolves itself into the development of a well-balanced, integrated, harmonious self. It is to this end, social adaptability, perhaps more than to any other, that we place music among the most important elements in the training of the feeble-minded. As they are almost invariably lacking in social adaptation, anything which will become functional to this end must be included in their program of instruction. The personality of the typical mental defective is more or less incongruous, incoherent, heterogeneous, non-integrated. Thus they are prevented at the outset from making a happy, successful adjustment to their environment, except possibly under conditions of the utmost simplicity. Experience has shown that music makes a definite contribution in terms of a beneficial behavioristic influence on the average subnormal individual.

Music, viewed as organized sound, with qualities of an æsthetic and even moral nature, provides a sensory situation producing physical as well as mental reactions, reflected in a modified conduct on the behavior side of the activities of the feeble-minded, and this to such an extent that we may say there is a tendency for music to lead him to a momentary, more or less fuller integration of self and a more normal adjustment to his environment. Sense satisfaction is one of the sensory goals of consciousness, and music appeals most intensely and vividly, since it tends to satisfy the auditory sensory needs of the most elementary human individual as well as of the more refined, the more socialized person. Through music an appeal often can be made to the feeble-minded

---

[1] M. S. Purdie: *Subject Matter in Reading for Younger, Low-Grade Children.*

who may not show any interest in any other sensory situation except food.

With individuals mentally handicapped, music stimulates activity, brings about the temporary rejection of abnormal habit reactions, overcomes inhibitions, and results in sound being interpreted in terms of reality. Music causes these individuals to concentrate themselves within the limitations of their mental capabilities, to make a more efficient use of all the forces (inner urge) dominant within them, to give up their personal biases and peculiarities to a more efficient, coördinated effort toward sociability. In other words, music, as a sensory situation, awakens emotional desires and prompts the individual to seek supplementary sensorial experiences. Music, then, is to be brought to the special school as an activity by the children and for the children.

Since the feeble-minded child, even of a very low mental order, enjoys these musical activities, we should not be too anxious to underrate his "power" of criticism. These powers or qualities appear to be developed rather keenly. The children enjoy even the more meager endeavors at performance of their mentally handicapped companions, whether those attempts be vocal or instrumental. By thus giving satisfaction to those inner urges for sensory experience, music furthermore tends to improve tone and to intensify the sensation of happiness. The satisfaction coming through participation in these musical activities arouses the desire to have them repeated over and over again, repetition of a thing once learned seeming to add zest to the occasion.

From the viewpoint of musical technique, group singing seems to be the most practical and fruitful form of music-making. Nearly all the upper imbecile and moron groups have singing voices good enough for group work; but the main objective is not voice culture especially but more particularly group participation, coöperative activity and effort, and social adaptation — including right enjoyment. It is the mental effort which is most worth while, and usually the artistic rendition of a selection is therapeutically of much less importance than is even a crude endeavor to strive for a new achievement. Music may therefore serve to cause two basic and apparently divergent reactions: it may serve as a constructive stimulant in many situations; it may work in terms of a soothing, beneficial stabilizer.

Sensory impressions do not appear to enter consciousness separately but rather as groups of varying tones. Experiences bury themselves more or less, and most of them seem to be forgotten. Music melodies, chords, rhythms, once registered in the mental equipment, act when sounding again as a veritable psychic lever, that is, as a stimulation to memory. The arousal or recall of musical memories is noticed, activating and rejuvenating the self again, and thus tends to restore the mental equilibrium of the feeble-minded.

Any artistic tendencies represent æsthetic sublimations of the inner urge (Freud's "libido") — psychic manifestations of that creative energy working within us. The sexual and the artistic tendencies appear to be closely allied, and they may include religious impulses as well. Thus, artistic activities with their pleasurable effects on the individual are outlets for the overflow of this creative yet pent-up energy. Music, as the representative of the artistic endeavors and activities, seeks as its goal the supplementation of life and the environment with that degree of completeness which seems to be the objective of all effort, of which perfect beauty, be it in concrete or abstract form, is the outward expression. Likewise, the flow of melody and harmony is a direct aid in establishing a proper sequence of words and actions. Music of any kind arouses the interest of the feeble-minded child whom it has been impossible to reach in any other way, and it is seldom that a child who enjoys music cannot make music of some kind himself. The desire to do is often two-thirds of the actual doing, hence the child who wants to make music, unless handicapped in some exceptional way, will usually find his way out if given an opportunity.

Some members of the group who cannot read words can learn to hum tunes; some possess rather good voices and sing correctly in time; some can learn to play easy selections on the piano, the violin, mouth harp, or different band instruments, including the drums, in which they seem to take special delight even in hearing. Because of this musical ability possessed by many of these children, parents many times find it hard to accept the verdict that such individuals are mentally incapable in other respects.

The music of a band makes an especially pleasurable appeal to the feeble-minded child because of the loudness of the tones; the orchestra holds the attention well, although not so well as the band, since its music is softer and of a finer quality and therefore does not strike upon his mind with the same impact. The child will invariably choose a selection in either band or orchestra which is lively, loud, and with an air easy for him to "catch."

Singing, with the feeble-minded child as a listener, does not ordinarily hold his attention as well as does the band or the orchestra. The child loves to sing, but is unable to rest content for any length of time unless taking part in it himself. If the song to which he is listening is lively, with a simple air, and with words he can grasp, he will listen with much interest many times, clapping his hands with the movement of the selection, or even humming the tune. On the other hand, when the music is soft and slow, he soon becomes restless and uneasy, in all probability giving his attention to something else.

A humorous song will always make its appeal — as will songs of the seasons, of flowers, birds, animals, occupations, or anything indeed with which he has an actual acquaintance. He likes to be able to sing the popular songs of the day, and to sing them with band or orchestra accompaniment is among his greatest delights. Although he perhaps prefers to know the words of the song, yet he will many times sing on to la-la-la and seem perfectly happy and contented.

Musical Training for the Feeble-Minded. — The work in music should proceed along three general lines, not including band or orchestra work: (1) rote singing; (2) rhythmic drill, in connection with physical education, reading, and certain occupations; and (3) musical appreciation.

(1) *Rote Singing.* — It seems to be pretty well agreed that the best way to teach a song is by rote, the idea in mind being to build up a repertoire of good songs which result in the mental and

moral uplift of the feeble-minded child. These may be taken from various sources, and different types of songs may be used — for example, patriotic songs, folk songs, hymns, familiar old-time melodies, and the popular songs of the hour. These children could perhaps get a song by note, but it is a slow and tiresome process on their part; and while they never tire of repeating a song once learned, they tire very quickly if a long time must be taken to learn it. Singing by note, however, is good practice for the mentally subnormal child, since it gives him some degree of independence — something which he lacks perhaps more than anything else so far as singing is concerned.

The feeble-minded child learns best by imitation; he can follow many apparently intricate processes and parallel them absolutely. This seems to account for the fact that in the teaching of a song by rote he learns primarily by imitation. Anything in which the child takes an active part interests him, and for this reason action songs are particularly valuable. Any simple action, as clapping the hands or moving the head, feet, or entire body, in time with the music, not only keeps him interested and attentive but tends to develop a sense of rhythm.

The following list of songs is intended to be suggestive merely:

(*a*) Patriotic Songs. — *Star-Spangled Banner; America; Columbia, the Gem of the Ocean; Battle Hymn of the Republic; America the Beautiful.*

(*b*) Folk Songs. — *Old Folks at Home; Old Black Joe; My Old Kentucky Home; Annie Laurie; Blue Bells of Scotland; Robin A'Dair.*

(*c*) Familiar Songs. — *Juanita; Love's Old Sweet Song; Long, Long Ago; In the Gloaming; Carry Me Back to Old Virginia.*

(*d*) Hymns. — *Battle Hymn of the Republic; Onward, Christian Soldiers; Abide with Me; Silent Night; Hark, the Herald Angels Sing.*

(*e*) Popular Songs. — *Tuck Me to Sleep; Old-Fashioned Garden; Smiling; Sweet Adeline; Put on Your Old Gray Bonnet.*

(2) *Rhythmic Drill.* — Rhythmical expression may be combined with the folk songs used in physical education and with numerous reading exercises. As suggested above, these songs

should first be taught by rote, perhaps in connection with the reading exercise or with dramatics. The accompanying rhythmical activities may be practiced during the physical education periods, and later the two may be combined. Phonograph records of the various songs may be used with either the rhythmical drill or the rote singing, or with both. For example, as an exercise in reading, the children learn the words of a chosen song; in the gymnasium they learn the rhythmical expressions or activities of that song, without perhaps knowing the relationship of the two; in the music period the record is played on the phonograph; then, line by line, verse by verse, slowly but surely, the pupils sing the words to the particular melody. Later, the rhythmical activities and the actual singing are combined into one integrated activity. Thus the work is motivated, the children are active participants, and the speaking and reading vocabulary is improved.

(3) *Musical Appreciation.* — "The habit of respectful attention is of great importance in life, and if established in school, may be retained in after-years." The singing periods may be interspersed with a weekly listening period. As the content of the music records, orchestra or band selections, are of a nature that the child can understand and enjoy, and have a familiar and easy appeal, he listens willingly.

Compared with the other major school expenses, how inexpensive is a well-organized musical department in the special school! What is there necessary? Merely a number of song books, a piano in the gymnasium and, if possible, a small portable piano for use in assembly, kindergarten, and class rooms, a phonograph with some well-selected records, orchestra and band instruments, including drums, and a sympathetic teaching staff.

Summary. — Music is an excellent means for arousing and keeping attention, stimulating the various activities of the children, developing motor coördination, training the voice, improving articulation, developing a sense or feeling of group consciousness, providing an ethical and word culture and background, adding to the speaking and reading vocabularies, and perhaps the most important of all, training the feeble-minded child in social adaptation. It should constitute a major phase of the special-school program, for, with the F. S. S. as an example of what it can do, it gives real enjoyment to the children, and more especially maximal opportunities for training in the right habits, attitudes, and interests of school and out-of-school life.

4. *Dramatization*

Dramatization as a Factor in the Training of the Feeble-Minded Child. — Dramatization seems to be an essential and necessary factor in the life of every child, and to this the feeble-minded are no exception. They begin it almost before they know it, for, after all, children are "born imitators," irrespective of what we may feel concerning the origin of that psychological entity commonly known as "imitation." In substance, dramatization has been found to be one of the very best means for developing interest, motivating subject matter, expressions, and grace of gait and carriage. Hence, its utility in the training of the feeble-minded; it tends to develop, activate, and invigorate just those characteristics or functions in which are exhibited the greatest and most obvious weaknesses.

Dramatization as an Aid to Other Subjects. — Dramatization as an aid in the teaching of reading may begin very simply with the nursery rhymes and fables, such as *Little Miss Muffet, Little Boy Blue, The Hare and the Tortoise, The Fox and the Stork*. The first form of dramatization in the schoolroom is that of expressive reading. The dialogue form of reading should be used at the outset, since it is in reality a practical aid in obtaining expression. The actual reading of the exercise may be preceded by a story, better told at first than read by the teacher, using the same events and characters that the children themselves will read somewhat later. After the story has been once told by the teacher, she retells it, but this time with the assistance of the class; that is, the teacher tells the necessary facts, calling upon the children for the conversational elements of the story. Later, a number of the children may take the parts of the several speakers. This brings the work very close to that of actual dramatization. The use of the dialogue results in a great deal of pleasure through actual though elementary participation and aids the general tone of the work very much.

Next comes the story, so selected as to answer the needs intended. It should be told if possible with all necessary action. As the children learn to carry out simple dramas, the specific method of conducting the dramatization will vary greatly. In any case, the children should be led to suggest, discuss, and decide the best places for holding the play, the positions of the various characters, and the objects to be substituted for articles used during the play. The suggestions and directions should be very simple — indeed, naïve, as a rule. When the children have once grasped the thought content of the rhyme or story, which many times they will be able to do, they will work out the setting and action, aided by the suggestions of the teacher. The text will be read then with clearer understanding and better expression.

Dramatization also serves as a closely related ally to music and physical education. A well-worked-out correlation of the reading story, the accompanying rhythmical expression, and the individual participation in this form of socialized activity is pedagogically and psychologically sound, as experience at the F. S. S. has shown. Likewise, the work in manual training and occupational activities is motivated, since dramatization only begins as an aid to reading. It reaches its climax, as we may say, in the actual presentation of plays, in which every department of the school has its parts, so interrelated, so coördinated, so integrated, that every child within the scope of the play sees the necessity of coöperative effort and social participation. Whatever calls for original invention, whatever is given and received with pleasure, that will prove educative in its influence.

By no other means within the power of the instructional staff can the restraint of the special-school atmosphere be removed so well as by the dramatization of a relatively simple and easily understood play — especially if it involves music and action — or even by the suggestion of a quick dramatization of a simple review story. Not only does it awaken interest and serve as a useful outlet for motor activity, but it serves as an adequate means of discipline. For some misdemeanor a child may be dropped from the cast; for more serious misconduct he may not be allowed to witness the play.

The feeble-minded child must be given the right incentive to act and read the part that will suit him best. To one who has not witnessed the presentation of a light opera at the F. S. S., any portrayal in words can hardly suffice for the physical, mental, social, and emotional results there obtained — incalculable in terms of the future life of its children. If the plays are properly selected and presented in an intelligent, enthusiastic manner, dramatization in the special school is sure to be worth while.

5. *Language and Composition*

Purpose of Language Teaching. — The purpose of language instruction in the special school is to give each mentally subnormal child a tool for use in those social and industrial situations which he is most likely to meet. Such situations, in comparison with those of the typical normal child, will be relatively simple, lacking those more complex elements or contacts of the more ordinary type of individual. In our language training we aim to increase the vocabulary of the feeble-minded child, which, by virtue of circumstances, is exceedingly limited in most instances. Furthermore, skillful teaching of language establishes correct habits of organization and expression of ideas.

In whatsoever situations the feeble-minded child has a vital interest, situations which for him have a strong appeal, under those conditions there will be a tendency toward self-expression or at least an endeavor. It follows, therefore, that in our teaching work provision must be made for a very wide range of firsthand experiences, with nature, the home, the neighborhood, the playground, school activities, with all those experiences and contacts which these children are likely to undergo, especially after leaving school. Through these numerous acquaintanceships the symbols taught in the proper associations with their objects will come to take on meaning; and if a situation arises having identical elements with some previous situation, the feeble-minded child has self-expression, that is, he now has a means of communication between himself and his associates.

Much time must be devoted to speech improvement and the correction of speech defects, for many of the mentally subnormal children are subject to slovenly, inarticulate, defective, and incorrect speech. A considerable part of speech training must find its way by means of reading, spelling, language, vocal music, and dramatization; however, it has been found necessary to give separate corrective exercises according to individual requirements and needs.

Content of the Language Program. — As indicated above, the language work of the special school, in order to meet the needs of these mentally subnormal children, should consist of: (1) conversation based on first-hand experiences; (2) story-telling, either by the teacher through the medium of pictures or by means of simple fables, folklore, or fairy tales — or by the children themselves through dramatization or the retelling of the story told by the teacher; (3) drill on correct usage of simple conversational phrases; (4) study of word meanings by the use of the picture dictionary on large cards and of the suitable setting for story illustrations; (5) sentence-building and writing from dictation; and (6) punctuation.

Much of this drill will take place in most of the academic work offered by the special school, but, in order that the child's language content may be functional even though simple and limited, it must be used in all possible experience and activities of the individual.

Purpose of Composition Teaching. — Feeble-minded children of the mental development necessary for the special school are naturally handicapped in composition writing. The defect is due to their limited degree of comprehension and to the narrowed range of experiences, activities, and interest. Even the boy or the girl who can retell a story with a considerable degree of accuracy is very often unable to reproduce the thoughts involved in writing. To those mentally inferior children who in adult life are to be expected to make any practical use of the composition work learned in school, perhaps the art of letter-writing will prove most valuable. Elementary exercises must necessarily precede, both for the sake of a foundation of later composition work and to the advantage of those whose mental thoughts do not necessitate letter writing as a medium of expression.

Content of the Composition Program. — It will be noted that much of the work included in composition belongs to language study and training. This includes in its most elementary presentation: (1) oral composition — original stories made up by the children, free dramatization, sand-table setting for story illustration, and the recognition of sentence completion preparatory to written composition — all particularly important to the feeble-minded child; (2) written composition, including the teaching of proper indentation, capitals, periods, and margins, and the writing of a few simple statements of a personal nature; (3) vocabulary building, including the use of the picture dictionary; (4) memorization of quotations and poems; and (5) drill in correct usage.

For mentalities eight or nine years or over, written composition would become somewhat more complex in content, including letter writing, properly motivated, writing directions, further vocabulary building through new experiences, additional drill in correct usage and memorization of poems. Letter writing, perhaps the culmination of the training of the high grade of feeble-mindedness, should be motivated by genuine experiences, such as letters to absent classmates, an invitation to class affairs, letters of thanks, requests for information or illustrative material, letters of application, and simple business letters. In most instances, pictures, vacation experiences, accounts and illustrations of class projects vitally motivate written composition, but special care should be taken not to overdo this with these children who are easily wearied by instructional procedure. Further vocabulary building may be brought about through discussion of new experiences, and correct usage by means of arousing a desire in the children to watch themselves and others for verbal improvement. In some groups it will sometimes be possible to arouse a competitive interest in the weekly acquirement of new words.

The following outline of an instructional program in language and composition is suggestively offered:

First Grade — Six-Year-Old Mentalities

Sentence building
Capital letter at beginning of sentence
Use of period and question mark
Retelling stories
Learning one poem a month

Second Grade — Seven-Year-Old Mentalities

Learning one poem each month
Retelling stories
Picture stories
Common abbreviations in their vocabulary
Writing sentences from dictation

Third Grade — Eight-Year-Old Mentalities

Picture stories from imagination
Retelling stories
Use of *haven't, any, were you, isn't*
Direction, east, west

Fourth Grade — Nine-Year-Old Mentalities

Common imaginary stories of things of interest
Picture stories
Dictation work
Common abbreviations
Letter writing
Punctuation

6. *History, Geography, and Civics*

The Feeble-Minded and Historical Content. — In considering the aims or objectives of the special school, we took occasion to state that the habits, attitudes, and skills attained by and through the instructional process for the feeble-minded are of much greater ultimate value and of considerable more importance than are the knowledge and the informational facts thus derived. From this viewpoint, the study of history presents particularly good opportunities. For our purposes it should be taught by means of stories concerning important events and men, that is, through biography as a basis, not only because the teacher can easily interest the feeble-minded child in these lives and experiences, but also because of the potentialities of this subject in terms of its objectives. In the historical survey of men and women, the teacher should dwell at considerable length upon all interesting details concerning life and its various experiences, making a strong point of positive personal characteristics, what was done, in what spirit it was done, and the results to the world at large — all in terms of the students' limited mental endowments and future probable activities.

Thus, the outstanding points in the discovery and growth of our country as revealed in the lives and deeds of important men may be motivated and taught through interesting stories told or read in the class, by the use of pictures, oral reproduction, written composition, and assigned or suggested readings, such as simple historical fiction.

In the special-school program, as typified by the F. S. S., the study of history begins in the fourth grade. The object in view is not, then, the acquisition of historical facts, *per se*, but the presentation in an elementary manner of how men lived, the spirit and motives of their work, and what they actually accomplished for some one other than themselves, by means of history in the form of biographical content. Through the acquisition of right habits, attitudes, ideals, and skills, there will come a social adaptation and a coöperative spirit, if consciously striven for by the teacher, which, after all, are the fundamental results for which the special school should strive.

Geography for the Feeble-Minded. — The geography of the special school should be presented in the third and fourth grades especially and in terms of the child's probable future experiences. The chief purposes are to arouse the imagination and stimulate the interest of the mentally subnormal child through excursions, observations, interesting stories, projects, the use of picture charts, and, to a considerable degree, a knowledge of local geography. Since it is rather unlikely that any of these children will travel far, their first lessons or exercises in geography should begin with places and things near at hand. Following the principles so carefully worked out by Dr. Fernald at the F. S. S., we are presenting the following course of study in this subject:

Third Grade — Eight-Year-Old Mentalities
Oral drill
Position — place under, over, etc.
Idea of distance
Local geography
Direction — east, west, etc.

Fourth Grade — Nine-Year-Old Mentalities
Surface — rough, smooth, even, uneven, etc.
Definitions — mountain, river
Common occupations
General knowledge of United States and Europe

Civics for the Feeble-Minded. — Civics may be taught in connection with history or geography, or as a separate study, although our special-school program does not call specifically for such designation. Even the individual of defective mentality can be taught in general his place in community life by emphasizing his place in the home, school, city, state, and nation. Of equal, if not of greater, importance are the knowledge and the understanding, where the latter is possible, of certain concepts and ideals, of which the following are representative: To know and obey the laws; to save money and time; to get a job and hold it; to keep clean and well; to be polite; to be honest; to keep up a good appearance; to get along with and consider others; to observe traffic rules and fire laws (*i.e.*, to turn in the alarm); and to have some general knowledge of public and private property, including taxes. That these and similar principles can be taught so as to function is well illustrated by the results of the training process at the F. S. S., which we shall attempt to present in Chapter VI, *The Results of the Salvaging Process.*

7. *Moral Training*

The Need for Moral Training of the Mentally Defective Child. — There is a much greater need for the moral training of the feeble-minded child than there is for the normal individual, and fortunately most of the mentally deficient make an adequate response to such training. The fact that there is greater need on the part of the subnormal child is not because the mental defective is morally worse than the average, although this seems to be a rather common point of view, but rather because his mental condition makes him more susceptible to suggestion and imitation. Hence, possible evil surroundings are likely to bring about harmful results, and even under favorable environment the feeble-minded are apt to go astray unless carefully trained and supervised. It is a generally recognized fact that, when disease, a congenital defect, an acquired deficiency, or an iniquitous environment, weakens the inhibitory control, the baser motives are most likely to assert themselves. Even with good surroundings these lower motives may become accentuated.

It follows that with the inhibitory control defective and the influence of suggestion almost always at hand, unless there is instituted some intelligent and judicious control, the mentally defective child is likely to meet with disaster early in life. It seems evident, then, that moral training of some sort, as well as physical, academic (mental), and industrial training, must of necessity be a part of the instructional program for the feeble-minded.

Methods of Moral Training Available. — The first method commonly suggested may be termed *expository*, consisting as it does in furnishing enlightenment concerning moral relations and obligations, virtue and vice, the difference between right and wrong, specific actions to be avoided, and particular responses to be acquired. If this method is followed, it must be made as concrete and practical as possible by means of stories, simple and easily understood, fables and parables, and illustrations of concrete or specific occurrences in the life of the school. Thus, from this approach, history, civics, and reading offer especially good opportunities for the presentation of material concerning right living, the ideal of coöperation, of social adaptation, etc. With the feeble-minded individual, as well as with the normal, "actions speak louder than words" and "practicing is better than preaching." Better from a functional standpoint, then, is daily training in correct modes of behavior, in actual doing of desirable things, and in the forming of fixed habits of response. Our chief and best means of developing socially acceptable behavior on the part of mental defectives must not be through expository instruction — that is, promises, good intentions, resolutions — or even through "good will"; rather, it must be through habit formation. Good conduct must be made a matter of habitual activity. The child can thus be trained to actually do the right and the polite thing — to be punctual, industrious, obedient, to talk distinctly, to help the still weaker children, to coöperate, to tell the truth, to clean his teeth, and to do many other essential things. We thus see that each phase of the instructional process has its contributions to make in the moral training of these children. The teacher must be the personification of all these positive attributes, not only in attitude, actions, and thought, but even in dress as well.

As a general principle of procedure in moral training, it is always better to emphasize the positive aspects rather than the negative, to stress that which is right rather than that which is wrong. A few years ago, Dr. Fernald, in discussing the training of the feeble-minded, expressed his belief that the sense or feeling of inferiority is one of the most serious factors in preventing normal activity in such retarded children. If a feeble-minded child is taught that he has within himself the ability to do the right and this is so emphasized that the child finally becomes aware of the fact, it will strengthen him mentally and physically and so help in character formation. Thus, as noted in the preceding paragraph, the choice of the teacher is not simply a question of ability to impart information of a rather specific nature, but carries with it a consideration of what may be in time of supreme importance for the child — moral qualifications and the capacity to impress them upon the child to a very considerable degree.

In a question of moral discipline, there is one attitude that must always be assumed. The mentally subnormal child must be led and not compelled, in the usual sense of compulsion. A display of force may compel apparent obedience, but the complexes and inhibitions thus aroused often result in the child's becoming secretive, more or less retiring, and so less amenable to future moral development and training. Above all other individuals, these children need sympathy and love, coupled with firmness, so that they may trust themselves to the one in charge. The feeble-minded child finds out practically as quickly as does the normal child to whom obedience must be rendered, and, having found this out, if such obedience is the result of confidence, the child will become immediately susceptible to moral training and support.

In the moral training of children of this degree of mental capacity, some system of modified rewards and punishments is effective. Although the modification must be such as is suited to individual needs, it is the general principle of rewards and punishments which is in need of modification. There is a vast difference between a possible reward for well-doing and the purchase of obedience. The latter is a habit easily acquired but always harmful in its results. A reward given after the act of obedience is completed is a far different matter. In the case of mentally deficient children with their enlarged capacity for sympathy, commendation is often the best reward that can be offered. No class of children need love and sympathy as do these; none have their capacity for it developed to such an extent; to deny them what they most need and what they have capacity for is almost inhuman, for it costs but little to give it and to withhold it may mean the stifling of moral growth in the child who needs it most to round out his very life.

Punishments must be, as a rule, by harmless deprivation, applied in such a way that the child is made conscious only of the fact that he has done wrong. From whatever angle we may view the subnormal child and punishment, the fact that the child is mentally deficient should not deter us from instituting such training as will teach him to have a regard for others, and the mere fact that he is deficient need not make him totally irresponsive to control. However, too much stress should not be placed upon the intellectual qualities of the child as a barometer of his capacity for moral consciousness, because a lack of this does not necessarily indicate an intellectual deficiency.

No matter how brilliant are the results which follow any system of training for the deficient child — whether it be academic, manual, or moral — there can never be a disregard for constant and confined after-care. These methods, although they have been found very gratifying, are not wholly permanent unless the proper supervision is maintained over a long period — in fact, in many instances it must embrace the entire period of the child's life.

8. Mental Hygiene and Mental Defectives

Mental Hygiene and Creative Activity. — In the training program for the feeble-minded, all instruction and school activities should be organized in accordance with the requirements of an adequate system of mental hygiene, so that the child's whole personality may be harmoniously developed; his instinctive tendencies to reaction and emotions properly controlled, sublimated, and inhibited; economical and desirable habits of feeling, thinking, doing, and studying formed; healthy and right attitudes toward the problems of life engendered; wholesome interest in objective realities developed; and the child freed from selfish fixations, mental and physical inhibitions, misconceptions, superstitions, repressions, and conflicts — all for the purpose of releasing his energies for creative, constructive, and purposive activities. Education for the mentally defective is therefore a deliberate and conscious endeavor on the part of the school for systematic training in adjustment to environmental factors and situation. "Integration is the essential characteristic of normal mentality."[1] It is an equally important ideal toward which to strive in the training of the feeble-minded. Adjustment to environment and the integration and coördination of the individual's personality are, then, the dominant characteristics of the mental hygiene program of the special school.

[1] W. H. Burnham: *The Normal Mind*, pp. 27–29. D. Appleton and Company, 1924.

9. *Summary and Conclusions of Chapters III and IV*

The Problem of the Future Education of the Feeble-Minded. — On the entrance of the mentally deficient children to the work of a grammar-school grade, the problem of their future education has narrowed itself to a rather definite point, the utilization of their academic instruction and training in industrial ways; for experience has shown the futility of leading them into departments of knowledge which result in development of a one-sided nature. Thus, a boy with a remarkable memory may lack moral balance; a girl who has a considerable mastery of manipulating figures in mental arithmetic may be incapable of self-respect. The industrial training begun by hand, sense, and object work is still furthered by "sloyd." After the half day of school work, the pupils pass into the workshop and learn, among other things, bread-baking, cobbling, brush-making, carpentering, and painting. Likewise, they do house-painting, assist in bricklaying and mason work, and become fair farmers. At the F. S. S., the outdoor work or occupations include the training of the lowest grades of mental defectives to dig ditches, make roads, or merely carry stones from one pile to another. Likewise, the girls are engaged in household duties, such as laundering, bed-making, cooking, cleaning, etc., or lace-making, stocking-making and darning, embroidery, sweater-making and similar pursuits. Much of the outdoor as well as some of the indoor occupations may not be feasible as a part of the special-school training which we advocate; much, perhaps all, will depend upon the presence or lack of necessary facilities and upon the mental level of the children in the particular community or school.

Previous School Education and Occupational Training. — The foregoing school education equips the higher grades of the feeble-minded for manual work to the same extent (if we may compare small things with great) that four years at college fit the graduates for business pursuits. Only on this ground can the education of these mental defectives be justified beyond the rudiments of the academic instruction outlined.

The Instructional Program Summarized. — In Chapter III we considered the sense-, physical-, manual-, and occupational-training programs for the feeble-minded, showing the relationship of these to each other and their connection in the attainment of the aims or objectives of the special school. In the Appendix we have placed the record sheets for various tests and a syllabus of the academic instruction as carried on at the F. S. S., the content of which we advocate for adaptation in the special school. Since this has been considered in Chapter V from a specific point of view, further discussion seems unnecessary.

Results of Special-School Training. — At this point the question may well be asked, "Will the instructional and training process which has been advocated function in real life? That is, does it insure quantitative and qualitative results? We believe it does, and shall, therefore, consider these in detail in Chapter VI under the title *The Results of the Salvaging Process.*

A SYLLABUS OF ACADEMIC INSTRUCTION RECOMMENDED FOR ADAPTATION IN THE SPECIAL SCHOOL

I. Kindergarten Things We Cannot Do

1. Gifts 6 and 7
2. We do not do the creative work on any of the gifts
3. Peg boards ⎫
4. Sewing ⎬ Very little original design
5. Weaving ⎬
6. Folding ⎭
7. Cutting — Very little free-hand work
8. Games — Requiring originality and initiative.

II. Kindergarten Things We Can Do

1. Gifts 1 to 6 — also 8th and 9th. No self-creative ability shown Doing work by imitation
2. Peg boards ⎫
3. Stringing ⎬ Getting the primary steps of the work
4. Cutting ⎬ Practically all work done by imitation, very littl
5. Sewing ⎬   free-hand or original work.
6. Weaving ⎭
7. Folding
8. Coloring

FOR THE FEEBLE-MINDED? 103

9. Painting
10. Modeling
11. Songs
12. Games { Mostly formal games, little imagination being shown
13. Stories

III. Primary Things We Do in the Kindergarten

1. Tracing letters with crayon, peas, or clay
2. Tracing figures with crayon or yarn
3. Tracing name with crayon or yarn
4. Counting objects with crayon
5. Ruling
6. Letter boxes
7. Color number — form cards
8. Beginning telling time — hour and half-hour
9. Picture reading cards
10. Picture number cards

IV. Things We Expect to Do in Our First Grade with Our Six-Year-Old Mentalities

Number:

Count by 1's to 100, 2's to 20, 5's and 10's to 100
Write numbers to 10 — names and figures
Do four processes to 10, first with, then without objects
Simple concrete problems of one step
Learn pt., qt., in., ft., cent, nickel, and dime

Reading:

Complete use of letter boxes
Obtain a First-Reader vocabulary
Blackboard reading of First-Reader material
Read from Primer and First Reader

Spelling:

Learn to spell words used in Readers
Learn to spell 100 one-syllable words
Learn to use words in sentences

Writing:

Proper position — form letters on blackboard and paper
Write name and short sentence — first from copy, then from dictation
Easy Palmer movement

Drawing and cutting:
>Free-hand drawing and cutting of plain forms and objects represented by these forms, as cart, flag, bag, etc.
>Filling in outline of fruits, etc.
>Much use of colored pencil and crayon to represent object and form, by tracing and free hand

Language:
>Sentence building
>Capital letter at beginning of sentence
>Use of period and question mark
>Retelling of stories
>Learn one poem a month

V. THINGS WE EXPECT TO DO IN OUR SECOND GRADE WITH OUR SEVEN-YEAR-OLD MENTALITIES

Number:
>Count by 3's to 100
>Learn Roman numerals to xii
>Do four processes to 20
>Name and express in figures and words to 50
>Learn coins from one cent to one dollar
>Learn — ft., yd., qt., and gal.
>Add columns within 50 limit
>Subtract without borrowing 97 — 35
>Do concrete problems of one step

Reading:
>Obtain a Second-Reader vocabulary
>Blackboard reading of Second-Reader material
>Read from Second Reader

Spelling:
>Spell words used in Reader
>Use words in sentence
>Learn to spell at least 125 second-grade words

Writing:
>Using simple Palmer method, write all small and capital letters correctly
>Also copy and write from dictation a short sentence

Drawing:
>Free-hand cutting and drawing all forms
>Drawing of objects to represent forms

Use of ruler
Begin straight lettering

Language:
Learn one poem each month
Retell stories
Picture stories
Common abbreviations in their vocabulary
Writing sentences from dictation

VI. THINGS WE EXPECT TO DO IN OUR THIRD GRADE WITH OUR EIGHT-YEAR-OLD MENTALITIES

Number:
Learn units, tens, hundreds
Write in numbers in figures and words to 100
Learn $\frac{1}{2}$, $\frac{1}{3}$, and $\frac{1}{4}$
Read numbers to 100
Multiplication tables to 7
Do problems in four processes in hundreds
Do short divisions
Do a two-step concrete problem

Reading:
Obtain a Third-Reader vocabulary
Blackboard reading of third-grade material
Read from Third Reader; aim to go through book

Spelling:
Learn 200 new third-grade words
Use words in sentence

Writing:
Special attention to position
Frequent Palmer practice

Drawing:
Straight line letters, from $\frac{1}{2}$ in. to $1\frac{1}{2}$ in.
Free-hand cutting and drawing — things in season, twigs, buds, etc.

Language:
Picture stories from imagination
Retell stories
Use *haven't any; were you; isn't*
Common homonyms, *blue — blew*

Geography:
  Oral
  Position — place, over, under, etc.
  Idea of distance
  Local geography
  Direction — east, west

VII. Things We Expect to Do in Our Fourth Grade with Our Nine-Year-Old Mentalities

Number:
  Learn Roman numerals
  Complete addition and subtraction drill
  Multiply and divide by numbers of 2 and 3 orders
  Drill in long divisions
  All multiplication tables
  Add and subtract simple fractions
  Frequent use of ruler and yardstick
  Add and subtract in dollars and cents
  Concrete reason problems of three steps

Reading:
  Obtain a fourth-grade vocabulary
  Read from Fourth Reader, elementary
  Geography and history

Spelling:
  Spell all words in fourth-grade vocabulary
  Use words in sentences

Writing:
  Practice in Palmer method
  Write legibly from dictation

Drawing:
  Straight-line letters — all sizes
  Free-hand cutting and drawing of things of season

Language:
  Telling imaginary stories of things of interest
  Picture stories
  Dictation work
  Common abbreviations
  Letter writing
  Punctuation

History:
  Stories of important men and events

Geography:
  Surface — rough, smooth, even, uneven, etc.
  Definitions — mountain, river
  Learn occupations
  General knowledge of Massachusetts, New England, and Europe

CHAPTER V

THE OBJECT LESSON

A. The Nature of the Object Lesson

The object lesson is a teaching device which aims to increase knowledge by the direct study of materials, processes, or conditions. It is a means of getting children to use their senses and their minds, to look carefully, to count, to observe such things as forms, shapes, colors, to get through the five important senses clear impressions and ideas with respect to objects and life in the world about them, and then to think over what they have seen and be able to answer questions put by the teacher, because they have observed carefully and reasoned to the extent of their intellectual powers or capacities. It is an application of the concrete; it is an attempt to subordinate the printed page to the use of the individual's senses, and the repetition of mere words to relatively clear ideas concerning things. Such a lesson may be given in nature study or elementary science with the fruits, vegetables, or flowers present to observe; in physiology, concerning the human body, through a talk by the teacher, supplemented by charts, pictures, and the like; in geography, through an observation lesson in which the pupils see for themselves the various forms of land and water, or the action of water upon rocks and soil; in history, through the use of interesting stories read or told in the class, through pictures, and dramatization, or by means of actual excursions to points of historical interest; in arithmetic, by means of the "play store" or self-corrective games. A visit to a shop, a mill, a store, or a ship, to see what is actually done and how the work is performed, is an object lesson. Trips to the aquarium, the museum, the zoo, the botanical garden, and the various lessons in the school garden, all belong to this category, as do also many of the lessons in cooking, sewing, and manual training.

Through this type of work, mentally deficient children gain a rather close and intimate acquaintance with a wealth of concrete material in their environment. The resulting knowledge should be all the more clear because the several senses have been active in acquiring it. Sight and hearing in particular, and taste, touch, and smell, frequently add their quota to the intellectual fund. The importance of sense training, as discussed in Chapter III, is thus distinctly shown, since upon this development rests the outcome of teaching by means of objects. Story-telling, and reading, and picture and chart study are essential accessories to this instructional process; yet even these cannot impart the vividness, the realization of details, and the interest that come from actually seeing, feeling, or touching things for one's self, and from being an active participant in the processes and conditions which bring these results about.

B. The Teaching of the Object Lesson

It is evident that the object lesson is to be conducted for the purpose of mastering some value. Thus there must be preparatory steps to arouse in the minds of the children a noticing attitude or feeling of need that will find satisfaction. The various objects studied must be related to knowledge already possessed, that is, taught in terms of common or identical elements, situations, or activities. And since the ideas are gained or derived from a more or less analytic study of the material itself, it is clear that this type of teaching procedure involves at least the first two steps of the inductive lesson: preparation and presentation. Frequently the information desired from this study of concrete materials and processes is used as a basis for comparison, generalization, and application, and, in such a case, all the formal steps are employed. To what extent this will be done in teaching the feeble-minded will depend upon the factor of mental ability, as well as upon the materials at hand, the teachers' skill, and the desires and needs of the pupils. The presence of a motive, then, serves to guide and to limit the observations and activities in presentation. Without a clear aim an object lesson in geography, for example, is a pretty poor proceeding, often resulting in much disorder and little information. In teaching the feeble-minded, the *aims* in any one lesson should be few and distinct, and the attention of the class held closely to an observation of the facts which relate to them. Other questions will presumedly arise, but they should be reserved for a future lesson or else deferred until the particular objectives at hand have been covered.

Too much study of details often defeats the underlying purpose of the lesson, particularly in the case of the mental defective. Even an excessive consideration of the concrete in any one class recitation may result in hazy and confused impressions. With the feeble-minded, only a few facts should be presented at a time, the observations made limited to relatively few considerations, and these should be thoroughly mastered before proceeding to new objects. In instructing children of this mental disposition, it is absolutely necessary that, rather than have them lost in a maze of actual activities and experiences, the teacher should proceed cautiously and slowly, yet conscious at all times of the ultimate objective in view.

Excursions and similar lessons give opportunities for group study as well as for individual activity, where the latter is possible. Certain phases of such lessons are observed by all the children in the group, whereas individuals or small groups have special assignments to note and report on. It is clear that such procedure calls for definite planning on the part of the teacher, since with subnormal pupils nothing can be presented in an aimless, haphazard, or purposeless manner. One of the outstanding reasons for this is that, in the case of such individuals, it is not so much the knowledge gained that is of most value as it is the habits and attitudes which will function in their daily contacts for social adaptability and coöperativeness. To the pupils, therefore, it must be made clear at the outset that such excursions are not mere pleasure outings but that they are lessons calling for obedience, careful work, and responsibility for results.

When such observations have been made, the pupils should be held accountable in some way for the results. The question or questions with which the recitation started should be answered. A satisfactory account of what has been seen or done should be given in oral form and, where possible in case of the feeble-minded, in written form; in any event, the main points should be made prominent.

As has already been suggested, the object lesson requires careful planning on the part of the teacher. If the class in geography is to have an outdoor lesson, the teacher should inspect the place beforehand, decide upon the various elements to be studied, the best places for observation, the route to be traversed, and similar details. If a demonstration lesson is to be presented, the materials and apparatus should be prepared and gone over by the teacher to be sure that everything is in satisfactory working order. Many a lesson has been interrupted and spoiled because there was a forgotten piece of apparatus or failure to ascertain beforehand that the materials or apparatus were not in working order. If the lesson is the usual exercise in the classroom, the teacher should be foresighted and make the necessary preparations for it so that when the lesson hour arrives the materials may be at hand, ready for use.

The Teacher and the Object Lesson. — The object lesson calls for real teaching ability — particularly, though not entirely, since dependence cannot be placed on the words of any text. Oral instruction of a group of feeble-minded boys or girls, using real objects, necessitates high instructional technique. The class must be kept naturally interested and under control; the dominant elements to be taught must be kept clearly in the mind of the teacher, who must ask the right questions at the right time and in proper order to carry the class's thinking to the right conclusions; and since so much of this type of training procedure is not written in books, it is necessary that the teacher have a broad basis of knowledge, not only of the subject presented, but of the psychology of the feeble-minded child as well.

The teacher must know both how to organize and to direct. Class lessons must be determined in advance in all their essential steps, and for this, teacher-preparation, or training for teaching the feeble-minded, is an absolute necessity. The teacher is emancipated from dependence on the words of a text; she is able to stand before a class full of her subject, ready to question freely. Thus, the teacher of the object lesson may become conscious of a new strength and a professional skill unknown to teachers whose sole or main dependence is on "textbook reciting."

The Object Lesson and Sense Training. — As we have already pointed out, the chief function of sense training for the feebleminded is mental, developing what we have chosen to call the "sensory consciousness" of the child. Therein it was noted that, when properly conducted, sense training should increase the speed, accuracy, and range of observation, should help the child to discriminate more fully between stimuli, to notice small differences, to acquire facts regarding various situations, to compare and contrast facts, to draw correct inferences and conclusions from the facts thus compared, to classify facts and organize them in logical sequence, and to give the right names to those facts observed. Indeed, one of the most important objectives of sense training is the development of systematic and methodical observation. We considered, also, the technique of instruction, and the materials involved in, and necessary for, sense training.

At this point we wish to note specifically, for purposes of illustration, the concrete materials necessary for training in color-sense and in sight.

Materials for Training of Color Sense

1. Color charts (Magnus and Jeffrey) with envelope of discs
2. Manual for color charts
3. Color names and color blindness (Magnus and Jeffrey)
4. Colors in schoolroom
5. Colored cambrics (Books)
6. Box of colored silks, wools, ribbons, etc.
7. Color instruction (Bradley). Teacher's Sample Box #2
8. Box of colored square cards, showing shades and tints
9. Box with eight colored compartments
10. Box with three colored compartments
11. Assortment of colored shapes and figures to use with colored boxes (9–10)
12. Oblong solids — red, yellow, blue, green, orange, purple
13. Cubes (1″) — red, yellow, blue, green, orange, purple

14. Cubes (2″) — red, yellow, blue, green, orange, purple
15. Oblongs (1″ × 1″ × 8″) — red, yellow, blue, green, orange, purple
16. Oblongs (2″ × 2″ × 8″) — red, yellow, blue, green, orange, purple
17. Large strips of colored cambrics (16″ × 24″) — green, light blue, dark blue, purple, heliotrope, red, orange, yellow
18. Small squares of colored cambrics (4″ × 4″) — green, light blue, dark blue, purple, heliotrope, red, orange, yellow.
19. Samples of colored cambrics bound
20. Kaleidoscopic top
21. Seguin cup and ball

Materials for Training Sense of Sight

1. Box of colored squares of cardboard (1″)
2. Box of colored forms of cardboard (1″) — square, oblong, oval, triangle, diamond, star, etc.
3. Package of color and form cards in same box (these forms to be pasted on cardboard)
4. Cubes (2″ × 2″ × 2″) in all colors
5. Oblongs (1″ × 1″ × 2″) in all colors
6. Oblongs (1″ × 1″ × 8″) in all colors
7. Oblongs (2″ × 2″ × 8″) in all colors
8. Colored pieces of cloth (16″ × 24″)
9. Box of colored ribbons, silks, wool, etc.
10. Bright colored worsteds or spools
11. Squares (6″ × 6″), oblongs (6″ × 9″), diamonds, triangles, circle, sphere, cube (6″), oval, cylinder — 2 each of these for form work
12. Form boards (Seguin; Dearborn; Shaw)
13. Colored baseballs, to be used in games
14. Everything in the cabinet and in the room, for drill purposes

A study of the above materials gives some indication of the interrelations existing between the training of the various senses, more especially with respect to the activities concerned. It is likewise to be noted that everything in the cabinet and in the room (Seguin) is to be used. Later, we shall endeavor to point out the organization of the materials.

The Object Lesson and the Kindergarten. — When a sufficient degree of progress has been reached in the sense-training room, the feeble-minded child enters the kindergarten, where the occupations and games are largely modified to meet the needs and capacities of these mentally defective children. As would be expected, there is not such a wide or marked line of deviation between the kindergarten and the primary school at the F. S. S. as there is in the regular public school, a principle which of necessity should be carried out and paralleled in the type of special-school training advocated in this discussion.

Although the object-lesson materials of the kindergarten will not be markedly different in the special school from those in the regular school, we would note specifically what these are at this time.

Object-Lesson Materials for Special-School Kindergarten

1. One box, colored sticks ($8'' \times \frac{1}{8}'' \times \frac{1}{4}''$)
2. Peg boards
3. Kindergarten beads
4. Kindergarten cubes
5. Painted blocks ($8'' \times 2'' \times 2''$)
6. Painted blocks ($7'' \times 1'' \times 1''$)
7. Painted blocks ($2'' \times 2'' \times 2''$)
8. Painted blocks ($1'' \times 1'' \times 1''$)
9. Color boxes (3 colors; 8 colors)
10. Form and color cards
11. Buttoning strips
12. Bean bags
13. Darning frames
14. Lacing strips
15. Horse peg boards
16. Small horse peg boards
17. Large horse peg boards
18. Box of colored cubes
19. Weighted blocks, A–C–E
20. Box of spools and twine
21. Shoes (4) mounted for lacing
22. Box of bits of paper to pick up

Having developed the various senses in a more or less rudimentary manner in the first phase of the special-school training process, a work of a somewhat similar although a considerably more advanced nature is carried on in the kindergarten. Through the use of objects, the training of the feeble-minded is made highly concrete, since in no other way will the instructional process of these individuals function. In order that this work might be particularly concrete, Dr. Fernald devised, for example, the idea of teaching lacing by means of actual models. Thus, the child learns the art of lacing either by means of shoes mounted for this purpose or by lacing and unlacing the shoe of a comrade. To the normal child such matters as lacing a shoe or tying a bow-knot come about rather "naturally"; he grasps the idea readily from one or two exposures. But with the feeble-minded child it is an entirely different process; lacking muscular coördination, deftness of finger manipulation, a sense of direction and position, he finds lacing a shoe a very intricate operation. But with the hand training and the sense training previously described, he gradually becomes able to cause his muscular reactions to work in harmony with his mental capacities, and so becomes able to do what any normal child does in this matter. The training involved in the "buttoning strips" presents a similar condition to the mental defective; but having learned how to do this, together with lacing his own shoes, he grows to the ability of performing those matters in dressing himself.

When a new child is placed in the kindergarten at the F. S. S., he is seated, ordinarily, beside one who has already learned or who has become familiar with the various games and occupations involved; and although he receives direct and individual instruction from the teacher, much of his acquired ability comes through watching his neighbor. The inner urge of desire to do as others are doing leads him on to his best efforts, and as time passes he is found to be doing whatever the others are doing or what the nearest child happens to be doing. Sometimes the entire class will be engaged in the same occupation; at other times, the work is fairly well individualized. By the time the defective has reached the low first grade, each of his senses has been somewhat developed, although not necessarily in terms of equality; considerable motor coördination of the kind required in upright walking, getting over or around obstacles, picking up articles such as pins and bits of paper has been attained; and he is now ready for academic or literary instruction and for either an introduction to, or still further training in, some simple industrial work or some more or less purely physical work, as the physical training in the gymnasium.

At no time, however, may it be said that training along occupational, physical, and academic lines is taking place as entirely separate processes. Each one is a distinct yet closely related element of the final mental equation. As will be shown presently, from the viewpoint of mental function in general, and of the object lesson in particular, each of these three elements of the training process is a contributory factor, contributing not only in mental terms but in purely material ways as well. It will be shown, likewise, that an object lesson may be a means of pure academic instruction, as in the case of vocabulary building in reading; but it will also be shown that an object lesson, or the project in its elementary form, although functioning as a teaching device in arithmetic, or reading, or geography may not only involve literary instruction but may be a contributory factor to other subjects of the curriculum, including those of an industrial and physical nature as well. That is, any object lesson which shall be presented may be construed as functional in terms of many subjects or phases of curricular activity as well as in terms of the particular subject mentioned.

C. The Object-Lesson Program

Keeping in mind the above conditions, we shall endeavor to present this phase of our discussion in three sections: first, a classified object-lesson program for purposes of special-school training; second, a series of object lessons for arithmetic, reading, geography, etc.; and third, a proposed daily object-lesson program for a typical school year. Although these will be presented at some length, no attempt will be made to make the discussion absolutely exhaustive, since each school must take away from or add to according to its equipment, materials at hand, needs, interest, and capacities of its pupil; and in some instances by virtue of its very location.

FOR THE FEEBLE-MINDED? 117

1. *Classified Object-Lesson Program for Special-School Training*

The following is a classified object-lesson program involving the materials, activities, and common experiences of the everyday life of feeble-minded boys and girls. It includes, as a rule, the objects — such as charts, envelopes, and stencils — necessary for presentation.

(1) FRUITS AND VEGETABLES (in classroom)
Objects: 2 apples, 2 pears, 2 quinces, 1 bunch of grapes, 2 peaches, 2 plums, 2 oranges, 2 bananas, 1 muskmelon, 2 potatoes, 2 carrots, 2 parsnips, 2 turnips, 2 beets, 2 onions, 2 cabbages, 1 head lettuce, 1 bunch of celery (with leaves), 1 summer squash, 1 Hubbard squash, 2 cucumbers
Also eight or more tin plates (according to size of class) and one knife for dividing one object of each kind into quarters

(2) FRUITS AND VEGETABLES (in vegetable cellar)
Visit vegetable cellar
One basket artificial fruit

(3) FRUITS AND VEGETABLES (in garden)
Visit vegetable garden and orchard

(4) COW
Objects: Cows (from the object table or school cabinet), steer's horn, backbone joint, churn
Envelope: Animals, domestic
Charts: Bancroft's "Animal Kingdom," Charts 1 and 2
Picture: Dissected ox
Stencils: Cow; cow and calf

(5) MILK, BUTTER, AND CHEESE
Objects: Milk, butter, cheese
  (Milk to be in glass jar so class can see cream rise)
Stencils: Cow; cow and calf

(6) GOAT
Objects: Goat (alive if possible or from school cabinet)
Pictures: Prang's, in frame, picture books
    Small picture in folders
Stencil: Goat
Chart: Bancroft's "Animal Kingdom," Chart 4

(7) PIG
Objects: A live pig, if possible, thoroughly cleaned, and in crate; otherwise, a toy pig from school cabinet
Pictures: Prang's Animal Chart
Stencils: Pig and small ones
    Wild hog

(8) HORSE AND ZEBRA [1]
   Objects: Horse and zebra from school cabinet
   Stencil: Horse; mare and colt; zebra
   Pictures: Prang's in frame. Picture book
   Chart: Bancroft's "Animal Kingdom," Chart 5
(9) COMPASS AND MAGNET
   Objects: Compass, in box of measuring instruments; magnet
   Pictures: Ship; hunter
(10) GARDEN FLOWERS
   Objects: One or more of several varieties of flowers brought by the children
   Stencil: Bouquet of flowers, with leaves
   Pictures: Picture books, Bancroft's "Mineral Kingdom"
      A visit to typical flower garden
(11) THE ZOO
   Visit the Zoo; or, where possible, visit a large stock farm
(12) PEAS AND BEANS
   Objects: Pea and bean vines; specimens of the fruit
   Charts: Two charts
   Stencil: Peas and beans in various forms and conditions
(13) CORN
   Objects: Cornstalks, 2 ears of corn, 1 can of corn, corn for planting
      Corn cake and corn-meal mush made in the Domestic Science Department by requisition
      Cornfield and silo (visit where possible at seasonable period of the year)
(14) THE SQUIRREL
   Objects: Two squirrels (alive if possible, or from school cabinet)
      Nuts eaten by squirrel
   Stencil: Squirrel on branch of tree eating a nut
   Pictures: Prang's, in frame, and small pictures in folder
      Prang's envelope — "Squirrel Family"
(15) NUTS
   Objects: Glass jar and coconut shell; common nuts
(16) HARNESS
   Objects: Single and double harness
      Single and double teams from school cabinet, fully harnessed; leather, buckles, etc.

---

[1] Likewise: (1) Raccoon and Woodchuck; (2) Alligator and Crocodile; (3) Rat and Mouse; (4) Cat, Lion, Tiger, and Leopard; (5) Dogs; (6) Monkeys.

FOR THE FEEBLE-MINDED? 119

Stencil: Horse harnessed
Pictures: Picture books, Bancroft's "Animal Kingdom";
Business catalogues
(17) WINTER HOME OF ANIMALS
   Lesson talk by teacher
   Picture: Prang's "Farmyard"
(18) WHEAT, OATS, RICE, SAGE, AND TAPIOCA
   Objects: School specimens of each in glass jar
   Chart: Calkins and Wilson, "Cereals"
   Bancroft's "Vegetable Kingdom," Chart 1
   Picture: "The Reaper"
(19) TREES
   Objects: Specimens of apple, cherry, peach, plum, and other fruit and forest trees
   Leaves of each variety
   Stencil: Forest
(20) RACES OF MEN (Charts and Pictures)
   Objects: Dolls of each race
   Charts: (1) Patagonian; (2) Eskimos; (3) Zulus; (4) Chinese; (5) Australians
   Scrap Book showing homes, etc.
   Envelope: Races of men
(21) RACES OF MEN (Dolls)
   Objects: Dolls of each race
   Swedish shoe, Dutch shoe, straw hat, huts and houses, etc.
(22) RELATIONSHIPS
   Objects: School chart
   Envelope: Relationships
(23) ELECTION DAY
   Objects: Torch; ballots and posters
   Acting out election in classroom or school
(24) OCCUPATIONS IN GENERAL
   Charts: Pictures and frame
   Envelope: Occupations
   References: Book of trades
(25) CAMEL
   Oibjects: Toy camel from school collection
   P ctures: Book on elephants, horses, and camels; picture books; card of camel pictures
   Stencil: Camel as a beast of burden
   If several toy camels are available, use sand table, showing the camel as the "Ship of the Desert."

(26) WOOL AND WOOLEN FABRICS
   Objects: Sheep, sheep's skull; wool, woolen fabrics showing various stages from raw wool to completed garment; carding comb; wristers or sweater made by children or at home.
   Envelope: Domestic animals
   Chart: Bancroft's "Animal Kingdom," Chart 3
   Pictures: Prang's table used in frame. Colored picture books.
   Stencil: Sheep

(27) COTTON AND COTTON FABRICS
   Objects: Cotton ball with seeds, raw cotton, absorbent cotton, cotton waster, cotton plant; box of Clark's O. N. T. cotton; cotton cloth
   Chart: Calkins and Wilson, Chart 22
   Bancroft's "Mineral Kingdom," Chart 11
   Envelope: Occupations
   Fabric book and fabric box

(28) SILK AND SILKWORM
   Objects: Fabric Box I, Division I, Silk in various stages
   Chart: Bancroft's "Animal Kingdom," Chart 9; "Vegetable Kingdom," Chart 4

(29) FLAX AND HEMP [1]
   Objects: Flax, hemp, flaxseed, and rope samples
   Charts: Johnston's Chart 1
   Calkins and Wilson, Chart 22
   Bancroft's "Vegetable Kingdom," Chart 12

(30) LOOM-FABRIC BOOKS — PATTERNS — DYES — ETC.[2]
   Objects: Loom for hand-weaving (Todd loom)
   Fabric Books
   Envelope: Occupations
   Charts: Calkins and Wilson, Chart 22; Plants used for coloring
   Bancroft's "Animal Kingdom," Chart 12

(31) POULTRY
   Objects: Rooster, 2 hens, hen and chickens, eggs
   Pictures: Prang's "Farmyard Pictures," Chart 8, with frame
   Colored picture books
   Envelope: Prang's "Envelope 1," Scratchers
   Stencils: Chicks (large), hen and chicks, rooster

[1] Likewise: (1) Bricks and Tiles; (2) Logging.
[2] Likewise: (1) Paper and Printing; (2) Basket weaving; (3) Bookbinding.

FOR THE FEEBLE-MINDED? 121

(32) TURKEY
Objects: Plucked turkeys with heads and feet; live turkey in cage; carving knife, fork, and steel; 2 platters, 2 skewers, tin plates; basin and towels
Reference: Book of directions for carving
Lesson given by one teacher to all classes, either in the gymnasium or in the Domestic Science Room, both morning and afternoon

(33) SPICES
Objects: Block B; bottles of spices
Pictures: Cards of spices
Envelope: Spices
Charts: Calkins and Wilson, Chart 22

(34) RABBIT
Object: Live rabbit in cage; or object from school collection
Envelope: Rabbit
Stencil: Rabbit
Pictures: Prang's, to be used in frame; colored picture books

(35) BUILDINGS
Objects: Stone building blocks; miniature house, garage, etc.
Envelope: Buildings, exterior and interior

(36) QUARRIES
Objects: Stone specimens from school collection
Envelope: Quarries
Charts: Bancroft's "Mineral Kingdom," Charts 7 and 8

(37) WOOD SPECIMENS
Objects: Wood specimens from school collection
Envelope: Trees
Charts: Bancroft's "Vegetable Kingdom," Charts 5, 6, 8, and 9

(38) ENGINE AND CIRCULAR SAW
Objects: 2 engines, bottle of alcohol, circular saw, belt; matches; small pieces of wood
Note: Place engine on slate to prevent fire. Put water in boiler, and empty after demonstration.

(39) CARPENTER
Objects: Carpenter's tool chest with tools
Pictures: Prang's, to be used in frame
Envelope: Occupation

(40) REINDEER
Objects: Wooden reindeer in box
Envelope: Pack animals

122   WHAT SHALL THE PUBLIC SCHOOLS DO

  Stencil: Santa Claus and reindeer
  Pictures: Prang's envelope (solid-boned animals and cud chewers); Prang's large picture with frame; Picture books
  Story: "'Twas the Night Before Christmas"

(41) GLASS
  Objects: Window glass; plate glass; spectacle glass; putty, putty knife; window frame
  References: Glass, putty
  Envelope: Glass
  Chart: Sand, Bancroft's "Mineral Kingdom," Chart 10

(42) KITCHEN FURNITURE [1]

(43) WHALE
  Objects: Whalebone; tin whale in box; basin of water
  Envelope: Whale
  Stencil: Whale
  Chart: Bancroft's "Animal Kingdom," Chart 6

(44) BUILDING RAILROADS, STATION, SIGNALS, ETC.
  Objects: Sand boxes in schoolroom; large blocks (8″ × 2″ × 2″); Kindergarten blocks (gifts 3 and 4), stone building blocks; R. R. track; station
  Envelope: Railroads
  Pictures: Photographs

(45) MAIL AND POST-OFFICE
  Objects: Mailbag; letters; postal cards; stamps
  Envelope: Mail and post-office

(46) ELEPHANT, RHINOCEROS, AND HIPPOPOTAMUS [2]
  Objects: Large elephant; small elephant; rhinoceros; section of elephant's tusk
  Pictures: Prang's elephant in frame; picture books
  Envelope: Elephant, rhinoceros, hippopotamus
  Chart: Comparative size of animals

(47) GENERAL INSPECTION OF INSECTS [3]
  Objects: Insect specimens from school collection, nest
  Envelope: Insects
  Charts: Bancroft's "Animal Kingdom," Charts 18 and 19
  Stencil: Horse fly, etc.

(48) BEVERAGES IN GENERAL — CHOCOLATE [4]
  Objects: Sample box of chocolate, with book; chocolate

---

[1] Likewise: (1) Living-room furniture; (2) Dining-room furniture; (3) Chamber furniture; (4) Laundry furniture.
[2] Likewise: (1) Bears; (2) Seals and Walrus; (3) Beaver
[3] Similarly: (1) Reptiles; (2) Turtles; (3) Frogs and Toads.
[4] Likewise: (1) Tea (made in classroom); (2) Coffee (prepared in D. S. Room).

made in Domestic Science Room; tin trays, spoons, small glasses, sugar
  Envelope: Beverages
  Charts: Johnston's Chart 10
      Bancroft's "Vegetable Kingdom," Chart 3
  Pictures: Cocao

In a similar manner of presentation, the following "object" lessons are suggestive: Occupations interpreted by means of the plumber (pipes, piping, and soldering), baker, sailor, blacksmith, grocer, butcher, shoemaker, surveyor (with tools); forms of water; lighting and heating; lighthouses, lifeboats, and preservers; fish and fishing tackle, shellfish, canned and dried fish; sponges, coral, and seaweed; telegraph, telephone, and speaking tubes; sugar maple, sugar beet, sugar cane; passenger trains, electric cars, automobiles; and paints and varnishes. The previous forty-seven object lessons, together with the above, give us some idea of the very numerous opportunities to present common and everyday materials in simple, concrete, and objective ways to the mental defectives. These materials should be kept in a well-arranged school cabinet, centralized or individualized in terms of each class group, each article of equipment having its special point of placement. None of this objective teaching material used need necessarily be expensive; indeed, outside of the stuffed or presented animal specimens and possibly a few of the charts, these objects, envelopes, and picture books may be homemade or purchased at a five-and-ten-cent store. The more of the material the children themselves make, the more purposive and meaningful the work becomes to them, and so to them comes a clearer and better understanding upon presentation to the class group. The main thing to bear in mind is simple, concrete, objective presentation with much drill and repetition, not the intrinsic value of the equipment of training.

  2. *Some Typical Object Lessons for Literary Instruction*

It will be noted in considering the typical object lessons which follow, and in contrasting them with those which have gone before, that there is no real line of demarcation between the two groups. Whatever variation there is may be said to exist in the fact that the first group illustrates certain activities and experiences of everyday life which the subnormal child is likely to meet during and after school training. The second group, those for "literary instruction," may be said to have as its purpose instruction in certain fundamental concepts concerned more especially during the school period with educational advancement of an academic nature; in after school life, more particularly with those activities and experiences of the nature of the first section.

(1) *Arithmetic.* — In our previous discussion of the teaching of numbers, it was stated that all number work must of necessity be presented to the feeble-minded in simple, concrete, objective terms; it must be based upon activities and experimental situations similar to those which are likely to be met in their everyday life; and must be given to these children in terms of their interests, needs, and capacities. It was further suggested that although much drill and repetition is essential, yet accuracy must in no way be subordinated to speed, since the mental defective unlearns with the same degree of difficulty as he learns. We attribute the success of the Fernald system of training not only to the principles enumerated in the previous chapters and above, but to the conscious application of fundamental psychological principles of the learning process of the feeble-minded. If one principle were to be mentioned, we feel it should be the principle of reintegration, or the law of common elements. The commonality of the elements of that training process and everyday experience is so great and broad that, as we have seen, the number of absolute failures is rare indeed.

Thus, the problems presented to the mental defective should be of a simple, practical nature, none very highly involved with intricate possibilities, based upon such daily activities as earning, saving, and spending of money; the cost of domestic art and manual training materials; the estimating of cost prices of clothing, food in the home, and fuel; and the like. By the use of these object lessons, or simple projects, the children of the special school should acquire a working knowledge of the usual units of measure; the common fractions and those decimals involved in the use of money should be taught; and the square, circle, triangle, rectangle, etc., may be used in various kinds of "measuring problems."

The following suggestions may prove helpful:

(a) *Money.* — Have one child act as clerk of a store, one as cashier, etc. The remaining members of the group with money in the form of small cards with various amounts printed thereon can buy the groceries, meat, candy, wearing apparel, and other items.

The children may find out the prices of articles of home consumption — fuel, food, clothing, for example — and make out lists to purchase within the range of an assumed income.

Drill should be given in making change — either "formal," or with the use of "money cards."

(b) *Clock Game: Telling Time.* — Have a large clock dial of heavy cardboard with movable hands. On a large number of small cards draw four-inch clocks without hands. On each of these draw hands indicating a different hour, half-hour, or minutes after the hour. On the opposite side print (or write) directions — such as "Make the hands say 12 o'clock." Each child is given an equal number of cards; reads the directions; sets hands of large dial; and looks at correct position on small card. If correct, the card is discarded, the one getting rid of his cards first winning the game. (The game may be modified to suit local conditions.)

(c) *Self-Corrective Games.* — Use flash cards involving combinations of each of the four fundamental operations, with answers on the back enabling class groups working together to check their answers.

Boxes divided into compartments (made by boys in manual training shop) with small cards may be used for number drill. Individuals may work separately; or two or more groups may work for accuracy in placing cards in proper compartment. They then exchange places and check the work of each other.

Another device is a cardboard wheel with elastic bands to hold small cards in place. The number cards are placed in the spaces, the child turns the wheel, gives the answer to the card at the pointer, and checks by comparison with answer on back of card. If correct, he keeps the card, the one getting the largest number of cards winning the game.

Cards containing number drills for accuracy and speed have spaces cut below them for answers, the child writing the answer only. By turning the card over and fitting it over space, he may check his work by comparing it with the correct answer on the reverse side.

For children of lowest mentality doing number work in the school, cards containing number facts with answers cut off in irregular lines may be used. The problem is to fit the answers in the right spaces.

(*d*) *Units of Measurement.* — To learn the liquid measure, the pupils may measure and sell milk (water) at the "store," using the pint, quart, and gallon measures. Bottles may be used, if preferred, and the three units compared.

For the linear measure, the boys may construct a doll house in the Manual Training Room; the class will measure the material for the house and furniture. The girls may arrange the house. As a further exercise in number work, bills may be made out for materials used.

The class group may measure the school garden, dividing it into smaller plots and estimating the cost of preparing and planting. Where a school garden is not available, the sand table or classroom may be used.

The girls may measure materials for sewing, the boys wood for toy building, both finding cost per foot.

At the model store, ribbon may be sold and the price determined.

(*e*) *Number Games.* — Adding scores in dominoes, ring toss, and the like will prove valuable. These devices are intended to be suggestive only, and in some cases it will be found necessary to modify them according to the degree of academic progress the class has already made, the mental capabilities of the individuals concerned, and the equipment of the school.

(*f*) *Work with Fractions.* — Make rulers for use in handwork, marking them off into inches and fractional parts of the inch.

Measure one-half, one-quarter, or one-eighth squares. Cut out rectangles eight squares wide, ten squares long. Draw and cut letters for posters, names, etc.

At the model store, weigh sugar (sand), buying and selling in fractional parts of a pound.

(2) *Reading, Vocabulary Building, Language, Spelling.* — Reading may be classified into two chief divisions, one having to do with the ability of the individual to read and know the meanings of words; and the other with the rate of reading and the degree of comprehension shown. Specifically, then, the first is primarily vocabulary building; the second, understanding and speed. In teaching the feeble-minded to read, the first and most important consideration is the development of a reading vocabulary covering the common terms met in their daily life and occupational contacts, including the automatic recognition of the words and the interpretation of the thought matter within the realm of their comprehension. They should be taught to read and understand notices, street signs, figures, the months and days of the year, simple orders and bills, their own signatures, and like matters of everyday concern.

With these objectives in mind, let us turn to the recitation room of the typical special school as illustrated by that of the F. S. S. The classroom is bright and airy; on the walls there are a few well-selected pictures; just above the blackboard, encircling the room, is an objectified alphabet (that is, beneath or directly adjacent to the A, for example, is a very large apple in colors; for B, a ball; for G, a girl; for T, a turkey; and for W, a wolf). Either beneath the blackboard, or at some vacant place on the wall, other objects made of heavy cardboard or paper are placed, most of which may be made by the children, assisted by the teacher. The class which we desire to present is a low first grade made up of twenty-five boys. Directly in front of the class there is, at their right, a movable blackboard upon which is written a simple verse of poetry or prose containing the following words: *baby, boy, squirrel, nest, hat.* At the left there is a long oblong table upon which are placed objects for teaching reading and arithmetic. About in the center is a small, round table upon which are objects or pictures representing the previous word list. First, the teacher and class read what is written on the blackboard; then the particular words are pointed out and pronounced. Upon printed cards (4″ × 8″) are the words, *baby, boy, squirrel, nest, hat*. A card is held before the attention of the class, and a boy is named who comes forward, takes the card from the teacher and matches the word with a like one on the blackboard. Similarly, all the words are matched.

Similar cards may be used as the stimulus for pointing out, identifying, or matching with objects and actions connected with the classroom, office, playground, neighborhood, streets, cars, newspapers, etc.

In learning to read, these children become familiar first of all with the alphabet, one of the training devices being that of placing a letter and an object together in proper order and relationship about the room. With this mastered, phonics is used, of which the following object lesson has proved its worth. On the movable blackboard the teacher pins a cardboard house, in whose center there is $\frac{1}{4}″ \times 2″$ opening with a protruding flap, or tongue, on which are printed several letters — such as *c*, *m*, *t*. The teacher then says, "We are going to learn something about the *ap* family." While speaking she writes *ap* at the right of flap. Then by pulling the flap to the proper position, the letter *c* is brought opposite to *ap*, spelling *cap*. Likewise, the *m* is brought into view; then the *t*; and so on.

Should the teacher desire to vary the exercise in reading by turning for the moment to arithmetic, the following objective presentations for purposes of drill have been found interesting to subnormal children. At a point within view of all, the teacher places two wooden soldiers, calls upon a child, who, placing his finger upon each soldier in succession, says, "One, two"; two other soldiers are placed in marching form, and a second child is called upon, who says, "One, two, three, four." The same procedure is useful for teaching to count by 2's, 5's, etc. Another "game" which these children enjoy is as follows: the teacher calls upon a boy who stands in front of the class; at some signal, he stretches out his hands and says, "Five, ten" (referring to the fingers on his hands); another boy approaches, faces the first boy, and pointing first to the latter's right hand, then the left, says, "Five, ten." Then, facing the class and standing next to the other boy, he adds, "Fifteen, twenty." Of course, these lessons do not proceed smoothly at all times, and when confusion of facts arises, real teaching skill is particularly essential.

(3) *History and Civics.* — History, in so far as the feeble-minded are concerned, should be approached by means of stories concerning important events and men, not only because the teacher can rather easily interest the child in these lives and experiences, but also because of the possibilities of this subject in forming worthy habits, attitudes, and ideals. For these, to the mental defective, are generally recognized as being of greater worth than the mere acquisition of information. Hence, from this point of view, the teacher should spend considerable time upon interesting details concerning life and its various situations, making a strong point of positive personal traits, the doing of the right social and moral act, the spirit in which it was done, and the results — all in terms of the interests, needs, and capacities of these children.

A few typical object lessons in history and civics are outlined below:

(1) STORIES OF THANKSGIVING
    Envelope: Thanksgiving, holiday stories
    Pictures: Prang's turkey in frame
    Stencil: Turkey
    Stories: "The First Thanksgiving," Thanksgiving Proclamation
(2) STORIES OF CHRISTMAS
    Envelope: Christmas
    Objects: Christmas tree, decorated; holly and mistletoe
    Stories: Stories of Christ; "Nellie's Christmas Eve"; "Three Christmas Boxes"; "The Night Before Christmas"; "The Little Match Girl"; "Little Roger's Night in Church"
(3) THE STORY OF FLAG DAY
    Objects: Flags to decorate school building
    Envelope: Flags of different nations
    Stencil: George Washington
    Picture: Betsy Ross making the first flag
    Stories: Any suitable for the occasion

Historical object teaching may likewise be presented through dramatization, oral or written reproduction, and the study of selected characters, such as Columbus, Magellan, Sir Francis Drake, Henry Hudson, Washington, Lincoln, Roosevelt, Henry Fulton, Morse, Bell, Edison, and Marconi. Each should be selected for a definite purpose, as noted in the introduction, and should be presented at some more or less definite period of the school year, for the sake of historical continuity. Local history, especially, is of value, and where conditions allow, considerable study may be made in terms of historical periods or movements.

(4) *Geography.* — In general, geographical content should be local, broadening in territorial scope with the future needs of the children and their capacities for the assimilation of knowledge. We are presenting two types of object lesson in this subject — one, that of transportation, rather general in content; the other, somewhat more specific, but illustrating the nature of a lesson in geography which involves practically all curricular activities.

In the first type, the various classes of power are discussed — hand and wind power, and steam, gasoline, and electricity. For objects, models of sailboats, steamboats, submarines, motorboats, rowboats, and canoes may be used, together with bicycles, wheelbarrows, sleds, baby carriages, trucks, automobiles, wagons, trains, and aëroplanes.

Stencils and pictures illustrating these transportation methods will prove helpful.

In the second type of lesson, a trip may be taken to a near-by town, with the purpose of teaching the children how to read a time-table, what and how to pack for a journey, how to check a trunk, how and where to purchase a ticket, and whom to ask for information. They gain also a knowledge of the country through which the trip takes place, and learn why the railroad was built along that particular way.

For objects, railroad folders containing maps may be used, as well as a small trunk or traveling bag, real or facsimile railroad tickets and baggage checks, and a few articles of wearing apparel.

In this project, geography may be taught through a study of

the map of the country passed through and guide-book accounts of the products and industries. Reading may be taught by means of the folders and other literature concerning the journey; while any number of related assignments to teach language — oral and written — will be discovered by the able teacher. For training in arithmetic, the miles between the stations, the total distance, the length of time consumed in traveling, the average number of miles per hour, and the meaning of A.M. and P.M. may be stressed. For the spelling lesson, the common words used in the journey will provide material. Hygiene may be emphasized by noting the necessary articles to take on such a trip to insure cleanliness, and the ordinary precautions to take against germs and dirt. Social adaptation through the pupils' attitude towards their fellow passengers will come in their observance of the rights of others, and all acts of courtesy.

(5) *Nature Study.* — The purpose of nature study is to awaken an interest in and give information concerning plants and animals. We should emphasize the fact that what we eat, drink, and wear comes from the soil. We should talk of home, finding out if vegetables, fruits, or flowers are grown there, and discussing the various varieties; we should study the animal pets about the home, the animals in the parks and zoo, their habits and uses. Seasonal activities should be studied, showing the dependence of one upon the other, and their relation to various flowers, fruits, and vegetables.

All these may be presented through the object lesson by means of the objects in the school collection, and excursions to farms, gardens, the zoo, and the like — the latter being planned in accordance with the purpose in need, the available materials, and the season of the year. A study of the common birds, the building of bird houses, and the use of window boxes will help to create interest in this phase of the work.

(6) *Dramatization.* — "A child does not get hold of an impression or idea until he has done it; he acts the thing out before he takes it in." Dramatization has been found to be one of the most successful means for developing interest, motivating subject matter, and gaining expression and grace of gait and carriage.

Thus, its place in the training of the feeble-minded is very large, since it tends to develop, motivate, and invigorate just those characteristics or functions in which they show the greatest and most obvious weaknesses. Dramatization as an aid to reading, and to the other subjects of the course of study for mental defectives, has been shown. In fact, there is practically no subject in which dramatization cannot play a part, and since our foregoing discussion concerning the object lesson has shown this, further consideration appears needless.

(7) *Music.* — In a similar manner, the place of musical instruction and expression has been shown in the training program for the feeble-minded. As in the case of dramatization, no specific object lesson need be discussed here, especially because of music's relation to the drama and to physical training.

3. *A Proposed Daily Object-Lesson Program for the Special School*

The object-lesson materials and procedure of presentation have been shown in their relation to sense training, the kindergarten, and literary instruction, together with a series of object lessons for the grades. The latter may be given to any of the class groups, either boys or girls, but must be presented in terms of the stage of development — mental, physical, and scholastic — of the particular group concerned. It will be noted that the lessons are organized to some extent in terms of seasonal activities and conditions, thus making them more purposeful and interesting. It will be seen also that they do not apparently follow a "logical" order of presentation; the purpose of this is to avoid monotony.

We are, therefore, presenting the object-lesson program as an indication of what the special school may accomplish during the school year.

September
General harvest talk
Garden flowers
Fall wild flowers
Fruits and vegetables

FOR THE FEEBLE-MINDED? 133

Storing of winter food
Sense training — smell
Spices

October

Squirrels
Nuts
Migration of birds
Pig
Horse and zebra
Harness
Autumn leaves
Wheat and other cereals
Trees
Pack animals
Winter homes of insects, animals, reptiles

November

Cotton and cotton specimens
Cotton fabrics
Silk and silkworm
Flax and hemp
Loom and spinning wheel
Sense training — taste
Honey and bees
Building
Bricks and brick-making
Quarries and stones
Surveying and tools
Logging, tools, sled, pictures
Engine and circular saw
Wood specimens, manual training
Glass, putty, sand
Trees, winter buds
Poultry
Thanksgiving

December

Carpenter, tools, and tool chest
Wooden building material
Fastenings
Light and heating
Blocks
Forms of water

Animal charts, comparative size
Plumbing and soldering
Reindeer
Evergreen trees
Christmas in other lands

January

Water transportation, hand, wind
Bedroom furniture
Kitchen furniture
Dining-room furniture
Water transportation, steam
The human body
Races of men
Relationships, the family
Occupations in general
Sheep, wool, and woolen fabrics
Camel

February

Laundry furniture
Railroad station, signals, etc.
Freight train
Passenger train
Gardening in boxes
Lighthouse, lifeboat, life preservers
Paints and varnishes
Printing
Whale
Fish and fishing
Blacksmith
Roads, bridges
Vehicles (man power)
Automobile, truck
Ambulance
Express wagon
Ice and ice team
George Washington

March

Scratchers
Common birds
Nests and eggs
Elephant, rhinoceros, hippopotamus
Rochester box of minerals

Seal and walrus, fur
Maple sugar
Animals (Mountjoy's Chart)
Beaver
Pine trees and cones
Measuring instruments
Metals
Mail and post-office
St. Valentine's Day (Make valentines)
Daniel Boone
Edison
Mines and mining
Iron
Bears
Ostrich
Birds of prey
Waders

April

Birds (Mountjoy's Chart)
Wasps and hornets
Moths and butterflies
Ants, beetles, spiders
Grasshoppers, dragon flies
Mosquitoes
Reptiles
Poisonous plants
Roots and leaves
Gypsy moth
Leaves, twigs, buds
Sugar (maple, beet, cane)
Salt
Shells, shell fish
Sponges, corals
Canned and dried fish
Farm and farm tools
Insects (Mountjoy's Chart)

May

Tea (from D. S. Room)
Rubber
Handwork
Musical instruments, stringed (Music teacher to demonstrate)

Paper
Liquid measures
Scales
Musical instruments, wind (Music teacher to demonstrate)
Cat family (Prang's Envelope)
Shoemaker and tools
Dog family
Flower shapes
Foreign flags
Fire truck
Fireflies
Animals (Bancroft's Chart)
Minerals (Bancroft's Chart)
Coffee (from D. S. Room)
Turtle
Frogs and toads
Spring flowers
Cream, butter, cheese
Cocoa (from D. S. Room)
Geography chart

June

Weasel family
Vegetables (Bancroft's Chart)
Alligator
Porcupine
Races of men
Rats and mice
Monkey
Kangaroo
Stork
Flag Day (June 10)
Bunker Hill story (June 17)
Story of our flag
Peacock
Memorial Day story
Memorial Day
Independence Day story

D. Summary and Conclusions

The object lesson has been defined as a teaching device which aims to increase knowledge by the direct study of materials, processes, and conditions. Thus, through these lessons the feeble-minded gain a rather close and intimate acquaintance with a wealth of concrete material in their environment.

In teaching the feeble-minded, the aims in any one lesson should be few and distinct, and the attention of the class held closely to the observation of relevant facts. The fundamental principles underlying this teaching device are that the training process should be simple, direct, concrete; and the steps between the various stages of informational advancement very small indeed.

The technique of instruction involved in the object lesson calls for real planning on the part of the teacher, as well as for real teaching ability, since dependence cannot be placed on the words of any text. Further, oral instruction of a group of feeble-minded boys or girls, using real objects as the basis of instruction, necessitates teaching skill. Thus the teacher must know how to organize and direct, and so teacher-training for those who instruct mental defectives becomes an absolute necessity.

The place of the object lesson in training the senses and in the kindergarten has been shown; likewise, the materials for such have been determined.

The object lesson in its relation to general and specific curricular activity has been discussed in three sections: (1) a classified, object-lesson program for purposes of special-school training; (2) a series of object lessons for number work, reading and related subjects, history and civics, geography, nature study, dramatization, and music; and (3) a proposed daily object-lesson program.[1] In no case has an attempt been made to make the series absolutely exhaustive, but an endeavor has been made to make the discussion serviceable as a guide in training the feeble-minded.

Since the worth of any training process is ultimately determined by the results attained, our attention will next be centered on the "Results of the Salvaging Process," or the social, occupational, and economic efficiency of 1,116 feeble-minded boys and girls trained and developed under the system we have discussed here in some detail.

[1] See Appendix I for the object-lesson materials.

CHAPTER VI

THE RESULTS OF THE SALVAGING PROCESS

A. THE SOCIAL AND ECONOMIC POSSIBILITIES OF THE FEEBLE-MINDED

RECENT studies and experiments have already begun to show the social and economic possibilities of the feeble-minded as contrasted with their well-known anti-social and uneconomical proclivities of attitude and behavior if left to themselves. As we shall point out presently, there are bad defectives and good defectives,[1] but up to the last ten years much intellectual and physical material has gone to waste, with little hope that this could be reclaimed and its potentialities made use of. For our purposes, it is the more significant that the majority of these important studies and experiments have been made with institutional, and hence the least hopeful, cases.

Borrowing a simile used by the late Dr. Pearce Bailey, former Chairman of the New York State Commission for Mental Defectives, the idea concerning the care of the feeble-minded, which until rather recently has prevailed, was that of comparing the institution for such individuals to a placid lake which slowly received its influx of new waters and lost the contents only by slow evaporation. That is to say, formerly, the institution of the commonly accepted type slowly received its patients up to the point of capacity and kept them until death took them away. This was the familiar type of institutional care urged by the segregation program for subnormals. "It was a case of giving elaborate care to one irresponsible, contemplating on how much had thereby been accomplished, and letting nine or more others drift to disaster and add to a fast accumulating pile of social wreckage."

---

[1] W. E. Fernald: *After-Care Study of the Patients Discharged from Waverley for a Period of Twenty-Five Years*, p. 2. Reprinted from *Ungraded*, Nov., 1919.

To men of vision and faith in the potentialities of the mentally defective, such as Dr. Walter E. Fernald, the problem came to be not one of theorizing as to how well the situation might be controlled if permanent institutional care were provided for all; rather, it came to be a question of making the existing institutions of the greatest possible service. Thus, the newer conception of institutional training toward social and economic rehabilitation came to be that of a lake fed and likewise drained by a continuous stream, with provision for sufficient inflow and overflow.[1] The training process therein involved we have chosen to call the "salvaging process," a process in which the public schools, as the chief educational instrument of the public, must, especially in the future, have their part.

In this chapter it will be our purpose to consider the work of the Walter E. Fernald State School; and at this point, as elsewhere in this thesis, we are indebted to the late Dr. Walter E. Fernald, who gave us the initiatory impetus toward investigation concerning the possibilities of applying his type of special-school training to the public school systems of our country. We are further indebted to Miss Mable A. Matthews, former Head Social Worker of the above institution, for the data contained in Section C; and to Dr. Ransom A. Greene and his entire staff for their permission to include in this discussion the social and economic survey of the training process considered in Section D.

B. After-Care of Discharged Patients

In the 1916 annual report of the F. S. S., Dr. Fernald wrote: "It should not be forgotten that until within a few years the various synonyms of mental defect were used to include only what are known as the idiot and the imbecile groups. Particularly the whole of the so-called moron groups, of whom there are perhaps more than of the idiot and imbecile groups combined, and whose presence in the community is of far more sinister significance, were not then recognized as being mentally defective and irresponsible until improved diagnostic methods

[1] S. P. Davies: *Social Control of the Feebleminded*, Columbia University, 1923, pp. 85–86.

came into use."[1] Thus, a different question formerly confronted the superintendents of institutions for the feeble-minded from that which has arisen during recent years. The approach to rehabilitation was not by the method of physiological education with a view to curing idiocy, as it had been earlier, but by means of social education which would enable these mentally retarded individuals to get along by making the most of their innate capacities.

Perhaps the great importance of this study of Dr. Fernald's is that it includes many cases discharged from the institution during the period when segregation was considered the best policy. The majority of cases were discharged under protest; although some were allowed to go because "they seemed to have no vicious tendencies, and their friends were intelligent and able to look out for them." Indeed, as Dr. Fernald remarks, "We honestly believed that nearly all of these people should remain in the institution indefinitely."

The total number of discharges during this period was 1,537, of which 891 were not considered in the inquiry for the following reasons:

Directly transferred to other institutions for the feeble-minded 187
Directly transferred to hospitals for the insane 153
Directly transferred to hospitals for epileptics 89
Directly transferred to other custodial institutions 8
Directly returned to home state 175
Could not be located 279

This left 646 — 470 males and 176 females — whose history in the community could be obtained. Of this number, 54 males and 24 females had died, and 68 males and 33 females had been readmitted to Waverley.

Disastrous social consequences would be expected in sending these people, particularly the women, out into the world, if our judgment were to be determined by the concept of feeble-mindedness prevalent up to the time the study was made. However, histories were obtainable in 176 female cases. Of these, 27, or 15 per cent, had married men "whose social status was rather

[1] Annual Report of the Walter E. Fernald State School, 1916.

above that of their own parents." With one exception, an imbecile whose marriage had turned out badly, all were of the moron groups. Eleven of these 27 married women "were living useful and blameless lives; had neat and attractive homes, bore good reputations in the community, went to church, and apparently were making good in every way." These 11 women had 34 children, all of whom, in the view of the social workers, seemed normal. Three of the 11 were discharged without protest at the request of responsible relatives; the remaining 8 were discharged only upon a writ of habeas corpus issued by the Supreme Court and against the advice of the Waverley authorities. All of the group were apparently feeble-minded and before admission had been immoral, giving difficulty while in the institution by reason of their active sex interest. Yet, after their discharge, and previous to marriage, they had apparently led blameless lives. Of the 27 married women, 16 were behaving badly, every one having been discharged contrary to the best judgment of Dr. Fernald and his associates. "In these sixteen unsuccessful marriages, the women turned out about as we had predicted, with a record of sex promiscuity, alcoholism, thievery, etc."

Concerning the total 176 discharged females, 48 had a history of known sexual immorality, including the 16 married women, 11 unmarried mothers, and 14 subsequently committed to other institutions. In practically none of these social failures were there responsible relatives or friends to give advice and supervision. That is, the women who got into trouble after leaving the institution were those who were left to drift, everything contributing, as it were, to social failure and nothing making for social success. Dr. Fernald concludes: "Apparently the women who had friends capable of understanding them, and of properly protecting them, did not have illegitimate children and did not become sex offenders."

Twenty-nine of the 176 "drifted" into other institutions after discharge; 4 to hospitals for epileptics; 10 to hospitals for the insane; 1 to prison; and 3 to girls' reformatories. In the period of 25 years, only 4 out of a total of 176 had been sentenced to penal institutions.

On the economic side, out of these 176 discharged women, not including the 11 successfully married women, 8 others were "fully and independently supporting themselves in the way of getting their own jobs and paying their own bills as ordinary working women do." All of this latter group were morons. Thirty-two others, as a rule of the low moron and high imbecile groups, were capable workers at home and, although probably not capable of earning a living wage, were nevertheless in no way an economic burden. Thus, approximately 30 per cent may be counted as economic assets, being capable in whole or in part of earning their own living. "These cases had friends able and willing to protect and care for them." Lastly, there was the group of 23 cases of the imbeciles and idiot type; 10 of these were more or less troublesome, the remaining 13 being quiet, well-behaved, and able to do very simple housework. The character of the home and the intelligence of the family largely determined the result.

To summarize the discussion thus far, we quote from Dr. Fernald's report (p. 5):

"To sum up, for 176 discharged female patients, we have the following report:

Married (11 doing well)	27
Self-supporting and self-controlling, unmarried	8
Working at home under supervision	32
Living at home, not able to do much work	23
Committed to other institutions	29
Died	24
Readmitted to Waverley	33
	176

"Of the 90 discharged females now at liberty, 52 are apparently giving no trouble, viz.:

Married, living at home	11
Self-supporting	8
Of those working at home	20
Of those living at home	13

"In the following tables, some persons are counted in more than one classification, so that the totals do not apparently check. The following groups have behaved badly, viz.:

Married women, sex offenders. 16
Unmarried mothers 11
Sex offenders not included above 21
Sent to other institutions 29
Of those working at home 12
Of those living at home 10
Readmitted to Waverley 33

In interpreting the results of the preceding records, consideration should be given to the fact that they were, to begin with, an unfavorable group; and that in the majority of cases they were discharged under protest. The findings, not fully looked for by even Dr. Fernald himself, gave relatively little support to the previous sweeping statements concerning the usual antisocial tendencies of the mentally subnormal. Thus, in publishing his report, Dr. Fernald led the way to a better understanding of the possibilities, social and economic, of the feeble-minded. That is, when the results from a purely unselected and highly negative group, who were discharged in most cases under protest and without any further supervisory control, were considered, it became apparent that there were vast possibilities of salvaging many of these heretofore hopeless individuals, of restoring them to community life through careful training and careful selection. In addition to the system of training and selection used by Dr. Fernald, a trial period was instituted, during which time the patient would have the close supervision of the institutional social worker and, where possible, the home. Such a program appeared worthy of very minute consideration.

The survey concerning the 470 males, all of whom were morons, was even more encouraging, although "few seemed capable of self-support while at the school."[1] Thirteen, or less than 3 per cent, had married; and there were but 12 children by these marriages. The homes were neat and clean, the children well-behaved and apparently normal. Only two of these men, able to support themselves without supervision, had proved failures, having been sentenced to the reformatory for larceny. The weekly wages of this group ranged from $8.00 to $36.00, and in occupation they were teamsters, elevator men, city laborers,

[1] W. E. Fernald: *After-Care Study of the Patients Discharged from Waverley.*

factory workers, farm laborers, soda clerks, tinsmiths, carpenters, painters, chauffeurs, machinists, etc. One was in business for himself, as a painter, a trade he had learned at the school;[1] one had saved $2,000; another owned a house. Concerning these, Dr. Fernald says, "These 28 men seemed to have a blameless record in their community. They are good citizens, regarded as simple-minded men and recognized as such by their employers, and by their wives, for where they had married normal women (as they nearly all did) the wives spoke very kindly of the mental limitations of their husbands."

As a second group, we may consider 86 of the discharged men, nearly all of whom were morons, with the exception of a few high-grade imbeciles, who were "steadily working for wages, living at home, closely supervised by their relatives." They were employed in 39 different occupations, the majority receiving from $7.00 to $16.00 weekly, although a few were receiving as low as $3.00 or $4.00 a week. Only a few were doing simple manual labor. The behavioristic reactions of this group were very favorable, none of them had been troublesome sexually or shown any criminalistic tendencies, and they appeared happy and contented. In brief, three factors were functional in making them useful and desirable members of society, outside of the training received at the F. S. S. — namely, good homes, careful supervision on the part of relatives, and steady work. Thus, where the feeble-minded are understood, their limitations recognized and considered, and where there is opportunity for proper training, they get along in the average community quite as well as most normal persons.

A third group of 77 males are described as being of the low moron and high-grade imbecile type, of various ages, able to do more or less work at home, but receiving no wages. Eight of these were attending public schools, not keeping up with the others yet learning a little slowly. We note that "these persons all seemed to be harmless and inoffensive. No record of sex offense could be ascertained. Where the members of this group lived on a farm or a small village, they were evidently happier

[1] *Mental Hygiene*, April, 1922, p. 338.

and did better in every way than those who lived in the city. In this group the lack of serious character defect and the fact that they were closely supervised were important factors in their behavior."

The fourth group consisted of 59 males of idiot and imbecile grade, living at home, unable to carry their own economic burden. Socially, however, the report concerning these is very favorable, due to favorable home conditions and the absence of disagreeable character traits in these individuals.

Of the fifth group no detailed comment is necessary; they were of the "bad defective" kind, being known to have been committed to penal or reformatory institutions subsequent to their discharge. "Without exception they were voluble, plausible, incorrigible, and apparently inherently criminalistic from early childhood." In addition, 23, 16 morons and 7 imbeciles, had been arrested for crimes or misdemeanors, but had not at the time of the report been sentenced to penal institutions. Both of these two latter groups were typical "defective delinquents" and should never have been released except under strict parole. Forty-three were committed to other institutions; 68 were readmitted to Waverley; and 54 died.

A summary of the 470 discharged males follows:

Earning a living without supervision	28
Working for wages, supervised at home	86
Working at home, no wages	77
Living at home, not able to work	59
Arrested, but not sentenced	23
Sentenced to penal institutions	32
Committed to other institutions	43
Readmitted to Waverley	68
Died	54
Total	470

It would appear, then, that a total of 250, or 53 per cent, constituted no serious menace at the time of the investigation.

The main point of variability in the record of the two sexes is in the matter of sex behavior, there being a better record in the case of the boys than of the girls. The study gives great hope that a considerable proportion of the feeble-minded, after a training such as is given at the F. S. S., can successfully take their place in the world outside. We can do no better in closing this section than to use Dr. Fernald's own words by way of summary:

> The results of this survey should be interpreted with great caution. As a rule, the most promising cases are allowed to go home. The parents have been properly instructed. Still many unpromising cases did well. There was a surprisingly small amount of criminality and sex offense, and especially of illegitimacy. We may hope for a much better record when we have extra institutional visitations and supervision of all discharged cases. Those with definite character defects, especially, those with bad homes, should be discharged with great caution. The survey shows that there are good defectives and bad defectives. It also shows that even some apparently bad do "settle down" and it shows much justice in the plea of the well-behaved adult defective to be given a "trial outside," for apparently a few defectives do not need or deserve lifelong segregation. It is most important that the limited facilities for segregation should be used for the many who can be protected in no other way.

C. Analysis of Report on Supervision of Trained Male Defectives

Another report of significance in this connection is that of Mable A. Matthews, Head Social Worker at the Fernald State School, entitled *One Hundred Institutionally Trained Male Defectives in the Community under Supervision*.[1] The defectives which Miss Matthews has included in her study were not a selected group but included all those who were within a given distance of the institution at Waverley. The boys studied had not been discharged, but were still under supervisory control, although they had been returned to their homes either because their parents or friends had asked that they might go out "on trial" or because they had been taken home for a vacation, and having secured work, were allowed to remain there. Two of these 100 boys had run away but were allowed to go on the list to report; 7 were considered sufficiently trained for purposes of self-support and were allowed to go out and take positions.

At the time of this study, 97 of these boys were living in the community; the remaining three had been returned to the insti-

[1] Reprinted from *Mental Hygiene*, Vol. VI, No. 2, April, 1922, pp. 332-342.

tution because of behavior reactions, inability to keep a job, and need of additional training.

The following outline shows the conditions of the 100 cases concerned in this study:

Boys with fairly high I.Q.'s., living at home and attending public school	5
Boys with mental age of less than 8 years — doing farm work	2
Boys with chronological age of 24 years, mental age of less than 8 years; semiparalyzed; living at home; of much assistance in the housework	1
Boys with mental age 6 years, living at home; of some assistance in house	1
In the Army	2
In the Navy	1
Taking Government vocational-training work	1
Out of work, due to "hard times," living at home and closely supervised	4
Sent to reform schools	2
Working and self-supporting	78
Total	97
Returned to institution	3
Total	100

Concerning the 78 boys reported as working and self-supporting, Miss Matthews says, "Notwithstanding the present scarcity of work and the fact that a number have had to find new jobs, 78 boys are working and self-supporting, although many of them have been reduced in pay or have had to take inferior positions."

Maximum and Minimum Wages Summarized. — The following outline of Miss Matthews reveals the relation of wages to mental age.

1. Maximum Wages (weekly) Earned by the Various Mental-Age Groups:

Defectives with M. A. of less than 8 years	$26.00
Defectives with M. A. of 8 years	28.00
Defectives with M. A. of 9 years	30.00
Defectives with M. A. of 10 years	32.00
Defectives with M. A. of more than 10 years	34.00
Average (Maximum Weekly Wages)	$30.00

2. Minimum Wages (weekly) Earned by the Various Mental Age Groups:

Defectives with M. A. of less than 8 years	$ 8.00
Defectives with M. A. of 8 years	10.00
Defectives with M. A. of 9 years	12.00
Defectives with M. A. of 10 years	10.00
Defectives with M. A. of more than 10 years	10.00
Average (Minimum Weekly Wages)	$10.00

Type of Work done by the Different Groups. — It is of value to consider briefly the type of work done by the various mental-age groups. The range of wages for those under eight years mentally was from $8.00 to $26.00 per week. In this group there were as many earning $24.00 a week as there were earning $8.00 a week, probably due to the fact that those earning $24.00 a week are hod carriers, roofers' helpers, or workers doing similarly hard or dangerous work, and are, therefore, paid more. These same scales have since been worked out with twice this number of boys and show practically the same results. Besides the types of work noted, some of these boys were working on farms, on milk wagons, or in factories, while one boy was learning to be an upholsterer.

The range of wages for those with eight-year-old minds was from $10.00 to $28.00 per week, the latter wage being that of a boy who is a fire-tender in a roundhouse. One receives $24.00 a week taking boards from the saw in a lumber yard; one repairs automobile radiators, and another nails boxes in a candy factory. In addition, we find helpers on machines, factory and farm hands, errand boys, stitchers in a tailor shop, and so on.

The range of wages for those with nine-year-old minds was from $12.00 to $30.00 per week, the latter including a painter and a machinist's helper. The majority of this group were working either on farms or in factories.

Of those boys with a mental age of ten years, the range of wages was from $10.00 to $32.00 a week. One as an employee of a railroad was earning approximately $32.00 each week, while the remainder of this group were truck and team drivers, errand boys, a canvasser, and so forth.

Concerning the last group, those of ten-year-old mentality, the range of wages was from $10.00 to $34.00 per week. In this group, there was a truck driver earning $30.00 a week, a painter receiving $20.00 a week, and at the other extreme a boy sixteen years of age who as an errand boy was earning $10.00 a week. As in the previous groups, the majority were evidently engaged as factory workers, one boy "directing stock" with seven men working under him.

As Miss Matthews notes, the largest number of working boys were factory workers and laborers, although another fair-sized group appeared successful in farm work. Likewise, another point is evident: with the increase in mental age, the wage earned increased.

With respect to the fact that these defectives were found to be successful, Miss Matthews says: "That these boys are a success is due to the fact that they are faithful, conscientious, methodical, unquestioning workers. While at Waverley, they were trained to work steadily and faithfully and to take pride in their work. They are painstaking with uninteresting details of their work, and it matters not how simple it may be, they take pride in doing it well. True, this pride needs to be stimulated by the interest shown by the one in authority. They will do the same thing in the same way day after day, and they will work until the bell rings. They seem to enjoy the monotony instead of tiring of the repetition. As a rule they will take a direction if they understand it and will follow it without questioning or stopping to debate whether it is really their job or whether it belongs to some one else to do it. They do what is expected of them. If they can only be made to feel that they are expected to do a certain thing, there is something compelling about this feeling, and they do the expected thing." Another reason for their success is that they crave respectability. They wish to be thought of as "somebody" and to be looked upon as are other men. Supported by charity, visited by the police in many cases, slow in school and in play, they have felt the "sting of scorn." Now, a "chance" has come to them; an opportunity to make good is at hand; and as a result they actually endeavor to suppress their antisocial traits and habits just as they were trained to do at Waverley. There they are taught the necessity of cleanliness; the officials of the institution have become their ideals of respectability as to mannerisms and dress, and having been taught to save, they take with them the conviction that in order to reach a high plane in society they must have a bank account, although probably few, if any of them, have any real idea concerning the necessity of saving.

Simple, wholesome amusements afford them recreational opportunities; few, if any, want or expect excitement, — "movies" once or twice a week; an occasional visit to the theater; baseball, gymnasium work, and athletics of various kinds; swimming; long walks on Sunday — with these they are satisfied, for thus they were trained at Waverley.

Miss Matthews concludes: "Their success seems to be due to the painstaking, constructive training received while at the school and to *proper supervision* after going out into the community. We feel that, with continued friendly, helpful supervision, free from humiliating circumstances, the average feeble-minded boy, properly brought up and trained, can live in the community and play his part there."

D. A Study of the Social, Occupational, and Economic Efficiency of the Feeble-Minded

As previously noted, the individuals concerned in this study were not a selected group. Some, who were felt to be sufficiently rehabilitated, socially, occupationally, and morally, were allowed to go out and take positions. In a very few instances, practically a negligible number, the cases reported were "runaways." Their admission to the school was the result of a desire on the part of the parents, who realized the incapacities of their children and the lack of opportunity offered by the public schools for their training, that these individuals have the advantages of the instructional process at Waverley; or of the efforts of social agencies working through Massachusetts; or of the efforts of doctors or hospitals. Both the boys and the girls reported came to the school at various ages — a rather large proportion, especially among the males, being brought at the age of eight or nine, and remaining there until the period of adolescence had passed, perhaps at the age of eighteen or nineteen. It will be noted that a considerable number entered late in life from the viewpoint of training possibilities and so, in some cases, do not reach the average economic status of their mental age. Many, likewise, remain beyond the twenties, until they have become more or less emotionally stable, occupationally fit, and socially adaptable.

Not always, however, will even the training process developed by Dr. Fernald at the F. S. S. accomplish these three aims, yet the cases of absolute failure are indeed rare.

A Study of Three Hundred Twenty-Eight Institutionally Trained Male Defectives. — For purposes of clearness of discussion, we have grouped the three hundred twenty-eight institutionally trained male defectives according to mental age.

The range of wages for the group under eight years mentally extends from $2.50 to $40.00, the latter being the wage of an individual with a mental age of seven years four months, acting in the capacity of truck driver, and the former the wage of a boy with a mental age of six years four months who works for newspaper publishers. One boy (M. A. 6/3) is a light tender in a railroad yard and receives $31.42 per week. Nine are doing general farm work with wages ranging from $15.00 to $75.00 a month. The more common earnings are $65.00 per month. Three are in either the United States Army or Navy; two are painters; while one works for an electric welding company. One, a deaf and dumb imbecile, earns $15.00 as a cigar maker, and two receive $15.00 and $20.00 per week in a photographer's studio. The remaining cases work in factories and in stores of various kinds.

The range of wages for those with eight-year-old minds is from $5.00 to $40.00. One boy (M. A. 8) who owns a truck earns $40.00 a week; a second, with a mental age of seven years two months, is a fire truck driver, having held the same position for six years and is earning $1,320 a year and room; a third earns $37.00 a week as a machinist; a fourth is an automobile mechanic with a weekly salary of $40.00; a fifth receives $4.00 a day as a steam fitter; and a sixth (M. A. 8/4) is an assistant to a city building inspector at a salary of $28.00 a week. As noted above, the minimum earning is $2.50 a week. Other than this, the lowest wage earned by the group is $10.00, the average for the entire group being $21.50. As in the first group, the farms and factories claim a considerable number; although the range of occupations is broader and seems to call for a greater degree of mentality among other qualifications.

The range of wages for our nine-year-old minds is from $12.00

to $40.00, with an average wage of $21.72 for the group. In this division, we note a floorman (shoe manufacturing company) receiving $40.00 a week; a vulcanizer earning $160.00 a month; a man working as head cutter for a plate glass company at $36.00 a week; and an automobile salesman (M. A. 9/2) earning $35.00 per week. There are, likewise, a painter at a weekly wage of $35.00, an express company employee at $25.00 a week, and a "professional barber" who earns $35.00 weekly. In this group are truck drivers, railway employees, hospital workers, auto mechanics, caretakers, and factory and farm laborers.

Of the group with a ten-year mentality, the average weekly wage is $23.12, the range being, as in Group III, $12.00 to $40.00. Of those receiving the maximum salary for the group, one is a traveling salesman for a picture company, and two are painters. The minimum wage is received by a porter in a cafeteria. One boy sells magazines for an agency at $35.00 a week, and another is a pick-and-shovel worker for a railroad at a weekly wage of $28.00. Practically all the unskilled and semi-skilled occupations are represented in this group.

The economic range of the wages of Group V, with mental ages of eleven years to eleven years eleven months inclusive, is from $10.00 to $43.00, the latter being the salary of a carpenter on a railroad, and the former that of a boy who delivers newspapers, although there is a difference of but two months in mentality between the two individuals. The average weekly wage for the group is $21.92, just slightly less than that of the ten-year-old group. One is an assistant foreman in a large manufacturing company and receives $33.50 a week; one is a truck driver at $30.00 a week; one is a box maker earning a weekly salary of $26.00; and another sells embroidery, receiving on sales a commission of ten per cent. A survey of this group from the standpoint of occupation reveals a somewhat greater range than heretofore, although the same industrial pursuits are dominant.

There are but two cases represented in Group VI (M. A. 12/11) and Group VII (M. A., 13 to 13/11 years). The former is a male defective with a mentality of twelve years who has

CHART III

AVERAGE WEEKLY WAGES OF THREE HUNDRED TWENTY-EIGHT MENTALLY DEFECTIVE MALES IN THEIR RELATION TO MENTAL AGE

(From Walter E. Fernald State School Data)

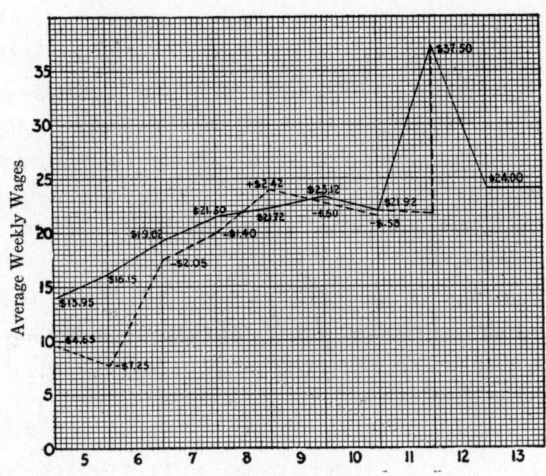

Mental Age in Years

———— Average Week Wages
-------- Probable Deviation from the Average

AGE	No.
5 to 5/11 years	9
6 to 6/11 years	17
7 to 7/11 years	50
8 to 8/11 years	99
9 to 9/11 years	84
10 to 10/11 years	48
11 to 11/11 years	19
12 to 12/11 years	1
13 to 13/11 years	1
Total	328

charge of the motor cars for a telegraph company, receiving for his services $150.00 a month and expenses. The latter is a boy who earns $24.00 per week as attendant in a state hospital.

Chart III gives a summary of each group of male defectives on the basis of the relationship of mental age and maximum and minimum wages, that is, the average weekly wage of three hundred twenty-eight mentally defective males in their relation to mental age, together with the P. E. deviation from the average. The general average weekly wage shows a constant increase from the mental age of five years to the mental age of eleven years, with a decrease in P. E. deviation from the average in the advance of the positive wage trend. The curve from eleven to twelve years, mental age, shows a decided upward trend, whereas from twelve to thirteen years, mental age, there is a downward tendency. Since in both instances but one case is represented, the curve is not truly representative from eleven years onward. Reference to the discussion concerning the range of wages and kinds of work shows a constant increase in the minimum wage from Group I through Group IV with a decrease in $2.00 per week on the part of Group V over that of Group IV. The maximum wage of $40.00 remains constant throughout the first four groups, that is, up to a mental age of eleven years, increasing by $3.00 in Group V, which is about what we would expect when considering the constancy of minimum wages in their relation to the general average wage of each group. Chart IV presents the average range of weekly wages earned by three hundred twenty-eight mentally defective males in their relation to mental age. Let us compare for a moment these two charts. They show very clearly that, although there is considerable variability between the factor of mental age and economic efficiency as measured by the range of weekly wages, there is a gradual rise in the average weekly wage curve as we advance along the mental age "ladder." It seems evident, therefore, that mental age or general intellectual capacity has a very close relationship and deciding influence in determining not only what occupation a mentally defective male individual will enter but likewise what wage he will receive therein. That is, mental age and occupational efficiency are

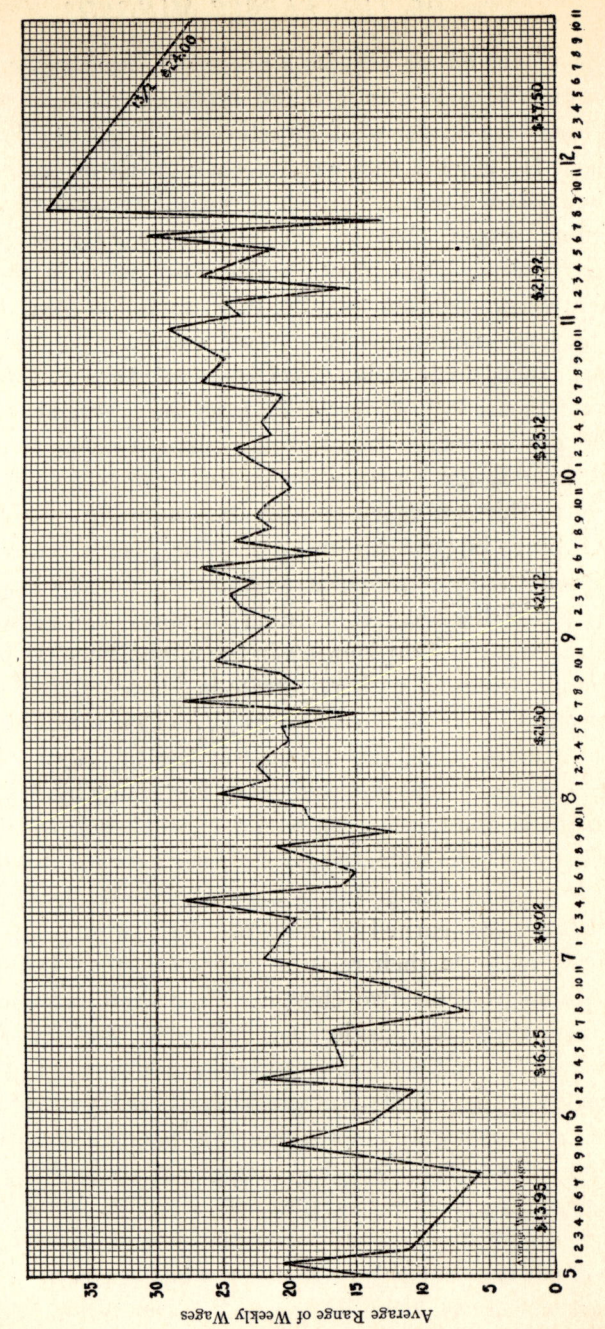

CHART IV

AVERAGE RANGE OF WEEKLY WAGES EARNED BY THREE HUNDRED TWENTY-EIGHT MENTALLY DEFECTIVE MALES IN ITS RELATION TO MENTAL AGE

very closely related. It is likewise evident that there are other factors at work — more especially, perhaps, the training of a particularized type, social adaptability, ability and desire to coöperate, mental and physical health, and personality. On the surface of our data, which factor or factors is most functional in the life-success of the mentally defective male is not shown; but down deep in this investigation one principle seems constantly functional — whatever may be the case with normal persons, with the feeble-minded tráining and environment are the chief determining factors in their social, occupational, and general economic success. However important may be heredity, the force which gives us our mental potentiality, we feel reasonably sure that, in the vast majority of cases, had not the training process been of the general nature described in the previous chapters been possible to the subjects of our study, the degree of social adaptability and occupational and economic efficiency would never have been reached. For — let us frankly ask ourselves — what has the *average* public school system to offer, outside of the more or less purely literary instructional program, to the mentally retarded children with mental ages ranging from less than five years up to approximately eleven or twelve years? Apparently there is not much; and so whatever may be the importance of heredity, and we do believe it to be very important, training and environmental situations of the right kind seem to be of greater importance to the typical mental defective at least.

A Study of Forty-One Institutionally Trained Female Defectives. — The same method of presentation of these forty-one institutionally trained female defectives was followed as in the previous section of our discussion.

In Group I — those with a mental age under eight years — the average weekly wage is $14.82, with a range of $12.00 to $20.00. The latter wage is received by a feeble-minded girl with a mental age of seven years three months who works in the diet kitchen of a large hospital; the former by a subnormal case with a mental age of seven years two months who shakes and folds clothing in a laundry. The third case in this group is a mentally defective female, with a mental age of seven years eleven months, who earns $12.50 a week doing housework at home.

In Group II — those with mental ages from eight years to eight years eleven months inclusive — the range of the weekly salary schedule is from $14.95 to $25.00, the average being $20.11. Two receive a salary of $25.00 a week — one as a second maid in a private home and the other as a baster and finisher on dresses. Two others do housework, receiving respectively $16.00 and $20.00 weekly. Of the remaining two, one earns $14.95 in a buckle factory, the other receiving the support of herself and baby. This latter case was recommitted once to Waverley some time after her first discharge.

In the third group — those with mental ages of nine years to nine years eleven months — the range of wages is from $5.00 to $21.00, considerably less than that for Group II. (See above paragraph.) The average wage here is $13.40. Six are doing housework; one is a presser in a hosiery concern; one is a mill operative, and two are factory workers.

For those with mental ages of ten years to ten years eleven months inclusive, the average weekly wage is $13.61, slightly in excess of that for Group III but less than for Group II. As in the preceding group, housework is the prevailing occupation, eight being thus engaged with a weekly salary scale ranging from $7.00 to $14.50. Two are hospital workers; two are factory workers; one is a waitress; and a fourth cares for children.

In Group V — those with mental ages of eleven years to eleven years eleven months — there are included six female defectives whose range of wages is from $10.00 to $22.00, an average of $15.40, the highest of any of the female groups studied. The highest salary is received by a girl with a mental age of eleven years three months, who works in a clothing store; the lowest wage is earned by a girl doing housework. Of the remaining four, two are factory workers; one is a sweeper in a large mill; and one does housework.

Chart V gives a summary of each of the above groups concerning the economic efficiency of forty-one defective females in terms of minimum and maximum wages in their relation to mental age. It will be seen that the average minimum wage shows great fluctuation, the high point being in Group II, where the mental age is eight years to eight years eleven months inclusive. From the nine-year level to the twelve-year level there is a constant and significant rise. The outstanding maximum wage is that of the eight-year-olds, with a decline through the nine- and ten-year levels, but with a rise in the eleven-year mental level. From this it seems evident that other factors besides mental age as we commonly think of it must be at work in determining what wage an individual of the nature of these female defectives is to receive. Chart VI presents a graphic study of the average range of weekly wages earned by forty-one mentally defective females in its relation to mental age. Contrasting Charts III and V, we find the same variation of wages according to mental age, which is not quite as great in the case of the girls as with the boys; in Chart V, however, we do not find the same gradual rise in wages as in Chart III. Chart VI is a graphic representation of the average weekly wages of forty-one mentally defective females in their relation to mental age. Whereas, in general, the average weekly wages of the male defectives increases regularly with mental age, with the female defectives there is a sharp rise at the mental level of eight years, a decline at nine years, but a gradual rise in the curve thereafter. Comparing Charts III and V with respect to the average salary earned per mental level and the nature of the curves thereof, it might be inferred that in the occupational world a higher degree of mentality is essential and necessary for success from a purely economic standpoint in the case of girls than for boys; or that possibly the training process had not been as functional with the former as with the latter. Neither of these inferences is probable. Our data show that the occupational range for girls is more limited than for boys; also, that, as a rule, those occupations open to girls are more poorly paid than those open to boys. This seems to be true also in the case of normal boys and girls, although perhaps not quite so much so, in spite of our democratic equality of sexes. Further, we do not feel this variation to be due to the training

CHART V

Average Weekly Wages of Forty-One Mentally Defective Females in Their Relation to Mental Age
(From Walter E. Fernald State School Data)

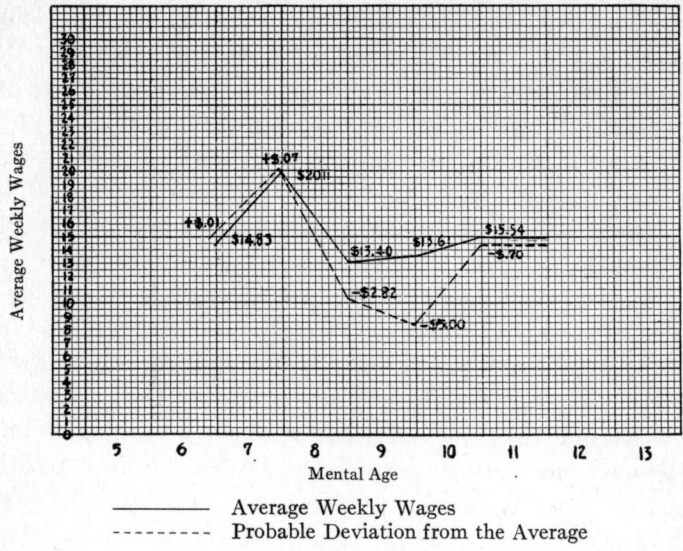

————— Average Weekly Wages
--------- Probable Deviation from the Average

CHART VI

Average Range of Weekly Wages Earned by Forty-One Mentally Defective Females in Its Relation to Mental Age

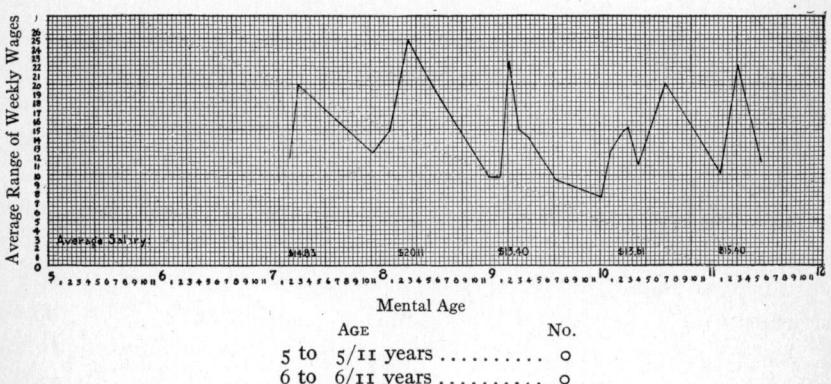

Mental Age

Age	No.
5 to 5/11 years	0
6 to 6/11 years	0
7 to 7/11 years	3
8 to 8/11 years	6
9 to 9/11 years	10
10 to 10/11 years	16
11 to 11/11 years	6
Total	41

156 A

process; there are other factors besides general intellectual capacity and training at work — such as emotional stability or lack of it, temperament, social adaptability, the willingness to coöperate, physical and mental health, and the like. We have reason to believe that, in addition to the more or less concrete determinants of relatively narrow vocational range and comparatively lower pay for defective females, all these rather subtle factors were at work with a strong tendency towards negative dominance. Properly trained, position for position, the defective female is quite as efficient as the feeble-minded boy. Contrasting the records before and after the training process had left its trace leaves no doubt in our minds but that Dr. Fernald and his staff have reaped a most amazing harvest in social and occupational efficiency among the feeble-minded girls and boys.

Thus we feel that, in the case of the feeble-minded student, although heredity furnishes the potentialities of mental endowment, what this becomes depends upon what is done with it; that is, upon the type of training and environmental situations furnished. Viewing those three hundred seventy as types, we cannot help but feel that training of the right kind is the dominating factor, although we do not wish to leave heredity out of the reckoning.

TABLE III

A Summary of the Economic Efficiency of Three Hundred Twenty-Eight Institutionally Trained Male Defectives in Its Relation to Mental Age

Mental Age	Minimum Weekly Wages	Maximum Weekly Wages
Group I, Mental Age — Under 8 years ...	$ 2.50	$40.00
Group II, Mental Age — 8 to 8/11 years ...	5.00	40.00
Group III, Mental Age — 9 to 9/11 years ...	12.00	40.00
Group IV, Mental Age — 10 to 10/11 years ..	12.00	40.00
Group V, Mental Age — 11 to 11/11 years ..	10.00	43.00
Group VI, Mental Age — 12 to 12/11 years ..	—	37.50
Group VII, Mental Age — 13 to 13/11 years..	—	24.00

TABLE IV

A Summary of the Economic Efficiency of Forty-One Institutionally Trained Females in Its Relation to Mental Age

Mental Age	Minimum Weekly Wages	Maximum Weekly Wages
Group I, Mental Age — Under 8 years . . .	$12.00	$20.00
Group II, Mental Age — 8 to 8/11 years . . .	14.95	25.00
Group III, Mental Age — 9 to 9/11 years . . .	4.50	22.00
Group IV, Mental Age — 10 to 10/11 years . .	5.00	21.00
Group V, Mental Age — 11 to 11/11 years . .	20.00	22.22

The range of the kinds of work is as wide and as varied as is the range of wages, especially among the male defectives. We find the largest group of boys working as laborers and factory helpers; they are able to manipulate fairly simple machinery and to do work of an automatic type which does not require much intelligence. Among these latter there is likewise a great variation. We find them working in piano, rubber, metal, hide, crayon, shoe, and candy factories, in knitting mills, bakeries, boat shops, machine shops, automobile repair shops, lumber mills, printing offices, cotton mills, and the like. Some are painters, masons, light tenders on the railroad, janitors, teamsters, restaurant workers, plumbers, cobblers, elevator operators, helpers in a laundry, silver platers, steamfitters' helpers, truck drivers, section hands on the railroad. Members of another group are successful at farm work and as gardeners. They are willing, desire to please, are plodders, faithful and earnest, and even though they may not like to arise early in the morning, as a rule, they do not think of objecting, taking it rather as a matter of coures. A number of these boys are semi-specialists, one receiving $1320.00 a year and room, driving a fire truck; a second is a vulcanizer, earning $160.00 a month; and a third receives a salary of $150.00 a month and expenses, taking charge of the motor cars for a telegraph company.

Among the defective females, housework and related occupational pursuits are predominant. A second group is made up of factory workers and hospital assistants, although we find an occasional one working in a clothing store or a shoe shop. The large amount of unskilled and semi-skilled work which these mentally subnormal boys and girls enter seems to give weight to our position in Chapter II that the training of the feeble-minded should be broad, basic, and fundamental, preparing perhaps more especially for the unskilled or semi-unskilled types of work, rather than too specific and highly specialized, preparing particularly for the higher occupational groups. Receiving very careful training under skilled leaders and teachers and given kinds of work which experience has shown best fit his or her mentality, the child is in most instances able to go directly from the special school to a position.

Summary and Conclusions. — Our study has included the results of three separate investigations concerning "The Salvaging Process" of 1116 cases as follows:

Study	Males	Females	Total
(1) Dr. Fernald's Study	470	176	646
(2) Miss Matthews's Study	100	—	100
(3) Our Own Investigation	328	42	370
Totals	898	218	1116

In each study the splendid work of the F. S. S., at Waverley, in the social rehabilitation, and in the economic-occupational efficiency program for mental defectives, so carefully and painstakingly worked out and planned by Dr. Fernald, has been more than substantiated. We can do no better than to conclude our present discussion with Dr. Fernald's own words:

"All of our experience with the feeble-minded indicates that if we are to manage adequately the individual defective, we must recognize his conditions while he is a child and protect him from evil influences, train and educate him according to his capacity, make him industrially efficient, teach him to acquire correct habits of living, and when he has reached adult life, continue to give him the friendly help and guidance he needs. If conditions are right, he may live at home and receive his training in the rural school or in the special class. If he is actually a social menace, he will need the institution. These advantages should be accessible to every feeble-minded person in the state and not to a few favored persons. The rights of the feeble-minded person and his family should be guarded jealously, as well as the rights of society."[1]

Indeed, these advantages and privileges of special-school training should not be denied any feeble-minded person in the United States.

[1] Walter E. Fernald: "The Inauguration of a State-Wide Public-School Clinic in Massachusetts;" Reprint § 149, from *Mental Hygiene*.

CHAPTER VII

THE TRAINING PROGRAM OF THE SPECIAL-SCHOOL TEACHER

IF the work of the special school is to result in permanent benefits to the individuals under its care, the classes for the mentally defective need superior teachers to carry on the training process. A study of the instruction of mentally subnormal children in the special classes of the public school systems of this country where the work has been carried on for any considerable period of time shows that, without superior and specially trained teachers, these mental retardates easily and readily fall into habits of idleness and waywardness, thus seriously jeopardizing their future conduct and usefulness. With good teachers, personally interested in the cause and in the children themselves, the general disposition, personality traits, and social tendencies on the part of these individuals show a marked improvement, not only with respect to their interests in the tasks assigned but also in the degree of efficiency with which they strive toward accomplishment. To the thoughtful it seems apparent that the training and instruction of this particular group of school children necessitates superior teaching ability as well as a thorough training of a somewhat specialized character on the part of the teacher engaged in this work. This is evident (1) because of the varied accomplishments along the lines of physical, industrial, and social training which these teachers must possess; (2) because of the particular methods of instruction and educational procedure and pace which must be used with children of low mentality in order to secure any permanent results; (3) because of the psychological problems which are constantly arising in the special school and which must be met with a knowledge of the mental and emotional reactions which they arouse, rather than in an experimental manner; and (4) because of the patience, sympathy, and understanding which these teachers must possess either in an inherent or acquired quality, and the love for the work which must be theirs by virtue of the service they can render.

A. Qualifications of the Special-School Teacher

What, then, are the specific qualifications of the special-school teacher which will tend toward success in the training and instruction of mental defectives? As a general standard of reference and rating, wherein the latter is considered desirable, we are presenting a summary of the essentials.

Good Physique. — Although under favorable circumstances the work of the special-school teacher is not excessively burdensome, yet she has more varied demands to meet than does the regular school teacher, and so must have endurance to meet and withstand them. It would be unjust and untrue to feel that there is a peculiar strain in special-school instruction which devitalizes the energies of the school teacher. Some of the healthiest and happiest teachers may be found among those instructing the mentally defective in special classes either in the public school or in state institutions. And there are many of these teachers who find such intellectual and spiritual compensations in their work that they would never contemplate returning to the regular classroom routine.

A Wholesome, Well-Balanced Temperament and Disposition. — Next in order of qualifications, if indeed not first, comes a wholesome, well-balanced temperament or disposition. This means the saving grace of common sense and good judgment. The special-school classroom is not the place for an overtemperamental individual, for the problems of the mentally deficient are too human, too real, too numerous, for such a person. These situations must be met as they arise; they must be appraised and reacted to in due proportion. All kinds of unforeseen and unpredictable situations and conditions are likely to arise; and although they do not require any transcendental wisdom, yet they do demand that ordinary good judgment which we characterize as "common sense" and that tolerant, perspective courtesy which we call "tact." If we but add to this a genuine sense of humor, we then have the foundation for special-school instruction in so far as the teacher herself is concerned. Given this triangular sense of values — common sense, tact, a genuine sense of humor — the problems of the special school may become even more interesting and significant than those of the regular classroom, where routine and group methods of instruction will tend to deaden the mental capacities of the teacher. A natively happy temperament, or even an acquired one, here, as elsewhere in the educational process, is an important asset.

Character and Personality. — Character should be mentioned separately, not because of any peculiar considerations of an ethical nature inherent in the work of the special school, but because of a certain spirit of self-sacrifice and undramatic professional heroism which lend satisfaction and strength to the teacher of mentally subnormal children. There are many rewards which are the accompaniments of special-school training; but a philosophy of life, a willingness to carry on in spite of discouragement, a feeling of respect for the dignity of the work — these and other more or less subtle factors go to make up that indescribable complex called character. It is difficult to define or measure character, but it is relatively easy to discern it. Lack of persistence and depth of character is the synonym of superficial special-school work. In addition to these qualities which we have termed character, there is that manifestation of the individual which is known as personality — including such qualities as poise and modest but correct address. Personality of a positive nature, as well as character, is an essential attribute of the successful special-school teacher.

Social Outlook. — Social outlook is a closely related qualification, since there is no specialty less narrow than the training process of the special school. Wrapped up and reflected in the special-school classroom are many of the great social and personal problems of life. The special school is a highly sociological institution, and the special-school teacher who has the ideals and attitudes of the social worker will be in a better position to make the necessary contacts with homes and community than will one who lacks these. Although such a social outlook is perhaps not indispensable to the everyday teaching work, yet a premium should be put upon it. It adds to the professional spirit and the value of a teacher. She is much more than a "pedagogue" to the subnormal mind; she is a social-welfare agent with a mission closely allied to that of a social worker; and as such we should look upon the teacher in the special school in a peculiar sense as a valuable servant of the state.

Skill in Teaching and Management. — These are essential and necessary attributes to complete success, for, after all, the teacher's most obvious responsibility is the daily care, nurture, and, indeed, the socializing of a group of fifteen or more exceptional children. Not only as a group, but as individuals within a group, they are exceptional children. Nowhere throughout the public school system are individual differences more marked than in the special school. Not only must the teacher possess an educational theory concerning individual differences among the mentally subnormal but an art to meet these mental variations. She must be able to abandon ordinary classroom methods almost completely and to try any plausible means of training and instruction at least once. If not, she is soon riding on the road to failure and disappointment. She must have almost a physician's diagnostic attitude, must be keen to interpret individual possibilities and limitations, to chronicle assets rather than liabilities, to bear in mind the fact that mentally defective children can learn something, and to find out what that something is and be satisfied only with the best the child can do.

Not only will her success depend upon her native mental and physical equipment and training, but upon whether she is interested in her problems. She cannot get along without a true sympathy for her pupils and a feeling for the humanitarian and socializing value of her work. Possessing such an attitude, she is likely to develop a family group atmosphere in her classroom, and conduct her work in a cheerful, parental kind of mood, to which rigidity, formalism, and disciplinarism are foreign characteristics. This parental attitude is not merely a question of sentiment; it is, as we may say, a hygienic attitude which lightens the burdens of the school day and permits a benevolent sense of humor to keep the values right. It is the formalistic type of teacher who attempts heroically to force her preconceptions upon her pupils who wears herself out and makes a failure of her work. Discipline is absolutely essential in the classrooms, shops, and laboratories of the special school; but discipline depends not so much upon a strict rigidity as on a psychological ability to interpret the mentally defective child, combined with sympathy and common sense.

Special Training. — It is apparent that many of the qualities considered above are dependent upon and the resultant of the general personality and innate mental and physical characteristics of the teacher. After all, perhaps, nothing can take the place of such native endowments. Even special training is subordinate to it; but, other things being equal or nearly so, preference should be given to the teacher who has undergone courses of special training. Only when the teacher is one possessing natural talent, who has had experience in kindergarten and primary work, and has an interest in and an acquaintance with mental defectives, can special training be safely dispensed with in assigning a teacher to the special school.

Special training has very much the same relationship to special-school teaching as it has to nursing. To be sure, there are excellent "practical" nurses, who have had for their training a more or less empirical form of experience; but the interests of public health and private nursing require a special course of training. Special-school teachers, like registered nurses, must have professional standards based on special training, since it is the equipping of the mentally defective children with right habits, attitudes, ideals, and skills, that is of the greatest importance in the training process.

B. The Major Subjects in the Training Program of the Special-School Teacher

A survey of the courses of instruction of both normal schools and colleges reveals a general inadequacy of opportunity, so far as specific training and preparation for special-school instruction is concerned, to the teacher who wishes to prepare herself for such work of a rather specialized nature. The fault does not rest, it would seem, with these professional institutions; it is only within the past few years that there has been a felt need for such training; it is but recently that the "salvaging process" for mental defectives has been shown to be not only possible but feasible as well. Special classes, designed more especially, it would appear, for educational "misfits," have existed during the past thirty or more years in some of our more progressive and far-seeing public school systems; but, although an endeavor has been made to train the child industrially, the major emphasis in practically all instances has been on the academic side of instruction. Ordinarily, the teachers of such special classes have been successful kindergarten or primary teachers, without having had specialized training for her particular work; yet to these pioneers who first taught mental defectives, the school, and indeed society at large, owes a great debt of gratitude, more particularly on the social side. With increasing information and a better understanding concerning the problems and the needs of the feeble-minded, together with an apparent growth in complexity of the entire question as to the training and instruction of the mentally subnormal, there has come, as was inevitable, a need for broader understanding on the part of special-school teachers than can be gained through the "school of experience" or even in the typical normal school or college. It is evident that when our public school systems begin the inauguration of special schools, the necessity of specially trained and qualified teachers will be seen, and perhaps only then will our professional schools see fully the value of courses of instruction involving the careful training necessary for the special-school teacher. Further, in order to draw into the ranks of the special-school staffs the proper kind of teacher, salaries must be made commensurate with the work, salaries equal at least to our better-payed high-school teachers. But we have faith in our professional schools as well as in our public school systems and those who are directly concerned in guiding their destinies.

The Normal School and the Special-School Teacher. — Taking Massachusetts as a type, it is found that out of the ten normal schools of that Commonwealth, but one, namely Salem, is doing anything by way of specialized training of teachers for the instruction of the mentally defective. At the present time, the courses of instruction in these normal schools are two, three, and four years in length, the three-year course preparing for junior high school work, the second for instruction in the commercial subjects. Thus, as analysis of the exact situation clearly shows, a teacher who desires to prepare herself for special-school work has a two-year course as her only means of approach. It is obvious, therefore, that when the usual preparatory courses to the teaching profession have been given due and adequate attention, but little time actually remains for a training admittedly of a highly specialized character. In the opinion of Miss Eleanor Walker, Supervisor of Special Class Work at the Salem State Normal, the only way to meet the present situation is to increase the preparatory professional course to at least three years, thus giving opportunity for one year of specialized study concerning the special school. This is in harmony with present educational trends, and it is probable that the day is not far off when our normal schools will become normal colleges with four-year courses of rather specialized natures leading to degrees. This will give opportunity for the type of teacher training which we believe necessary for adequate instruction of the feeble-minded.

What the Typical Normal School Offers. — When the normal school offers anything at all by way of preparation for teaching in the special school, it presents a general-methods course in the instruction of the mentally defective child, together with some opportunity for observation and apprenticeship teaching. Through necessity, probably for more than any other reason, the course in general methods considers rather briefly the more important phases appertaining to the mentally subnormal, including (1) the nature, cause, and consequences of feeble-mindedness, (2) general methods including means and materials of presentation which we have termed the object lesson, (3) classroom management in special-class work, with (4) opportunities to observe and participate in special-class instruction under supervision. It is evident that this marks a splendid beginning toward the solution of the special teacher training problem, and hence of this as such we must not be too critical; it is evident, nevertheless, that excellent as is this beginning, more must be done if the feebleminded child is to receive training commensurate with that of the normal individual. Under present normal school conditions, therefore, it is essential that adequate preparation should include the equivalent of one year's additional study in some institution of high learning, specifically, a school of education or a teachers' college.

What the Typical Normal School Should Offer. — It is not our purpose to outline in detail the course of instruction for training the special-school teachers, but rather to propose the major subjects which a three- or a four-year, normal, preparatory course should offer. With the present general methods of teaching mentally deficient children, including sense and industrial training, as a nucleus, the following is presented as indicative of the specific need: (1) Educational psychology and mental hygiene of the mentally deficient child, including the problems of the mentally deficient; (2) classroom management and control of the special school, dealing with the major problems and features of the work of the special-school class; (3) observation and apprenticeship teaching, under supervision, of special-school classes; (4) mental clinic, including the demonstration of typical cases of mental deficiency, with a discussion and analysis of their psychological, social, and educational needs; (5) the measurement of intelligence, emphasizing the practical aspects of mental testing; (6) literature of the mentally deficient, interpreted as meaning a survey of the literature in which the feeble-minded are especially interested; and (7) a general course in handwork, including the major occupational endeavors, such as bench-work, weaving, cooking, sewing, etc. It would be necessary, in order to make the training process highly valuable in a practical way, to have a model school in each normal school, including at least one section of mentally deficient children, which would be of benefit both to the teachers in training and to the children as well.

The College and the Special-School Teacher. — As a good illustration of what the college offers, we have selected, first, as more or less typical, one of the best known and finest of the New England colleges for women. The main course at this institution, which prepares definitely for any phase of special-school work, is known as "Specialized Education," and includes the general consideration of theory and methods of teaching the mentally backward, together with three rather specific phases — namely, practice teaching; field work and the study of individual mentally deficient children; and special study of the problems of the mentally defective. In connection with this course of instruction, under an expert supervisor and teacher of backward children, a well-equipped, separately housed, but small school is conducted — a combined educational endeavor on the part of the college and the city in which it is located. In this institution it is seen that there is a real beginning of the solution of training and instructing the feeble-minded in so far, at least, as the teacher-training problem is concerned.

For our second illustration of what the colleges are actually doing in this connection, we have selected a well-known graduate school of education in the East. Although the students who attend this school have presumedly prepared themselves by way of theory and practice in the art of teaching, and although there are many courses of real interest and value to the special-school teacher offered, the following are found to be of particular worth: (1) Individual Development and Education; (2) The Philosophy and Psychology of Play; (3) The Measurement of Intelligence; (4) The Clinical Study of Mentally Deficient Children; (5) Elementary Education, including the management of an elementary school and the elementary school curriculum; (6) Vocational and Educational Guidance; and (7) Motivation in Elementary Education. It is obvious that in order to have a clear understanding of the above courses, preliminary courses are necessary, as evidenced by the bachelor's degree, a prerequisite to attendance at this as at any recognized graduate school of education.

What the College Should Offer. — In presenting the following proposals concerning the training of the special-school teacher, it should be borne in mind that this discussion has to be primarily with the undergraduate work of the college student, since from the graduate schools will come more especially the special-school supervisors and principals, who, it is evident, must understand the theory and practice underlying the training and instruction of mentally backward children. These courses we would mention as follows: (1) General Methods and Theory of Teaching Mentally Deficient Children; (2) Educational Psychology, including Mental Hygiene and Individual Differences among the Feeble-Minded; (3) The Psychology of Play in its Relation to the Mentally Backward; (4) The Measurement of Intelligence; (5) The Mentally Deficient and the Socializing Process; (6) Educational Tests and Measures; (7) Special-Class Demonstration and Apprenticeship Teaching; (8) Physical Education and Games in their Relation to the Problems of the Feeble-Minded; (9) Underlying Principles of Industrial Training, including Actual Shop Practice; (10) The Nature, Causes, and Consequences of Mental Defect, including the Types of Feeble-Mindedness. In addition, in order to further this training process, a model school for demonstration and practice purposes should be maintained either within the particular public school system or as a definite adjunct to the college itself.

What, then, are the major subjects in the training program of the special-school teacher? In general, it may be said that for some time to come the majority of special-school instructors will be graduates of recognized normal schools, although some will come undoubtedly from collegiate circles. Further, as previously noted, special-school supervisors and principals will be graduates of college, doing either graduate or undergraduate work, or both. In this proposed program it is likewise assumed that each normal school or college will maintain, either directly or indirectly, a model school or facilities whereby the prospective special-school teacher will meet first-hand the problems and complexes of mentally deficient children.

The following program is therefore proposed as representative of what the training process should be: (1) The Nature, Causes, and Consequences of Mental Deficiency; (2) Educational

Psychology and Mental Hygiene of Mentally Backward Children; (3) General Methods of Teaching the Feeble-Minded; (4) Observation and Apprenticeship Teaching of Mentally Retarded Children; (5) Management and Organization of Special-School Classes, including the Major Problems and Features of Special-School Classroom Work; (6) Socializing the Mentally Retarded; (7) The Measurement of Intelligence; (8) The Clinical Study of Mentally Retarded Children; (9) Handwork and Occupations, including (*a*) the main types of manual and occupational training suitable for the mentally retarded, and (*b*) a general course of a practical nature in the industrial arts, such as bench-work, weaving, cooking, sewing, printing, and so forth; (10) Individual Differences among Mentally Backward Children; (11) Vocational and Educational Guidance of the Mentally Retarded; (12) Motivation in Elementary Education; (13) Physical Education and Games in their Relation to the Mentally Deficient; (14) Educational Tests and Measures; and (15) a seminary in the Major Problems of the Mentally Retarded, including actual field work and a case study of mentally defective individuals.

It is apparent, on the one hand, that no one student in the course of the usual educational teacher-preparation program could take all of the above-mentioned subjects; on the other hand, it is apparent that under present conditions no one college or normal school could offer the entire range of preparatory work for the special-school teacher. Thus, in either case, there must be selection or else a combination of certain of the above-mentioned courses. Nevertheless, this is the goal toward which the college may well aim in teacher preparation for the special school.

C. Summary and Conclusions

The training and instruction of mentally deficient children necessitates superior teaching ability as well as a thorough training of a rather specialized character on the part of special-school teachers. Thus, the specific qualities which will tend toward success in this particular instructional process are: (1) a good physique; (2) a wholesome, well-balanced temperament and disposition — common sense, tact, and a genuine sense of humor; (3) character and personality; (4) a broad social outlook; (5) skill in teaching and management; and (6) special training of a professional nature.

For this special training, fifteen major courses of study for the special-school teacher have been proposed.

CHAPTER VIII

A PROPOSED STATE PROGRAM FOR THE TRAINING AND INSTRUCTION OF MENTAL DEFECTIVES

A. THE MENTAL DEFECTIVE AND THE PUBLIC SCHOOL

WHATEVER may be their lot as adults, the responsibility for whatever training can be given the mental defectives as children is one that confronts educational authorities and the public school system in particular. With these rests the question of how best to provide for the subnormal children so that they may become an economic and social asset rather than a liability. How this can be done most effectively, as we understand the problem, has been discussed in the foregoing chapters, and the very fact that the public school system is providing one of the earliest means outside of the home for the development of future citizenship of the state naturally imposes upon it the responsibility of carrying into execution with all means at its command the solution of this very complex need.

The Mental Defective a Potential Social and Economic Burden. — It is generally recognized that the mental defective constitutes, together with his progeny, one of the great potential social and economic burdens of our modern civilization. Much information is available concerning the causation, prevalence, social and economic significance, and treatment of mental retardation, together with its influence as a source of unhappiness to the defective himself and to his family — as well as its bearing as a causative factor in the production of crime, pauperism, prostitution, and other extremely complex social conditions. An intelligent democracy, if it is to justify itself as a political institution giving equal opportunity to all, irrespective of mental status, can no longer persistently ignore a condition which involves a large number of persons, families, and communities, so large an aggregate of human suffering and misery, so great an economic-social cost and waste.

Reasons for the Lack of a Formal, Accepted Program. — Nearly every state in the union has made a beginning of an educational program dealing with mental defectives, either directly or indirectly. The development of this program varies greatly both in method and degree. Even the more progressive states have not as yet formulated a plan for the training and instruction of all educable subnormals; and it is probably safe to assert that no state has as yet taken cognizance, from the viewpoint of real education, of more than ten per cent of the mentally defective in the political unit. Little has been done as yet to define the problem of the feeble-minded — their number, location, or the exact nature and expression of their defectivity. The vast majority of these receive no training and instruction and no adequate supervision and protection.

But there are many reasons why we are without the definitely accepted and formulated program concerning the care, training, and supervision of these feeble-minded children. The problem itself cannot be solved by a simple formula which can be adequately expressed in one piece of legislation. It is extremely intricate, varying according to age, sex, degree, and kind of defect, the presence or absence of hereditary traits or criminal or anti-social tendencies, home environment, and the varying individuals in a community. The moron, the imbecile, the idiot present different needs and dangers, each having different complexes and troubles according to sex and age. Rural, sparsely settled communities with more or less homogeneous populations have conditions pertaining to the mental defectives which differ widely from those of urban industrial centers with their varied racial complications.

B. Proposed Program for the Salvaging of the Mentally Defective Child

Obviously, the problem of the mentally defective child is of such magnitude and overlaps so many different agencies and institutions that its solution becomes a coöperative venture on the part of the school, the court, the state, private institutions for the mentally incompetent, and all social and philanthropic organizations that are interested in the welfare of unfortunate children. From the viewpoint of this discussion — that is, in so far as the schools are to function with respect to this salvaging process — the main points of our proposed program for the training and instruction of mentally defective children may be summarized as follows:

(1) Early recognition of every mentally defective child in the community and in the public school.

(2) Training and instruction in terms of the child's needs, capacities, and interests, emphasizing the acquisition of socially accepted habits, attitudes, ideals, as well as skills, over and above the acquisition of mere knowledge.

(3) Long-continued industrial and vocational training. Thus, the organization of the special school, or the "junior school," as an integral part of the regular school system.

(4) Social service during the school life of the child and after-supervision and continued guidance.

C. The Early Recognition of Every Feeble-Minded Child in the Community and in the Public Schools

The Keynote of a Practical Program for the Training and Instruction of Mental Defectives. — There should be a mental examination of every child entering upon an educational career, as well as special mental examinations of all children obviously retarded in school accomplishment. The keynote of any practical program for the training and instruction of mental defectives is to be found in the fact, which apparently has been proved at the Fernald State School, that those retardates whose defects are recognized while they are young children and who receive proper training during childhood are, as a rule, not especially troublesome after they have been guided safely through the early period of adolescence. Thus, it seems feasible to advocate an extension of the present method of health examination of all school children so as to insure a mental examination of every child entering upon an educational career —

with a more detailed examination of all children obviously retarded in school accomplishment because of mental defect. It would be necessary, therefore, to give all children at least one mental examination; and to examine more carefully those children who are three or more years retarded in school work. Such an examination would probably isolate the mentally defective — perhaps from two to seven per cent of the primary-school population. However, a mistake in diagnosis would be almost a tragedy; indeed, it is a very serious matter even to suspect a child of mental deficiency. Therefore, any child who upon his first examination is found to be below the normal mental median must be diagnosed from two viewpoints: (1) the School Clinic Record, including more especially the "Ten Fields of Inquiry" and the "Correlation of Chronological, Mental, and School Age," the latter more particularly when the child has later shown signs of academic retardation, both at the opening and at the closing of the school year; (2) the Mental Clinic. In the urban communities, the mental examinations could be given by special examiners and at mental clinics. In fact, every special school should have at its disposal during at least one day each week the time of one psychologist. The rapid development of out-patient clinics all over the country will soon furnish facilities for such examinations — more particularly in the larger cities. Rural communities and small towns could be served by traveling clinics, whose personnel would consist of a psychologist, a psychiatrist, a social worker, and a secretary, as a part of the department of education of the state government. This clinical group, possibly even an individual clinician, could examine the presumedly defective children over a very considerable area, a visit being made to each community once every year. In addition, every institutional school for the mentally defective should conduct weekly mental clinics both at the institution and in the various towns and cities served by the school. At the conclusion of the examination, the parents should be informed with respect to the mental status of the child and of his need for special-school training and supervision.

Rural-School Training of Defectives and Instruction of Parents.
— Suitable manuals should be prepared by the state department of education. These manuals, to be placed in the hands of every teacher of mental retardates and also of rural school teachers, would describe the methods and materials of training and management of these exceptional cases. The public should recognize that the defective child is entitled, perhaps even more than the normal child, to an education according to his needs and capacities. The defective children who cannot be taught in the regular school classes should find their place either in the special school or in an institutional school, depending primarily upon the "type" of feeble-mindedness represented and environmental conditions present.

The proper division of the state department of education should further prepare simple, readable manuals of facts for the use of the parents of mentally defective children. These brochures — to be prepared in series, with special articles concerning young boys, young girls, older boys, older girls, and for other groups — would tactfully instruct the parents with respect to the limitations of these children in so far as scholastic possibilities are concerned, emphasizing the importance of the formation and development of habits of obedience and industry, and the necessity of protection against evil influences and companions. Emphasis would be made of the possible need, in certain cases, of institutional care in the future.

D. The Organization and Administration of Special Schools as Integral Parts of the Public School System

From the foregoing chapters it seems evident that no matter whether the number of mentally defective children be two or seven per cent of the school population, it is certainly large enough to present a very serious social, economic, and educational problem. Every city of any size has enough boys and girls who are unable to go beyond the fifth or sixth grade and who cannot profit to any appreciable degree by the usual type of elementary school training after eleven or twelve years of age, to constitute a successful school of the special type. We shall never do our duty toward these mentally backward children until we give them the kind of training that will prove useful to them in later life. The parents of such children, especially when they once understand the situation, are almost invariably appreciative and grateful for this sort of training provided for their children. The expense need not be great; simply-planned and bright airy quarters and comparatively inexpensive equipment are best for this purpose. The instructors should understand fully the mental-age limitations and the academic and the industrial possibilities of each child. The work should be simplified until it is within the comprehension of the children being taught; and here again, "the best the child can do is good enough."

The Special School and the Rural Community. — In the rural communities we face quite a different problem with respect to the training of the mentally defective child. Here, the mental retardates are usually scattered; and so few are found in any one school that the special school, organized and administered as we shall propose, seems somewhat out of the question under present educational conditions. Notwithstanding these difficulties, it is evident that something should be done. That the number of backward and mentally defective children in the rural communities is proportionately as great, compared to the number of population, as in the larger cities and towns is clear. At least, there are no data available to prove otherwise. Every objection that can be raised to the presence of the mental defective in the regular school grade of the urban community can be shown to have its application with equal force to his presence in the rural school. Just how this particular phase of the training aspect of the feeble-minded can be best solved is still an open question, although some suggestions can be offered in this connection.

(1) *The Consolidated Rural School.* — Consolidation of rural schools would go a long way toward the solution of this as well as of many other rural school problems. If, instead of the many isolated, one-room schools, with their small attendance, we had the well-equipped, well-attended, flourishing centralized schools such as are becoming more common in some of our states, it

would be possible to make adequate provision for the mentally handicapped child.

(2) *Country School Homes.* — Lacking in many states, at the present time, the consolidated rural school, one possible solution of our problem is the organization of country school homes for the care and training of the feeble-minded under the combined state and community auspices, with state aid. This plan seems feasible, provided the program includes the after-care and supervision of the special-school child when he leaves the country schoolhouse. For, in the greater number of cases, the success of any system of training and instruction of the feeble-minded rests upon the type of supervision exercised at the conclusion of the school career.

(3) *The Colony System.* — A third solution is the colony system, the practicality of which has been demonstrated at the Fernald State School and the Rome (New York) State School. Not only have these colonies maintained their own self-support but they have actually yielded a profit to the school. More important indeed than mere economic gain is the fact that the boys and girls at the colony centers are happy and contented, believing that they are actually doing work that is worth while. They give their supervisors but little trouble, apply themselves industriously to their tasks, and try faithfully to make their colony homes a success.

The consolidated rural school, it seems to us, offers the most ideal solution of the problem of the feeble-minded and the rural community; the other two plans, though offering better conditions, smack too much of the institution. A possible solution might be found in the country-day school for mental defectives, organized on the same principles as those in the special school of urban communities, and maintained by combined state and community aid. Nevertheless, as previously noted, the defective child, if given ordinary school opportunities, seems to get about all he is capable of getting in the way of academic instruction. As Dr. Fernald said: "He has a small dipper, and he gets that dipper full under very common and ordinary conditions." It would seem that for some time to come the mentally defective child is destined to receive his academic training in a manner similar to the rest of the school. Due to the usual high degree of individual instruction within a small group in the rural school and to the comparative simplicity of the average rural community, this may perhaps suffice quite as well as a more highly specialized form of academic instruction. The usual rural life, more especially that of the farm, furnishes first-hand experiences lacking in the life of the city boy or girl, and so to a considerable degree the lack of certain industrial types of training in the rural school is compensated for in the numerous environmental contacts and activities.

(4) *Traveling workshops.* — It would be possible to supplement this training by means of "traveling workshops"; that is, by equipping a covered auto truck with wood-working tools and benches, a lathe or two, shoe-repairing materials and tools, a blacksmithing equipment, etc., for the boys; for the girls, a similar movable laboratory of an industrial arts nature. Such equipment as this would serve the purpose of a comparatively large area at a relatively small per capita expense. It would necessitate, of course, the employment by the districts served of one instructor in manual arts and one in domestic arts. We would consider the money thus applied well spent, since the mentally defective child, not being to blame for his condition, is entitled to such training, treatment, and supervision at the hands of society as will best contribute to his happiness and usefulness.

Organization of the Junior School in an Urban Community. — Let us now turn to a discussion of the organization, equipment, and courses of study of the special school in an urban community.

(1) *General Standards for Assignment of Pupils to the Junior School.* — In a previous section it was pointed out that in terms of intellectual and educational capacities and possibilities, as a general standard for the assignment of pupils to the special school, we would limit such placement to those children whose I. Q.'s have varied from 30 to 75 or 80, whose mental ages have varied from 3 to 11 or 12 years, and whose educational potentialities have varied from a pre-kindergarten to a probable attainment of fifth-

or sixth-grade work. We should interpret this to mean that children near the limiting mental or scholastic borders and those whose diagnosis is uncertain, should be given the benefit of the doubt, in so far as special-school opportunities are concerned. This presumes the children admitted to the junior school to have been properly and thoroughly examined, not only with respect to their mental status by the use of standardized mental tests but in terms of "The Ten Fields of Inquiry" as well.

(2) *Enrollment.* — Ideally, the maximum number of pupils in any one section, assigned to one teacher for academic instruction, should not exceed fifteen. Circumstances and conditions may, however, necessitate the enrollment of twenty children to a section, but beyond this the numbers should never go. Class or section enrollment may be somewhat greater than this in the industrial and physical training work, depending somewhat upon materials and space available. Likewise, ideally, the total enrollment of the junior school should approximate one hundred twenty-five, with instructional divisions according to sex.

(3) *The Special-School Curriculum.* — The curriculum for the junior school, discussed in previous chapters, includes: (1) sense training; (2) physical training; (3) manual and occupational training; (4) moral training and mental hygiene; (5) music, drawing, and dramatization; and (6) academic or literary instruction, including number work, reading, penmanship, literature, history, civics, geography, language, and composition. Experience shows, however, that backward children who succeed in life do so because they become capable of doing something worth while with their hands. This kind of training begins, according to the age of the child and his mental age, with the use of pencils, rulers, crayons, water colors, paper-folding, paper-cutting, etc., and has for its ultimate aim actual work with tools and materials, such as carpentry, painting, weaving, basketry, cobbling, printing, etc. It is important that this work should be intensively carried on from the age of twelve until the child leaves school.

(4) *Physical Properties and Equipment of the Special School.* — Mentally retarded children are obviously the most helpless of

our school population, and rather than place them in small, poorly lighted, poorly heated and ventilated rooms with meagre equipment, they should have the very best of rooms so far as light, heat, ventilation, and equipment are concerned. The room for a mentally retarded class should be large enough, not including the customary cloakrooms, to allow at least twenty-five square feet of floor space to each child. The lighting of each classroom and shop should be from large windows, appropriately placed, and low enough so that the children may lower and raise the sashes. The heat should be such as to keep the temperature even and approximately three to five degrees below that required for normal children. The ventilation must be especially good, automatic or by means of windows. A movable, adjustable desk is perhaps best for the special-school child, and where the classroom has pupils of several sizes, each room should be equipped with desks of various sizes. Whatever furniture is used, including the teacher's desk, should never be fastened to the floor. Blackboard space should be abundant, and so located that the children can use all parts of it. The color scheme of the rooms and the pictures should be such as to make a cheerful effect. Growing plants in the windows, as well as paper decorations on the walls, will add much to this cheerfulness. A neat bookcase for books and supplies is a necessary piece of furniture, along with a movable phonograph or small piano to be used for marching, folk-dancing, or pure musical enjoyment. Textbooks and fiction of the best kind and suited to the mentality of the children should be supplied, and discarded as soon as they become badly soiled or torn. Drawing and painting materials, including paper, paints of various colors, colored pictures, pencils, etc., are very essential in the work of the special school, and also scissors, paste, and paper for cutting and folding.

The sense-training materials have been discussed in detail in Chapter III, and so need no further elaboration at this time. The physical-training equipment should consist principally of wands, dumb-bells, Indian clubs, basket-balls, bean bags, baseballs, and other baseball equipment. The occupational materials will vary according to the types of industrial endeavor present

FOR THE FEEBLE-MINDED? 183

in the particular special school and in any case will not vary materially from those of a well-equipped trade school.

The object lesson and its materials, together with a constructive program of organization and presentation, have been presented in Chapter V. It should be emphasized that although these materials should be available in considerable quantities, they need not be of an elaborate or expensive nature; indeed, many of these function best when constructed by the individuals who are to use them for actual training purposes.

(5) *The Daily Program — Length of School Day and Year.* — The special school for mental defectives, in so far as curricular activities are concerned, must be limited only by their intellectual and emotional endowments, and hence the educational process must not be merely a limited adaptation of the course of study planned for normal children. Many of the customary academic subjects must be presented either in a simplified form or else, when certain points are reached, omitted altogether. In any case they must be taught by a rather specialized method of presentation and at a very slow rate of progress or procedure. Likewise, special emphasis is to be placed upon sense, manual, physical, and occupational training and practice, for one of the main elements in the success of the feeble-minded child is that there shall be long-continued social, industrial, and occupational training fitting him to work on a competitive basis of equality with the unskilled and the semi-skilled. From the viewpoint of the daily program of the ordinary school, outside of the fact that there are regularly designated hours or periods for the various types of instruction, there is no "daily program" as commonly understood. It may be that the recitation periods assigned to the usual academic studies, as arithmetic, reading, or writing, will involve a particular literary pursuit in terms of concerted activity; it is equally possible, perhaps more probable, that a particular "recitation period" will find the group subdivided, more or less unconsciously, into small groups of three or four, each busily engaged in what they need most or in which they are, for the time being at least, most interested, with the teacher assisting each small group as required. In this respect the daily

program for mentally defective children is somewhat comparable to the Dalton Plan. Since the feeble-minded child is unable to follow one line of endeavor for any great length of time, it seems advisable to change the time devoted to academic work and the physical and industrial training as best fits the organization of the particular junior school involved.

It is essential that a maximum of school supervision be given mental defectives and that both work and play be carried on under the directing influence of the teaching staff. If this be true, as we believe it is, it is essential that the influence of the teacher should be extended beyond the hours of the usual school day. In practically all cases plans can be formulated for these children to do systematic work at home under the guidance of immediate members of the family. However, the teachers must keep in close touch with such work and assist the parents to arrange the training in a systematic, orderly manner. It is essential to the future success of the child that the parent realize that this homework should be carried on so as to provide an important phase in the child's training. It would seem especially advantageous to these mental retardates if additional hours, and hence a longer school day, of supervised work could be provided. Further, it would appear of distinct value — especially from social and later economic considerations — to provide a special school that would be in session throughout most of the year.

The school day, itself, should be divided about equally between physical exercise, industrial work, supervised play, and academic training, as the ability of the individual pupils shall render possible. The "long school day" must in no way become irksome to mentally defective children; it must be organized with a sufficient variety of activities and flexibility of plan to give the children a day of directed work and play and happily sustained contentment.

In the same general manner, the school year might well be extended throughout a considerable portion of the calendar year. Wherever conditions require, vacations might find their place, in a way similar to that of the regular school schedule; but feeble-minded children are, as a general rule, much better off when under the direction, care, and guidance of a trained instructional staff than they are in the home or on the street. Under such a proposed form of procedure, it is not presumed that the same subject matter is to be taught throughout the year; a variety of work is to be introduced so that the school shall not at any time become a place of pure monotony. Thus, the school garden can be developed during the spring and summer; "fall repairs" may well find their place in the curriculum; pageants and musical entertainments can always give place to or be interrelated with the usual school work.

Thus, the school day might be lengthened to seven or eight hours; the school year to forty-two or forty-five weeks, depending upon the environment, and the nature of the children being trained. Under these proposed conditions, it is realized that the junior-school teachers would be carrying a maximum burden; hence the community should not ask them to assume unaided the longer time schedule recommended above. That is to say, if the work of the special school is to be carried on with maximum efficiency, some means must be provided of securing assistant teachers for the junior-school staff.

(6) *Discipline in the Special School.* — The repression or complex of failure has faced most special-school children all their lives. The teacher should develop and approve their assets and not catalogue their liabilities. As Dr. Fernald has stated this matter: "Let him achieve success every day. His bad behavior is largely his attempt to compensate for a feeling of inferiority from repeated failures. He has failed so often that he expects to fail. His social attitude and behavior largely express his clumsy attempts to keep his own self-respect; in other words, a simple defense reaction."[1] It is the duty of the teacher, therefore, to avoid letting the children know they have failed; it is his duty to make them feel they are succeeding. We need to consider their viewpoint and give them an opportunity to do what seems to them at least worth while. Mentally defective children need immediate and tangible rewards, a word of praise

[1] Fernald, W. E., "The Subnormal Child," p. 5. Reprinted from *School and Society*, Vol. XVIII, No. 458, October 6, 1923.

frequently, but not too frequently given, a special privilege made for the purpose. The act worthy of praise may be ever so little — it is frequent occurrence that gives it weight.

Perhaps, above all other things, the teacher should be sure that the children understand her. Explanations and instructions are often made in terms which are not understood by the feeble-minded; an extreme sensitiveness, characteristic of many of these children, coupled with a lack of proper understanding, often results in what may seem at first sight to be stubbornness. When a mentally defective child is disobedient, the teacher should be firm in discipline but never angry, for anger in the teacher arouses a corresponding feeling in the child and causes him to close in upon himself.

That a certain act is wrong is not to be unduly emphasized. When the mentally subnormal child becomes angry or disturbed, he tries to show how angry he is by doing the very thing known to be considered bad. Experimentation has shown the utility of spending time in establishing those things which are right and good. The special-school child desires to be happy; and if an atmosphere conducive to happiness prevails in the classroom or elsewhere, school discipline will come of its own accord. Hence, the teacher must be kind, but firm; sympathetic, yet understanding; patient almost without limit, not acting until she knows the circumstances, encouraging the children when encouragement is necessary, remembering that with the mentally retarded child, as with the normal child, childhood should be a time of happiness.

If the special school sets out to have discipline as commonly understood, such discipline will never be attained; if it sets out to make the child happy, to enable him to achieve even a little success every day, the right kind of control will come as a natural resultant.

(7) *Qualifications of the Special-School Teacher.*[1] — In order that each mentally defective child may receive training and instruction commensurate with that of the normal child, each teacher of the special school should have had the academic and professional training given by any state normal school or by any

[1] Chapter VII.

recognized professional school, either collegiate or noncollegiate; and in addition one full year of special training in an approved institution in dealing with the problems of the mentally subnormal child — such training being included or not included as circumstances determine in the normal school or college. In lieu of one year's continuous training, special courses in approved summer schools should be accepted for such part of the work as they represent. Further, as soon as conditions permit, special-school teachers should be required to have had at least one year of successful experience in the instruction of normal children.

(8) *General Methods of Instruction in the Special School.* — Flexibility of program and adaptation of work to the capacities of these children are the vital factors to be considered in dealing with methods of instruction. The work must be graded to the mentality of the children in the school or in the particular section, being simplified until it is within the comprehension of the pupils being taught. Although the general principles of teaching the mentally defective are the same as for the normal child, the conditions are different, the rate of progress much slower. And to hold the interest of these subnormal children, objective teaching materials and methods must be used. Thus the children will do well in the junior school, provided they are understood by the teacher, the work is suited to their mental level, and the teachers are satisfied with the very best the child can do.

The Special School as a Training Unit by Itself. — For some time to come, it may be that circumstances and urban conditions, including those of a financial nature and that potent factor, "public opinion," shall determine whether the junior school is to be an educational unit by itself, or a "school within a school." Specifically, by the former type of organization is meant a school equipped and maintained for the very definite purpose of training and instructing mental defectives; by the latter is meant taking over a part of a typical grammar school equipped for both academic and industrial pursuits, or a trade school for recitation, industrial, and play purposes.

The main point of differentiation would seem to be not so much whether the actual form of instructional procedure of the one type is superior to that of the other, but whether or not, when the special school is an institution by itself, the feeble-minded tend to lose a certain necessary social contact by such an organization of educational affairs. It would seem very plausible to believe that this type of child would gain something very important of the nature of a social asset by virtue of opportunities for mingling with his more normal brothers on the playground, in the assemblies, and elsewhere. Yet the results shown at the F. S. S. draw us to the conclusion that even when the feeble-minded are trained more or less in isolation, as at that institution, the vast majority of graduates are able to make favorable and positive social contacts. As in the regular public school, they tend to keep to themselves; and, with the exception of the more loquacious individual, for some reason or other, they seem to realize their limitations, although perhaps not understanding them (a point stressed in no way at Waverley), so they manage to get along quite as well apparently as though they had been trained in a "school within a school." In fact, whether or not the average feeble-minded individual is a social asset to any community depends not so much on him himself, as it does upon a thorough understanding and sympathy for him upon the part of his employer or those with whom he comes in contact.

Ideally, what we most desire is one of two possible means of special-school training for the mentally defectives: (1) a separate building and playground, equipped, organized, and administered in a manner similar to that of a high-class trade school, junior high school, or even a technical or vocational high school, with a specially trained instructional staff; or (2) an integral part of a properly equipped grammar school or trade school — provided under such conditions the special school can be a "school within a school." Since the trade school, the junior high school, or the technical or vocational high school do not seem anxious to give over in any way their industrial advantages to the less well-endowed children, in spite of the results of the salvaging process, a purely practical consideration leads us to believe that the best, and in the long run the most economical, method of establishing the junior school is to construct and equip it avowedly without fear or apology for the express purpose of training mental defectives along social, industrial, economic, physical, and academic lines. The history of education has shown that the new educational venture must be constructed from its very foundations. Expediency must, of course, be considered.

In determining the name of the school, the word "feeble-minded" should, of course, not be considered; it carries a certain stigma that we wish to avoid. Thus, for the special school, we propose the term "junior school." Its purpose shall be the training of mentally backward children of the community in gainful and worth-while industrial pursuits and the formation of socially adaptable, law-abiding individuals.

The organization of the junior school for training and instructing the intellectually deficient calls for at least five well-coördinated departments: (1) A Seguin or pre-kindergarten department, so-called, perhaps, for the lack of a better name, in which children are placed primarily for purposes of sense training. It would include, in general, those who have a mentality of two, three, or four years, depending upon the nature and degree of mental retardation; (2) a kindergarten department which would continue the training of the senses and involve matters of the usual kindergarten work, including, in general, those who have a mentality of four or five years; (3) a more or less departmentalized group of classes with grades corresponding to "low," "normal," "high" sections, in which are placed the children of a post-kindergarten mentality and degree of acquisition, presumedly a mentality of four or five to eleven or twelve years inclusive; (4) an industrial section, which would include those children who have been or are taking work of an academic nature, with specific provisions for both boys and girls; (5) a physical education section; and (6) a music department.

In considering the special school as an integral part of the public school system, upon a basis of an approximate registration of 125, with class sections of 15, the instructional staff would consist of (1) a principal; (2) an industrial arts instructor; (3) a domestic arts instructor; (4) four instructors in academic work;

WHAT SHALL THE PUBLIC SCHOOLS DO

(5) a physical director; and (6) a music teacher, who would be a regular member of the physical education division and music staff, respectively, of the particular school system.

In any case, where there are enough special schools to justify the appointment, there should be a Junior School Supervisor, whose chief function would be not only to coördinate the work of these schools but also to act as intermediate officer between the special and the regular schools. Thus, so far as the general relation of the junior school to the entire public school system is concerned, the following presents a diagrammatic representation: —

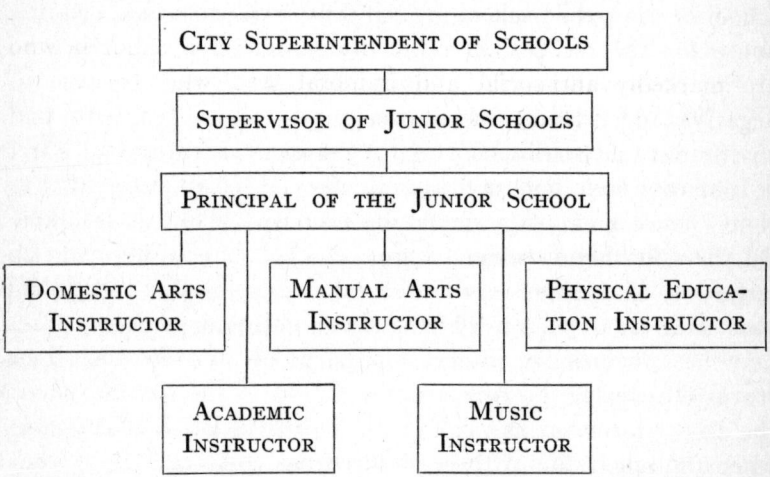

Social Supervision and Social Assistance. — Social service, in its highest and deepest sense, is probably the greatest need of the feeble-minded in the public school system. It would not seem difficult to supply this need; the teacher was the original social worker, and her objectives, methods, and results were similar to those of the social worker at the present time. In the public school system of today, the school nurse, the attendance officer, the visiting teacher, or the child's teacher — all these should be familiar with the life and the environment of the mentally retarded child. The social supervision and social assistance by school authorities up to the age of sixteen, when the child presumedly leaves school, almost assure us that he will have passed safely through the greatest dangers of adolescence.

However, not only to safeguard the highly emotional and easily influenced child, but to give him that which is justly his, some form of after-care and supervision must be formulated, either under the directing influence of the school authorities or of some other capable and well-informed agency. It should be able to deal with the problems and reaction complexes of the mentally subnormal when their school life has ended.

The Special School as a "Clearing House." — The special school of the public school system may well serve as a clearing house for the recognition of mentally defective children who are markedly anti-social and immoral, and who, because of negative and adverse social proclivities, and often with bad environmental conditions, need permanent institutional care. It is an easy step, however, from the special school to the institution; hence great care should be exercised before it is taken. On the other hand, while the special school should be made up largely of undoubted cases of mental subnormality, it should also serve as a laboratory wherein doubtful or problem cases may be assigned for observation purposes, and, as their true status is revealed, be permanently placed in the special school, the classes for the backward, or in the institution. In any case, when the school life of these children has come to a close, they should receive the benefits of follow-up and after-care assistance and help, since, in many cases, this means quite as much as does the training process itself.

Legal Provisions for the Establishment of Special or Junior Schools. — There should be a preliminary, state-wide, mental survey, followed by legislation requiring the establishment of special schools. Every city of any size has enough boys and girls, as indicated by preliminary surveys, who are unable to go beyond the fifth or sixth grade of the usual grammar school, and who receive practically nothing from an academic viewpoint after eleven or twelve years of age, to make a splendid, good-sized school of the special type. Following a preliminary, state-wide, mental survey by competent and qualified experts, having for its purpose the registration and classification of all mentally defective children, legislation should be enacted requiring the establishment of special schools in all communities whose number of feeble-minded children makes the inauguration of such a system of training and instruction feasible — this latter to be determined by the results of the mental survey. Whereas in most states it is required that a community shall establish a special class when there are ten (or fifteen) children three or more years retarded among the school population, so the special-school law might require the establishment of a junior school in every community having forty (or fifty) mentally subnormal children of compulsory school age.

The first step, in a rational program, would be, as noted above, the beginning of a complete and continuing census of all mental defective children under sixteen years of age in the entire state. This would necessitate the appointment by proper authorities of mental clinics in various strategic parts of the state. Legislation should make these mental clinics a permanent institution under the general direction of the state commissioner of education, although specifically under the control of an assistant commissioner (or commission) for the mentally subnormal.

Legislation should further embody the following general principles: (1) objectives and need for special-school training; (2) mental examination, upon school entrance, of every child; (3) conditions under which, including numbers, a special school should be established; (4) general standards of assignment to the special school; (5) a general statement concerning the special-school curriculum; (6) length of school day and school year; (7) qualifications of special-school teachers; (8) the general organization of the special school; (9) general means and methods of instruction; (10) social supervision and social assistance, including provisions for follow-up and after-care work; and (11) provisions for state aid.

It is to be noted that these legislative provisions should be stated in general terms, leaving each community to carry them out according to their means and needs. Likewise, legislation should be enacted more specifically for training mental defectives in rural communities, the general purpose of which has been discussed previously in this chapter.

E. Summary and General Conclusion

There is no panacea for solving the social, economic, industrial, and educational problems of mental defectives. There will always be mentally defective children in the school population of every state and country. All the experience at the Fernald State School indicates that if we are to manage the individual defectives adequately, we must "recognize them when they are children, protect them from evil influences, train and educate them according to their capacities, make them industrially and socially efficient, teach them to acquire habits of and attitudes toward true living, and when they have reached adult life, continue to give them the friendly help and guidance they need."[1] For the vast majority of the feeble-minded, these advantages can be wrought only by the establishment of the special school as a part of the public school system, thus making the opportunities accessible to every mental defective child in the state. Perhaps the most important result of such training would be the erection of barriers that would seek to prevent the class of defectives from perpetuating their decadent stock. The program for meeting the needs of these highly varied and heterogeneous groups must be as flexible and complex as the problem itself. It should and will be modified and developed as our knowledge and experience increase.

[1] Walter E. Fernald: "The Inauguration of a State-Wide Public-School Mental Clinic in Massachusetts." *Mental Hygiene* (Reprint), No. 149, p. 16.

APPENDICES

APPENDIX I

THE OBJECT-LESSON MATERIALS

(TO ACCOMPANY CHAPTER V)

Shelf I: The Sea
  Lighthouse
  Steam launch
  Canoe, birch
  Yacht, sloops
  Yacht, schooner
  Sailboat
  Rowboat
  Oars (pr.)
  Anchor
  Fishing line (2)
  Pictures (steamers)
  Staveboat, N. Y.
  Raft of splinters
  Steamboat
  Submarine boat
  Seaplane

Shelf II: Mechanical and Household Devices
  Circular saw
  Alcohol stove
  Electric motor
  U. S. mail box
  Cash register
  Two-piece steam engine

Shelf III: Vehicles
  Surrey
  Express wagon (2 horses) with contents, 2 bxs., 2 barrels, 1 trunk
  Hack (2 horses)
  Watchman and footman
  Steam fire engine (2 horses) with ladders
  Bicycle
  Wheelbarrow
  Sled
  Windmill
  Toboggan
  Coal cart
  Sleigh, double-seated
  Baby carriage
  Ice wagon
  Delivery wagon
  Mowing machine
  Horse rake
  Plow on wheels
  Automobile
  Automobile racer
  Truck
  Auto express
  Ambulance

Shelf IV: Railroad
  Engine
  Tender
  Passenger car
  Mail
  Baggage
  Freight
  Caboose
  Horse car and horses
  Cattle car with cattle inside
  Express car

Shelf IV: Railroad
 Electric car
 Track
 Small engine with one car
 Trunk
 Traveling bag
 Suit case
 Hatbox
 Truck

Shelf V: Specimens in Bottles
 Block A
  Indian corn
  Corn meal
  Sweet corn
  Rye
  Ryemeal
  Oats
  Oats, rolled
  Wheat
  Graham flour
  Wheat flour
  Barley
  Buckwheat
  Sage

 Block B
  Cloves
  Ground cloves
  Pimento
  Mustard
  Cayenne pepper
  Ginger
  Pepper, whole
  Pepper, ground
  Cinnamon — bark, ground
  Nutmeg
  Rock salt
  Coarse salt
  Fine salt
  Sugar

 Block C
  Starch
  Tea
  Coffee, raw
  Coffee, roasted
  Peas
  String beans
  Lima beans
  Colored beans
  Black beans
  Squash seeds
  Flaxseed
  Cocoa

 Block D
  Ammonia
  Turpentine
  Kerosene
  Alcohol
  Peppermint
  Cologne
  Lemon extract
  Vanilla extract
  Ink, black
  Ink, red
  Vinegar
  Castor oil
  Sperm oil
  Blueing
  Carbolic acid

 Block E
  Coal, hard
  Coal, soft
  Charcoal
  Ashes
  Tar
  Gravel
  Sand
  Camphor
  Mucilage
  Rosin
  Sachet powder
  Soap, soft
  Mercury (metallic)

Shelf VI   Tableware
 China

APPENDIX I

Glassware
Silver
Linen

Shelf VII: Dolls and Flags

Skeleton
Dolls of various nations
Flags of various nations

Radical Types — 5 charts

  Patagonians
  Eskimos
  Chinese
  Zulus
  Australians

Shelf VIII: Building Materials

Stone
Brick and mortar
Lumber
Glass
Pipe

Shelf IX: Insects and Reptiles

Insects
Reptiles
  (Book — Shellfish, insects, butterflies, etc.)

Shelf X: Sea Forms

Sponges
Corals
Shells I
Shells II
Shells III
Shells IV

Stencils
Pictures

Shelf XI: Birds

Birds
Eggs
Nests
Stencils
Pictures — large and small cards—robin, oriole, thrush, sparrow, hen, rooster, parrot, woodpecker, sea birds, swallow, warbler, blackbird, heron, bobolink, duck, goose, owl, eagle, swan, pigeon

Prang's Natural History Series in Envelope — Birds

  Scratchers
  Swimmers
  Waders
  Birds of prey

Shelf XII: Animals — Toy Models

Horse, saddled
Horse, harnessed
Horse and colt
Cow, large
Cow, small
Sheep
Dogs
Pigs
Sheep's skull
Backbone joint of animal
Steer's horn

Shelf XIII: Animals — Pictures and Books

Prang's Large Picture Cards (Use only with frame and glass)

        Cow   Pig
        Horse   Elephant
        Goat   Porcupine
        Sheep   Etc.

Prang's Natural History Series in Envelope
  Solid-horned ruminants
  Hollow-horned ruminants
  Cat family
  Weasel family
  Squirrel family
  Books
  Small picture cards
  Stencils
  Bancroft's Object-Lesson Cards

Shelf XIV: Animal Kingdom
  Including anatomy of Physiology I–V

Shelf XV: Vegetable Kingdom

Shelf XVI: Mineral Kingdom

Shelf XVII: Prang's Aids for Object Teaching
  Trades and Occupations
    Carpenter
    Shoemaker
    Tailor
    Farmer
    Etc.
  The Book of Trades
    Foods and food producers

Shelf XVIII: Wool
  Wool
  Fabrics
  Wool carding comb
  Books on fabrics

Shelf XIX: Household Furniture
  Kitchen
  Dining room
  Bedroom
  Living room

Shelf XX: Metals and Leather
  Metal sheets, $4'' \times 4''$
  Leather strips

Shelf XXI: Tools
  Farm tools
  Common tools

APPENDIX I

Shelf XXII: Weights and Measures
Shelf XXIII: Instruments for Measuring
Shelf XXIV: Sense-Training Materials
Shelf XXV: Form
   Set of color and form cards
   Teacher's set of forms and solids (Wood)
   Hammett's Box of Forms and Solids

Shelf XXVI: Color
   Color charts, Magnus and Jeffrey, with envelope of discs
   Color charts, Magnus and Jeffrey, with envelope of discs
   Manual for color charts
   Color names and color blindness
   Color in the schoolroom, Milton and Bradley
   Colored cambrics, book
   Box of colored silks, wools, ribbons, etc.
   Color instruction — Bradley System — Teacher's Sample Box
   Box of colored square cards, showing shades and tints
   Box with 8 colored compartments
   Box with 3 colored compartments
   Assortment of colored shapes and figures to use with compartment boxes
   Oblong solids — red, yellow, blue, green, orange, purple
   Cubes, $1''$ — red, yellow, blue, green, orange, purple
   Large squares of colored cambrics (7 colors: $16'' \times 24''$, green, light blue, dark blue, purple, heliotrope, red, orange, yellow)
   Samples of colored cambric (bound)
   Kaleidoscopic toys
   Seguin cup and ball

Shelf XXVII: Numbers
   Set of dominoes
   Pack of playing cards
   Set of colored number cards (homemade, 1 to 10)
   Teacher's set of number cards (homemade, 1 to 10)
   Pavirhs Primary Number Tablets, First Year A
   Pavirhs Primary Number Tablets, First Year B
   Aid to number: 1 to 10, 28 cards (Badlam)
   Aid to number: 10 to 100, 30 cards (Badlam)
   Desk number frame — 18 of these
   Box of kindergarten colored sticks
   Box of colored pasteboard soldiers
   Box of colored wooden soldiers

APPENDIX I

Shelf XVII: Numbers

Box of Jack and Jill. Ten pins, blocks, and balls
Cows, busy work pictures or cards in box
Paper dolls
Box of objects for number teaching

> Marbles   Iron tools
> Colored discs   Colored sticks
> China dolls   Colored cubes
> Shells   Colored pictures

Primary arithmetic cards
Figure cards
Primary number cards
Primary number game
Fraction balls (9 in box)
Fraction circles (12 in envelope)
Sloames Cards, Fractions (5 cards in envelope)
Object fraction rulers
Box of paper money
Aids to numbers: 10–20, Badlam (cards)
Number cards, large, cardboard, homemade
Number sticks
Arithmetic blocks
Combinations 1–10

Shelf XXVIII: Hand-Training Materials

Shelf XXIX: Primary Reading

Riverside chart sentences (Parker Word Builder)
Set (200) word cards in box
Set (40) word cards in package
Alphabet box with letters on cards
Story cards for primary classes, 20 lessons, #1
Story cards for primary classes, 20 lessons, #2
Story cards for primary classes, 20 lessons, #3
Graphic reading leaflets for primary classes
Thompson's busy work, No. 1, in box
Thompson's busy work, No. 2, in box
Thompson's busy work, Little Boy Blue, in envelope
Thompson's busy work, Old Woman in Shoe, in envelope
Thompson's busy work, Jack and Jill, in envelope
Primary school work bulletin in box
Script alphabet cards in box
The Three Bears, cards in envelopes
Word builders

APPENDIX I

The Little Mind Builders
Script Perception Cards — sight, touch, motion
Spelling board
Parker's Word Builder
Young printer
Letter box
Fox Educational Board
Picture word cards
Set of familiar words
Stencils of animals and birds with printed name

Drawer A: Kitchen Utensils and Household Articles
Drawer B: Building Materials
Drawer C: Nails, Screws, and Hooks
Drawer D: Hemps and Rope
Drawer E: Cotton and Flax
Drawer F: Miscellaneous Small Articles
Drawer G: Fruit and Vegetables
Drawer H: Hardware
Drawer I: Plants and Flowers

    Prang's large picture cards
    Prang's Natural History Series (in envelope)
    Shapes of roots, of flowers, of leaves
    Poisonous plants
    Rose — lily — pink families
    Spices and coffee (small colored cards)

Drawer K: Miscellaneous Brushes
Drawer M: Animal Stencils
Drawer O: Garden Tools
Drawer Q: Material for Color, Form, and Number Work
Drawer R: Geography Materials

    Stencils
    Charts — Island, peninsula, isthmus, cape, promontory, mountain, hill, volcano, valley, river, lake, pond, sea, gulf, bay, strait.
    Relief globe
    Pictures

Chart Cabinet

  1. Familiar objects represented by words and pictures
  2. Reading — first lesson

Chart Cabinet

3. Reading — second lesson
4. Reading — third lesson
5. Reading — fourth lesson
6. Reading — fifth lesson
7. Elementary sounds
8. Phonic spelling
9. Writing
10. Drawing — elementary, geometrical, perspective
11. Weights and measures
12. Forms and solids
13. Familiar colors
14. Chromatic scale of colors
15–19. Zoölogical specimens
20–22. Botanical specimens

APPENDIX II

"THE TEN FIELDS OF INQUIRY"

THE COMMONWEALTH OF MASSACHUSETTS
DEPARTMENT OF MENTAL DISEASES
SCHOOL CLINIC RECORD

_____SCHOOL CLINIC   No._____

SECTION 13, CHAP. 123, GENERAL LAWS. The department shall establish and maintain a registry of the feeble-minded *** but the name of any person so registered shall not be made public except to public officials or other persons having authority over the person so registered, and the records constituting the registry shall not be open to public inspection.

Name

School   Grade

Parents' name

Parents' address

Reasons for examination

Date of birth

Age

Mental age

I. Q.

Diagnosis

Advice given

Date of examination:

Examiner:

APPENDIX II

THE COMMONWEALTH OF MASSACHUSETTS
DEPARTMENT OF MENTAL DISEASES
SCHOOL CLINIC RECORD

FIELDS OF INQUIRY — SYNOPSIS OF FINDINGS

Name   Age   Date   No.

     Height   Weight   Circum.

1. Physical Examination:

2. Family History:

3. Personal and Developmental History:

4. History of School Progress:

5. Examination in School Work:

6. Practical Knowledge:

7. Economic Efficiency:

8. Social History and Reactions:

9. Moral Reactions:

10. Psychological Tests:

APPENDIX II

THE COMMONWEALTH OF MASSACHUSETTS
DEPARTMENT OF MENTAL DISEASES
SCHOOL CLINIC RECORD

CORRELATION OF CHRONOLOGICAL MENTAL AND SCHOOL AGE

NAME DATE NO.

Chronological Age	I. Q.	Mental Age	School Grade for Present Chronological Age	School Grade Work Finished					
				Reading	Arithmetic	Spelling	Writing	Geography	Language
16		16	H. S. II						
15		15	H. S. I						
14		14	J. H. S.						
13		13	VIII						
12		12	VII						
11		11	VI						
10		10	V						
9		9	IV						
8		8	III						
7		7	II						
6		6	I						
5		5	Kindergarten						
4		4							
3		3							
2		2							
1		1							

APPENDIX II

THE COMMONWEALTH OF MASSACHUSETTS
DEPARTMENT OF MENTAL DISEASES
SCHOOL CLINIC RECORD

PHYSICAL EXAMINATION

....

Name   Date of birth   No.

....

Height { Sitting / Standing   Weight

General appearance and nutrition

Sight   Face

Speech   Eyes

Hearing   Nose

Reflexes   Mouth

Genito Urinary organs   Tongue

Menses   Teeth

Cardio Vascular   Naso-Pharynx

Glands   Palate

Head   Ears
  (a) Length
                     Skin
  (b) Width
                     Hair
  (c) Circum.

                     Skeleton
  (d) Cephalic index
                     (a) Torso leg ratio

Extremities
                     (b) Spread of arms

Date of examination:

Examiner:

THE COMMONWEALTH OF MASSACHUSETTS
DEPARTMENT OF MENTAL DISEASES
SCHOOL CLINIC RECORD
FAMILY HISTORY

Name

1. Brothers and sisters, with names and ages (Use ▢ male, ◯ female) including those who have died, and miscarriages (Indicate *w. d.* and *cause*). Indicate any not sound in mind or body.

2. Age of parents at birth of child
    Father   Birthplace
    Mother   Birthplace   Maiden name

3. Occupation of Father

4. Did the parents or relatives of this child ever show any peculiarity of mind or body, such as: (indicate with an "x" and relationship).

    Paternal   Maternal
            Insanity
            Feeble-mindedness
            Epilepsy (fits)
            Convulsions
            Paralysis (age of)
            Sexual promiscuity
            Syphilis
            Gonorrhea
            Tuberculosis
            Alcoholism
            Criminal
            Pauper
            Drug habitué
            Blind
            Deaf
            Severe headache
            Extreme nervousness

5. Other facts concerning father, mother, or other relatives.

Date of examination:

Examiner:

APPENDIX II

THE COMMONWEALTH OF MASSACHUSETTS
DEPARTMENT OF MENTAL DISEASES
SCHOOL CLINIC RECORD

PERSONAL AND DEVELOPMENT HISTORY

Name

1. Date of birth.   Place of Birth.   No.
2. Was he born at full period?
3. Was birth difficult, prolonged, instrumental or unusual in any way?
4. Is there any history of convulsions? If so, describe, give date of onset, etc.
5. Describe fully any illnesses occurring before the age of 5 or 6 years.
6. At what age did he begin to walk?
7. At what age did he begin to talk?
8. When did the first teeth appear?
9. At what age did mental peculiarity manifest itself? Was he backward or peculiar from birth, or did symptoms of peculiarity develop suddenly? Describe fully.

10. As a baby did he "take notice," sit up, play with toys, etc., at the usual age?
11. Was he different from other babies in any other way?
12. Could he dress self at the usual time?
13. Does he wet the bed or day clothing?
14. Does he soil the bed or day clothing?
15. Has he ever masturbated?
16. Does he hide, break, or destroy things?
17. Is he able to go about alone and protect h self from ordinary dangers on the street and elsewhere?
18. What hospitals has he been in?   Where?   When?   Why?

Date of examination:

Examiner:

APPENDIX II

THE COMMONWEALTH OF MASSACHUSETTS
DEPARTMENT OF MENTAL DISEASES
SCHOOL CLINIC RECORD
HISTORY OF SCHOOL PROGRESS

Name   No

1. At what age did   he first attend school?

2. Where did   he attend school?

3. How long was   ne in the first grade?

   How long was   he in the second grade?

   How long was   he in the third grade?

   How long was   he in the fourth grade?

   How long was   he in the fifth grade?

   How long was   he in the sixth grade?

   How long was   he in the seventh grade?

   How long was   he in the eighth grade?

4. What does teacher say of h   school progress and behavior?

5. Is   he a truant?   If so, what is h   own reason for playing truant?

Date of examination:

Examiner:

APPENDIX II

THE COMMONWEALTH OF MASSACHUSETTS
DEPARTMENT OF MENTAL DISEASES
SCHOOL CLINIC RECORD
PRACTICAL KNOWLEDGE (I)

Name   No.

1. When is your birthday?
2. How long have you gone to school?
3. In what grade are you?
4. Do you study geography?
5. At what time do you go to school?   How long recess do you have?
6. In what state do you live?
7. What is your father's name?
8. What does your mother do?
9. What does your father do?
10. How do you know when a person is old?
11. What do you call this (cheek)?
12. Where is your stomach?   Brain?   Chest?

13. When are you hungry?

14. Are you more thirsty in summer or in winter?   Why?
15. What is a dream?   A pain?
16. When you get up tomorrow will it be morning or evening?

17. What is a janitor?
18. What things would you need to fry eggs?
19. How does one make a fire?

Date of examination:

Examiner:

THE COMMONWEALTH OF MASSACHUSETTS
DEPARTMENT OF MENTAL DISEASES
SCHOOL CLINIC RECORD
PRACTICAL KNOWLEDGE (II)

Name   No.

The following questions, always varied or modified to suit the particular case, only indicate the general line of inquiry likely to show the mental capacity and ability. The answers elicited will suggest queries.

How old are you?
What year were you born?
How old are your brothers and sisters?
What was your mother's maiden name?
Where do you live?
Is it a city or town?
How far from Boston (or the nearest large city)?
What is the trolley fare from Boston or the nearest large town?
What towns are near your own town?
Name some large cities in Massachusetts.
Name some rivers in Massachusetts.
Name some mountains.   Where are they?
What is made in Lynn, in Lowell, in Waltham?
Who is the Governor of Massachusetts?
Who is the President of the United States?
Who is the King of England?
Do you read any newspapers?   Which ones?   Which departments?
What news in the papers recently?
What books have you read? Tell the story of one.
How high is this door?
How long is this pencil?
How tall are you?
How much do you weigh?
What size shoe do you wear?
What does a pair of shoes cost?   A hat?   Gloves?
Name some flowers, vegetables, animals.
Describe streets, mills, buildings, etc., in your town.
What did you see on your journey this morning?
What job would you like?
Where have you worked?
Why did you leave your last job?
What wages did you receive?
What do you like to do best?
Do you play baseball?   What position?
How much does a baseball cost?
How long would you boil an egg?
How long would you bake a potato?

Date of examination:

Examiner:

APPENDIX II

THE COMMONWEALTH OF MASSACHUSETTS
DEPARTMENT OF MENTAL DISEASES
SCHOOL CLINIC RECORD
ECONOMIC EFFICIENCY

Name   No.

(This sheet does not apply to children under 14 years of age, as a rule, except to indicate helpfulness at home, but is most important in determining the mental condition of the adolescent.)

1. Has he ever earned wages?

2. Kind of work?   Wages?   Quality?   Reason for leaving?

3. What does employer think of h ?

4. How much supervision does he require?

5. If he has never earned wages, what kinds of useful work is he capable of doing in the home or elsewhere?

Date of examination:

Examiner:

APPENDIX II

THE COMMONWEALTH OF MASSACHUSETTS
DEPARTMENT OF MENTAL DISEASES
SCHOOL CLINIC RECORD
SOCIAL HISTORY AND REACTIONS

Name   No.

1. Environmental conditions:

    (a) Home

    (b) Neighborhood

2. Whom does he choose for associates?
3. Does he play with children of h own age?
4. Is he teased by other children, and if so, what are h reactions to being teased?
5. Is he accepted as an equal by boys and girls of h own age?
6. Is he a leader, or is he led by others?
7. What are h amusements, interests, and recreations?
8. Is he quarrelsome or cruel to other children?
9. Indicate any definite character traits, such as being:

Egotistical	Seclusive
Quarrelsome	Social
Passionate	Impulsive
Selfish	Emotionally unstable
Vain	Ill-tempered
Obedient	Resentful of authority
Suggestible	Over-affectionate
Stubborn	....
....	....
....	

(Underscore traits characteristic of child)

10. Remarks

Date of examination:

Examiner:

APPENDIX II

THE COMMONWEALTH OF MASSACHUSETTS
DEPARTMENT OF MENTAL DISEASES
SCHOOL CLINIC RECORD
MORAL REACTIONS

Name   No.

1. Does he lie?   Steal?

   Protectively?
   Maliciously?
   Imaginatively?
   Purposelessly?

2. Any evidence of abnormal interest or practice in sexual matters?

3. Has she borne illegitimate children?

4. Has he a court record?   Where?   Why?

5. Remarks.

Date of examination:

Examiner:

NOTE

The record sheets for examinations in school subjects and for psychological tests have not been included here. These should, however, be taken into consideration in estimating the mentality of any subnormal child. Although, in the actual examination of the child, it is possible that we may dispense with the tests in school subjects, from our point of view it is important that the child be given an intelligence test.

For the examinations in school subjects, almost any good standardized tests would prove of value. For the psychological tests, the following in particular are recommended:

Stanford Revision of the Binet-Simon Tests. Houghton Mifflin Company

Herring Revision of the Binet-Simon Tests. World Book Co.

Kuhlman Revision of the Binet-Simon Tests. Warwick & York

APPENDIX II

THE COMMONWEALTH OF MASSACHUSETTS
DEPARTMENT OF MENTAL DISEASES
SCHOOL CLINIC RECORD

CORRELATION OF CHRONOLOGICAL MENTAL AND SCHOOL AGE

NAME *Case I*   DATE   NO.

Chrono-logical Age	I. Q.	Mental Age	School Grade for Present Chron-ological Age	School Grade Work Finished					
				Reading	Arith-metic	Spelling	Writing	Geog-raphy	Lan-guage
16		16	H. S. II						
15		15	H. S. I						
14		14	J. H. S.						
13		13	VIII						
12		12	VII						
11	.69	11	VI						
10	.66	10	V						
9	.66	9	IV						
8	.64	8	III						
7		7	II						
6	.52	6	I						
5		5	Kinder-garten						
4		4							
3		3							
2		2							
1		1							

APPENDIX II 219

THE COMMONWEALTH OF MASSACHUSETTS
DEPARTMENT OF MENTAL DISEASES
SCHOOL CLINIC RECORD

CORRELATION OF CHRONOLOGICAL MENTAL AND SCHOOL AGE

NAME *Case II* DATE NO.

Chronological Age	I. Q.	Mental Age	School Grade for Present Chronological Age	School Grade Work Finished					
				Reading	Arithmetic	Spelling	Writing	Geography	Language
16		16	H. S. II						
15		15	H. S. I						
14		14	J. H. S.						
13		13	VIII						
12	.63	12	VII						
11	.67	11	VI						
10	.67	10	V						
9		9	IV						
8	.71	8	III						
7		7	II						
6		6	I						
5		5	Kindergarten						
4		4							
3		3							
2		2							
1		1							

APPENDIX II

THE COMMONWEALTH OF MASSACHUSETTS
DEPARTMENT OF MENTAL DISEASES
SCHOOL CLINIC RECORD

CORRELATION OF CHRONOLOGICAL MENTAL AND SCHOOL AGE

NAME *Case III* DATE NO.

Chrono-logical Age	I. Q.	Mental Age	School Grade for Present Chron-ological Age	School Grade Work Finished					
				Reading	Arithmetic	Spelling	Writing	Geography	Language
16		16	H. S. II						
15	.74	15	H. S. I						
14	.70	14	J. H. S.						
13	.73	13	VIII						
12	.78	12	VII						
11	.78	11	VI						
10		10	V						
9		9	IV						
8		8	III						
7		7	II						
6		6	I						
5		5	Kindergarten						
4		4							
3		3							
2		2							
1		1							

APPENDIX II

THE COMMONWEALTH OF MASSACHUSETTS
DEPARTMENT OF MENTAL DISEASES
SCHOOL CLINIC RECORD

CORRELATION OF CHRONOLOGICAL MENTAL AND SCHOOL AGE

NAME *Case "X"* DATE NO.

Chronological Age	I. Q.	Mental Age	School Grade for Present Chronological Age	School Grade Work Finished					
				Reading	Arithmetic	Spelling	Writing	Geography	Language
16		16	H. S. II						
15		15	H. S. I						
14		14	J. H. S.						
13		13	VIII						
12		12	VII						
11½	.78	11	VI						
10⁹⁄?	.69	10	V						
9	.64	9	IV						
8¾	.68	8	III						
7⁴	.52	7	II						
6			I						
5	.41	5	Kindergarten						
4		4							
3	.21								
2	.27	2							
1		1							

APPENDIX III

BIBLIOGRAPHY

Allen, F. D., *Educational and Vocational Guidance in the Providence Public Schools.* National Vocational Guidance Association Bulletin II, No. 4, January, 1924.

Baldwin, B. T., and Stecher, L. I., *Mental Growth Curve of Normal and Superior Children.* University of Iowa Studies, Vol. II, No. 1, January 1, 1922.

Barr, M. W., and Maloney, E. F., *Types of Mental Defectives.* P. Blakiston and Sons.

Beatley, Bancroft, *Standardized Tests and Scales in Secondary Education.* Harvard University Graduate School of Education, 1923. (Unpublished.)

Berry, C. S., *The Mentally Retarded Child in the Public Schools.* National Committee for Mental Hygiene, Inc., Reprint No. 168, 1923, 8 pp.

Brooks, F. D., *Changes in Mental Traits with Age.* Teachers College Contributions to Education, Columbia University.

Brown, Wm., and Thompson, G., *Essentials of Mental Measurement.* Cambridge University Press, 1921, 216 pp. (Cambridge Psychological Library.)

Burnham, William H., *The Normal Mind.* Appleton, 1924, 702 pp.

Carl, G. P., *A Study of High School Failures.* Harvard University Graduate School of Education, 1923. (Unpublished.)

Cobb, M., *The Inheritance of Arithmetical Abilities.* Journal of Educational Psychology, 1917.

Colloton and Rugg, *Constancy of the Stanford-Binet I. Q. as shown by Retests.* Journal of Educational Psychology, XII, pp. 315 ff.

Colvin, S. S., *Construction and Use of Intelligence Tests*, Twenty-First Year-Book, 1923. Public School Publishing Company. 275 pp.

Conklin, Edwin G., *Heredity and Environment*, Princeton University Press. 5th Edition, Revised, 1923.

Davies, S. P., *Social Control of the Feeble-minded.* National Committee for Mental Hygiene, Inc., 1923, 222 pp.

Dearborn, Walter F., *Intelligence Tests: Their Significance for School and Society.* Lowell Institute Lectures, 1925. To be published by Houghton Mifflin Company.

Dearborn, Walter F., and Others, Symposium, *The Nature of Intelligence.* Journal of Educational Psychology, XII, March–May, 1921.

Dearborn, Walter F., and Inglis, A., *Psychological and Educational Tests in the Public Schools of Winchester, Virginia.*

Dewey, John, *Individuality, Equality, and Superiority.* New Republic, December 13, 1922, pp. 61–63.

Dickson, Virgil, *The Reliability of the Binet Scale and Pedagogical Scales.* Journal of Educational Research, Vol. 4, No. 2.

Dickson and Norton, *The Otis Group Intelligence Scale Applied to the Elementary School Graduating Class of Oakland, California.* Journal of Educational Research, III, pp. 105–115, February, 1921.

APPENDIX III

Eaton, N. T., *Intelligence of Pupils Who Repeat.* School and Society, Vol. 17, No. 423, pp. 139–141, 1923.

Fernald, Grace M., and Keller, H., *The Effect of Kinæsthetic Factors in the Development of Word Recognition in the Case of Non-Readers.* Journal of Educational Research, 1921.

Fernald, Walter E., *Standardized Fields of Inquiry for Clinical Studies of Borderline Defectives.* Mental Hygiene Reprint, No. 8, 1922, 24 pp.

The Subnormal Child. School and Society, XVII, No. 458, 1923, 9 pp.

Inauguration of Public School Mental Clinic. Mental Hygiene Reprint, No. 149, 1922, 16 pp.

A State Program for the Care of the Mentally Defective. Mental Hygiene Reprint, No. 62, 1923, 8 pp.

After-Care Study of the Patients Discharged from Waverley for a Period of Twenty-Five Years. 9 pp.

What is Practicable in the Way of Prevention of Mental Defect. Mental Hygiene, 1922, 9 pp.

Feeble-mindedness. Mental Hygiene Reprint, No. 202.

The Salvage of the Backward Child. Reprint from Boston Medical and Surgical Journal, August, 1923.

An Out-Patient Clinic in Connection with a State Institution for the Feeble-minded. Mental Hygiene Reprint, No. 96.

Fernald, Walter E., State School Archives. (Waverley, Mass.)

Freeman, Frank L., *Interpretation and Application of the I. Q.* Journal of Educational Psychology, January, 1921, 10 pp.

Garrison and Tippett, *Comparison of Binet-Simon and Otis Tests.* Journal of Educational Research, Vol. VI, pp. 42–48, June, 1922.

Goddard, H. H., *Feeble-mindedness, Its Causes and Consequences.* Macmillan, 1923.

Gates, A. I., *Unreliability of Mental Age and Intelligence Quotient Based on Group Tests of General Mental Ability.* Journal of Applied Psychology, September–October, 1923.

Gesell, Arnold, *Special Provisions for Exceptional School Children.* New Haven, Conn.

What can the Teacher do for the Deficient Child? State Board of Education, Hartford, Conn.

Gregory, C. A., *Fundamentals of Educational Measurement.* Appleton, 1923, 382 pp.

Haines, Thomas H., *Special Training Facilities for Mentally Handicapped Children in the Public Day Schools of the United States.* Mental Hygiene, Vol. VIII, October, 1924, No. 4, pp. 893–911.

Harvard Psycho-Educational Clinic Archives.

Hewes and Others, *Mental Age and School Attainment of 1007 Retarded Children in Massachusetts.* Journal of Educational Psychology, April, 1924.

Holley, C. E., *Mental Tests for School Use.* Urbana, University of Illinois Bureau of Educational Research Bulletin, No. 4, 1920, 91 pp.

The Influence of Family Income and Other Factors on High School Attendance. University of Illinois School of Education, Seminary in Educational Administration.

Hollingworth, Leta L., *Special Talents and Defects.* Macmillan.

Holmes, Henry W., *Intelligence Tests and Individual Progress in School Work.*

Twenty-First Year Book of the National Society for the Study of Education, 1923, pp. 117–122.

Hopkins, L. T., *The Intelligence of Continuation School Children in Massachusetts.* Cambridge, Harvard University Press, 1924. (Harvard Studies in Education, Vol. V.) 132 pp.

Inglis, A., *Principles of Secondary Education.* Houghton Mifflin Co., 1918, 741 pp.

Irwin, Elizabeth A., and Marks, Louis A., *Fitting the School to the Child.* Macmillan, 1924, 335 pp.

LaPage, C. P., *Feeble-mindedness in Children of School Age.* Manchester University Press.

Lincoln, Edward A., *Beginnings in Educational Measurement.* Lippincott, 1924, 151 pp.

The Average Adult Mental Age Level. Journal of Educational Research, Vol. VI, September, 1922.

The I. Q.'s of Summer School Pupils. Journal of Educational Psychology, Vol. XIII, pp. 384–495.

Matthews, Mable A., *One Hundred Institutionally Trained Male Defectives in the Community under Supervision.* Mental Hygiene Reprint, No. 145, 1922, 11 pp.

Miller and Others, *The Administrative Use of Intelligence Tests in the High School,* Twenty-First Year Book of the National Society for the Study of Education, 1923, pp. 117–188.

Monroe, Walter S., *Theory of Educational Measurement.* Houghton Mifflin Co., 1923, 361 pp.

Myerson, M., *The Inheritance of Mental Diseases.* Macmillan, 1926.

Proctor, W. M., *Psychological Tests as a Means of Measuring the Probable School Success of High School Pupils.* Journal of Educational Research, Vol. I, pp. 258–270.

Psychological Tests and Guidance. Public School Publishing Company, 1923, 125 pp.

Parkhurst, Helen, *Education on the Dalton Plan.* Dutton, 1923, 278 pp.

Ruch and Stracham, *Intelligence Ratings by Group Scales and by the Stanford Revision of the Binet Tests.* Journal of Educational Psychology, Vol. XI, pp. 421–429, November, 1920.

Sayles, Mary B. and Nudd, Howard W., *The Problem Child in School.* Joint Committee on Methods of Preventing Delinquency, 1925.

Spearman, C., *The Nature of 'Intelligence' and the Principles of Cognition.* Macmillan, 1923, 358 pp.

Stenquist, John L., *Unreliability of Individual Scores.* Journal of Educational Research, Vol. IV, pp. 347–354.

Strayer, G. D., *Age-Grade Census of Schools and Colleges.* United States Bureau of Education Bulletin, No. 5, 1911.

Terman, L. M., *Uses of Intelligence Tests.* Journal of Educational Research, January, 1920.

Toronto, Ontario, Department of Education, Suggestions for Teachers of Subnormal Children, 1922, 1924.

Thompson, G., *The Hierarchy of Abilities.* British Journal of Psychology, 1919.

Thorndike, Edward L., *Psychology of Arithmetic.* Macmillan, 1923, 314 pp.

Tredgold, A. F., *Mental Deficiency.* 4th Edition, Wm. Wood and Co.

Twenty-Fourth Year Book, *Adapting the Schools to Individual Differences.* Public School Publishing Company, 1925, 410 pp.

Van Denburg, J. K., *Causes of Elimination of Students in the Public Secondary Schools of New York City.*

Wallin, J. E. W., *Education of Handicapped Children.* Houghton Mifflin Co., 1924, 395 pp.

Wentworth, Mary M., *Individual Difference in the Intelligence of School Children.* Harvard University Press. (Harvard Studies in Education, Vol. VII.)

Stecker, William A. - Physical Training Lessons. John Joseph McVey, Phila, Pa. - 1924.

Zwarg, Leopold F. - Apparatus Work for Boys and Girls - 1923.

Stecker, W. A. - Handbook of Lessons in Physical Training and Games.
- Book No 1 - First and Second Grades
- " " 2 - Third and Fourth "
- " " 3 - Fifth, Sixth, Seventh, Eighth "

Stecker, W. A. - Physical Training Lessons for Backward Classes. 50¢. (In Three Grades of Difficulty).